Cities
and
Churches

Cities
and
Churches

READINGS ON THE URBAN CHURCH

Edited by
ROBERT LEE

493

Philadelphia

THE WESTMINSTER PRESS

PRINTED IN THE UNITED STATES OF AMERICA

To
my former students and colleagues
at Union Theological Seminary,
New York City

1384

CONTENTS

FOREWORD

The growth of cities and the influence of urban civilization on contemporary life give new urgency to a consideration of the role of the church in the modern metropolis. American Protestantism has too long abdicated its responsibility for the city. In large measure, this is so because we have failed to understand the processes of urbanization which have revolutionized many aspects of our life and thought.

This book makes an important contribution to the understanding of the church in the urban setting. Prof. Robert Lee has compiled and edited a rich body of materials which should aid churches in understanding their relationship to an emerging urban culture. The selections he has chosen from a variety of sources represent the ragged growing edges of creative thought.

The appearance of this volume should stimulate more serious study of the role of religion in urban society. In view of the scattered nature of the materials relevant to this concern, this work should find a ready welcome: seminary instructors will find it of immediate value as a classroom text; urban church institutes, lay study groups, and training centers will find it a useful and helpful resource; and urban pastors in search of fresh insights and stimulation will find it indispensable.

This collection of basic readings for urban churchmen

was a project encouraged by the Department of the Urban Church of the National Council of Churches. It has benefited from the counsel of leaders in the field and has been tested by classroom use. Readers will find here an important point of departure from which they might proceed in the search for better insights.

JOHN C. BENNETT
Dean of the Faculty
Union Theological Seminary
New York City

PREFACE

This book of readings is presented at a time when there is renewed concern for the urban church and when urbanization has become a "permanent revolution" in American life. For too long Protestant churchmen have adopted an irresponsible attitude and policy toward the city. The traditional pattern of evasion has become obsolete. Fear and flight in the face of dynamic urban changes can be only self-defeating. The trend toward urbanization continues and quickens as 70 per cent of the nation's population are city dwellers and 130 cities claim a population of 100,000 or more. Urbanization is so characteristic of modern society that for Protestants to be uninvolved in the city is to be standing on the sidewalk watching the passing parade march by.

Fortunately, there are signs of a realization that the church which remains aloof from the city is cutting itself off from the wellsprings of civilization. The renewal of city churches is both a cause and a consequence of the recent spate of literature on the urban church. Moreover, in urban centers across the nation various church experiments have sprung up. And professional church researchers and planners, whose numbers are growing in denominations and councils of churches, are searching for new strategies to relate the church to the modern metropolis. These developments testify to the renewed concern for cities and

13

churches. Perhaps the moment has arrived to lift up into a single volume selections from among the abundant literature that has emerged in this field.

Surely it is a risky task to select a group of readings that seek to cover the major facets of the life and action of the urban church. Yet this risk must be taken, even with the full knowledge that much valuable material will necessarily be excluded. There is a desperate need for a compilation of writings on the urban church to be brought together into a single volume, since some of the best documents are found in fugitive sources and difficult-to-reach journals.

Anyone who has taught a course on the urban church, either in seminary or in a pastors' institute, realizes that teaching aids and textbooks are woefully inadequate. This book grew out of my efforts to teach "Church and Community" courses to seminary students and to practicing clergymen. Church executives and colleagues at other seminaries faced with similar responsibilities were most encouraging, as they urged me to fill a gap in this field by bringing together a body of significant literature.

Of course, a book of collected readings usually lacks an integrated theory or a sustained focus on one central theme. Yet there is an advantage to be gained from tapping the major insights and contributions of a wide range of authors. This is particularly true in view of the present status of scholarship in this field. So rich in complexity and extensive in scope is the urban church that no single person or book has yet to comprehend its various dimensions in any fully satisfactory way.

It is my conviction that before students of the urban church can construct a more adequate house of knowledge, careful attention must be given to the cultivation of building blocks. Hopefully, the present volume provides such a stimulus. Classic statements are included from the works of Wirth, Simmel, Park, H. Paul Douglass, and Kincheloe. Many of the selections are from the pen of contemporary urban church leaders who are writing out of their own experiences.

Each article has been selected with one guiding question in mind: does it provide a clue, a perspective, an insight for seminary students, urban pastors, and intelligent lay people to understand the church in its urban setting? In other words, will it stimulate reflection and critical self-awareness? Hence this book is not intended to be a "tool kit," a "do-it-yourself manual," which contains simple panaceas for problems confronting the urban church. To be sure, the imaginative reader will find concrete suggestions for church work in the city in many of the selections. But the larger intent of this volume is to stimulate and provoke the reader to do his own thinking and planning.

Since this work is intended primarily as a text for courses, some of the articles were chosen for their representation of an important concern of the urban church rather than for their unique contribution to scholarship.

Several glaring omissions should be mentioned. Because of space limitations, no attempt has been made to include the stimulating and provocative literature that is reaching these shores from abroad. Specifically, I have in mind the writings of Tom Allan, George MacLeod, T. R. Morton, E. W. Southcott, and E. R. Wickham.

Considerations of space also prevented the inclusion of pieces on research and survey methodology. The material on research techniques is so extensive and tends to be either overly simple or overly complex that it can best be handled by a separate book or research manual with detailed instructions. In no sense should either of these omissions be interpreted invidiously.

The editor's intention for this book will not be served if readers confine their study to the materials in this volume exclusively. Instead, the readings here should whet the student's appetite and drive him to the original sources. A reader is never a substitute for more extensive reading but merely a useful starting point.

Editorial comments are confined to brief chapter introductions which contain an abstract of each selection. These comments are held to a minimum so as not to interfere with the instructor's use of the documents. In addition to these readings, the seminary instructor may find it desirable to assign one or more of the following texts: Walter Kloetzli and Arthur Hillman, *Urban Church Planning* (Muhlenberg Press, 1958); Murray Leiffer, *The Effective City Church* (Abingdon Press, 1961); Ross Sanderson, *The Church Serves the Changing City* (Harper & Brothers, 1955); Frederick A. Shippey, *Church Work in the City* (Abingdon Press, 1952); Kenneth Underwood, *Protestant and Catholic* (The Beacon Press, Inc., 1957); Gibson Winter, *The Suburban Captivity of the Churches* (Doubleday & Co., Inc., 1961).

My indebtedness must be expressed to many friends for their help and encouragement: to Meryl Ruoss, who, as Director of the Department of the Urban Church of the National Council of Churches, encouraged this project for use in lay study groups and urban church institutes; to Arthur Stevenson, of the National Board of Missions of The United Presbyterian Church U.S.A., who initially proposed the idea; to Yoshio Fukuyama and Joseph W. Merchant, of the Board of Home Missions, Congregational Christian Churches; to Lauris Whitman, of the National Council of

Churches, and Leland Gartrell, of the Protestant Council of the City of New York. Also my thanks to John Bodo, of the San Francisco Theological Seminary, and Richard Tholin, of Union Theological Seminary's field work staff.

I am particularly grateful to my students at Union Theological Seminary who provided me with the opportunity to experiment with these course materials. These students have helped to close the gap between the dream and the reality of this volume.

I wish to take this occasion to express my great gratitude to John C. Bennett, Dean of Union Theological Seminary, New York City, for friendly offices and counsels.

A special appreciation is extended to the publishers and the authors who so kindly gave permission to reprint their works and to The Westminster Press for undertaking this publication venture.

ROBERT LEE

San Francisco Theological Seminary
San Anselmo, California

THE SETTING:
URBAN LIFE
AND URBAN CULTURE

Introduction

What is the city? What are its characteristic features? What impact does the city have on human personality and on social institutions?

These are the crucial questions discussed in Chapter I. The selections in this chapter depict the urban ethos, the social setting of the city dweller. They show how the city leaves its characteristic marks upon the psychological and social patterns of modern man.

In brief compass these selections provide a conceptual framework for understanding the city from a sociological vantage point. Questions of religion and theology are not dealt with directly. This is not to imply that these are unimportant issues. Theological concerns will appear in later chapters. At the outset it is essential for the urban churchman to have a clear understanding of the cultural context of urbanization. For this is the social setting *that every church caught in the urban surge confronts today.*

The three articles in this chapter that depict urban life and urban culture have long been recognized as among the classic writings on urbanization. Louis Wirth's "Urbanism as a Way of Life" is a perceptive analysis of the urban mode of life. The late professor of sociology at the Univer-

19

sity of Chicago wrote this article nearly twenty-five years
ago. It remains a fresh discussion of urban existence as
characterized by the absolute numbers of population in a
settled area, density of population, and heterogeneity. The
implications of these characteristics for social life and human interaction are vividly portrayed.

"The Metropolis and Mental Life," by Georg Simmel,
one of the seminal social theorists of the late nineteenth
century, is as timely today as was its first German publication at the turn of the twentieth century. Simmel's article
on the metropolitan style of life is a penetrating psychological analysis of urbanization. Here is a classic statement
of urban anonymity and impersonality, of the rapid pace
and multiple stimuli which impinge upon the urbanite.
One begins to understand the bases for the clock-bound
nature of city living, contractual rather than personal relationships, and the blasé attitude and reserve so typical of
life in the metropolis.

The final article is a brief excerpt from a long article that
Robert E. Park wrote in 1916. Park was an outstanding
American sociologist who taught at the University of
Chicago. The longer article is actually a research agenda
that stimulated generations of students into the exploration of different facets of urban life. Park reminds us that
the city is more than crowded buildings and peoples. It is
a state of mind, a body of customs and traditions, and a
peculiar setting where divergent types of people may find
a congenial environment for the full and free expression of
their talents and gifts.

Urbanism
as a Way of Life

Louis Wirth

A city may be defined as a relatively large, dense, and permanent settlement of socially heterogeneous individuals. On the basis of the postulates which this minimal definition suggests, a theory of urbanism may be formulated.

In the rich literature on the city we look in vain for a theory of urbanism presenting in a systematic fashion the available knowledge concerning the city as a social entity. Despite the multiplication of research and textbooks on the city, we do not as yet have a comprehensive body of compendent hypotheses which may be derived from a set of postulates implicitly contained in a sociological definition of the city.

In the following pages we shall seek to set forth a limited number of identifying characteristics of the city. We shall then indicate what consequences or further characteristics follow from them in the light of general sociological theory and empirical research. We hope in this manner to arrive at the essential propositions comprising a theory of urbanism.

There are a number of sociological propositions concerning the relationship between (*a*) numbers of population,

Reprinted in abridged form from *The American Journal of Sociology* (July, 1938), pp. 10–18. Used by permission of The University of Chicago Press. Copyright, 1938, by the University of Chicago.

21

(b) density of settlement, (c) heterogeneity of inhabitants and group life, which can be formulated on the basis of observation and research.

SIZE OF THE POPULATION AGGREGATE

Ever since Aristotle's *Politics*, it has been recognized that increasing the number of inhabitants in a settlement beyond a certain limit will affect the relationships between them and the character of the city. Large numbers involve, as has been pointed out, a greater range of individual variation. Furthermore, the greater the number of individuals participating in a process of interaction, the greater is the *potential* differentiation between them. The personal traits, the occupations, the cultural life, and the ideas of the members of an urban community may, therefore, be expected to range between more widely separated poles than those of rural inhabitants.

That such variations should give rise to the spatial segregation of individuals according to color, ethnic heritage, economic and social status, tastes and preferences, may readily be inferred. The bonds of kinship, of neighborliness and the sentiments arising out of living together for generations under a common folk tradition are likely to be absent or, at best, relatively weak in an aggregate the members of which have such diverse origins and backgrounds. Under such circumstances competition and formal control mechanisms furnish the substitutes for the bonds of solidarity that are relied upon to hold a folk society together.

Increase in the number of inhabitants of a community beyond a few hundred is bound to limit the possibility of each member of the community knowing all the others personally. Max Weber, in recognizing the social significance of this fact, pointed out that from a sociological point of view large numbers of inhabitants and density of settlement mean that the personal mutual acquaintanceship between the inhabitants which ordinarily inheres in a neighborhood is lacking. The increase in numbers thus involves a changed character of the social relationships. As Simmel points out:

[If] the unceasing external contact of numbers of persons in the city should be met by the same number of inner reactions as in the small town, in which one knows almost every person he meets and to each of whom he has a positive relationship, one would be completely atomized internally and would fall into an unthinkable mental condition.

The multiplication of persons in a state of interaction under conditions which make their contact as full personalities impossible produces that segmentalization of human relationships which has sometimes been seized upon by students of the mental life of the cities as an explanation for the "schizoid" character of urban personality. This is not to say that the urban inhabitants have fewer acquaintances than rural inhabitants, for the reverse may actually be true; it means rather that in relation to the number of people whom they see and with whom they rub elbows in the course of daily life, they know a smaller proportion, and of these they have less intensive knowledge.

Characteristically, urbanites meet one another in highly segmental roles. They are, to be sure, dependent upon more people for the satisfactions of their life needs than are rural people and thus are associated with a greater number of organized groups, but they are less dependent upon particular persons, and their dependence upon others is confined to a highly fractionalized aspect of the other's

round of activity. This is essentially what is meant by saying that the city is characterized by secondary rather than
primary contacts. The contacts of the city may indeed be
face to face, but they are nevertheless impersonal, superficial, transitory, and segmental. The reserve, the indifference, and the blasé outlook which urbanites manifest in
their relationships may thus be regarded as devices for
immunizing themselves against the personal claims and
expectations of others.

The superficiality, the anonymity, and the transitory
character of urban social relations make intelligible, also,
the sophistication and the rationality generally ascribed to
city dwellers. Our acquaintances tend to stand in a relationship of utility to us in the sense that the role which
each one plays in our life is overwhelmingly regarded as
a means for the achievement of our own ends. Whereas,
therefore, the individual gains, on the one hand, a certain
degree of emancipation or freedom from the personal and
emotional controls of intimate groups, he loses, on the
other hand, the spontaneous self-expression, the morale,
and the sense of participation that comes with living in an
integrated society. This constitutes essentially the state of
anomic or social void to which Durkheim alludes in attempting to account for the various forms of social disorganization in technological society.

The segmental character and utilitarian accent of interpersonal relations in the city find their institutional expression in the proliferation of specialized tasks which we
see in their most developed form in the professions. The
operations of the pecuniary nexus leads to predatory relationships, which tend to obstruct the efficient functioning
of the social order unless checked by professional codes
and occupational etiquette. The premium put upon utility

and efficiency suggests the adaptability of the corporate device for the organization of enterprises in which individuals can engage only in groups. The advantage that the corporation has over the individual entrepreneur and the partnership in the urban-industrial world derives not only from the possibility it affords of centralizing the resources of thousands of individuals or from the legal privilege of limited liability and perpetual succession, but from the fact that the corporation has no soul.

The specialization of individuals, particularly in their occupations, can proceed only, as Adam Smith pointed out, upon the basis of an enlarged market, which in turn accentuates the division of labor. This enlarged market is only in part supplied by the city's hinterland; in large measure it is found among the large numbers that the city itself contains. The dominance of the city over the surrounding hinterland becomes explicable in terms of the division of labor which urban life occasions and promotes. The extreme degree of interdependence and the unstable equilibrium of urban life are closely associated with the division of labor and the specialization of occupations. This interdependence and instability is increased by the tendency of each city to specialize in those functions in which it has the greatest advantage.

In a community composed of a larger number of individuals than can know one another intimately and can be assembled in one spot, it becomes necessary to communicate through indirect mediums and to articulate individual interests by a process of delegation. Typically in the city, interests are made effective through representation. *The individual counts for little, but the voice of the representative is heard with a deference roughly proportional to the numbers for whom he speaks.*

While this characterization of urbanism, in so far as it derives from large numbers, does not by any means exhaust the sociological inferences that might be drawn from our knowledge of the relationship of the size of a group to the characteristic behavior of the members, for the sake of brevity the assertions made may serve to exemplify the sort of propositions that might be developed.

DENSITY

As in the case of numbers, so in the case of concentration in limited space, certain consequences of relevance in sociological analysis of the city emerge. Of these only a few can be indicated.

As Darwin pointed out for flora and fauna and as Durkheim noted in the case of human societies, an increase in numbers when area is held constant (i.e., an increase in density) tends to produce differentiation and specialization, since only in this way can the area support increased numbers. Density thus reinforces the effect of numbers in diversifying men and their activities and in increasing the complexity of the social structure.

On the subjective side, as Simmel has suggested, the close physical contact of numerous individuals necessarily produces a shift in the mediums through which we orient ourselves to the urban milieu, especially to our fellow men. Typically, our physical contacts are close, but our social contacts are distant. The urban world puts a premium on visual recognition. We see the uniform which denotes the role of the functionaries and are oblivious to the personal eccentricities that are hidden behind the uniform. We tend to acquire and develop a sensitivity to a world of artifacts and become progressively farther removed from the world of nature.

We are exposed to glaring contrasts between splendor and squalor, between riches and poverty, intelligence and ignorance, order and chaos. The competition for space is great, so that each area generally tends to be put to the use which yields the greatest economic return. Place of work tends to become dissociated from place of residence, for the proximity of industrial and commercial establishments makes an area both economically and socially undesirable for residential purposes.

Density, land values, rentals, accessibility, healthfulness, prestige, aesthetic consideration, absence of nuisances such as noise, smoke, and dirt determine the desirability of various areas of the city as places of settlement for different sections of the population. Place and nature of work, income, racial and ethnic characteristics, social status, custom, habit, taste, preference, and prejudice are among the significant factors in accordance with which the urban population is selected and distributed into more or less distinct settlements. Diverse population elements inhabiting a compact settlement thus tend to become segregated from one another in the degree in which their requirements and modes of life are incompatible with one another and in the measure in which they are antagonistic to one another. Similarly, persons of homogeneous status and needs unwittingly drift into, consciously select, or are forced by circumstances into, the same area. The different parts of the city thus acquire specialized functions. The city consequently tends to resemble a mosaic of social worlds in which the transition from one to the other is abrupt. The juxtaposition of divergent personalities and modes of life tends to produce a relativistic perspective and a sense of toleration of differences which may be regarded as prerequisites for rationality and which load toward the secularization of life.

The close living together and working together of individuals who have no sentimental and emotional ties foster a spirit of competition, aggrandizement, and mutual exploitation. To counteract irresponsibility and potential disorder, formal controls tend to be resorted to. Without rigid adherence to predictable routines a large compact society would scarcely be able to maintain itself. The clock and the traffic signal are symbolic of the basis of our social order in the urban world. *Frequent close physical contact, coupled with great social distance, accentuates the reserve of unattached individuals toward one another and, unless compensated for by other opportunities for response, gives rise to loneliness.* The necessary frequent movement of great numbers of individuals in a congested habitat gives occasion to friction and irritation. Nervous tensions which derive from such personal frustration are accentuated by the rapid tempo and the complicated technology under which life in dense areas must be lived.

HETEROGENEITY

The social interaction among such a variety of personality types in the urban milieu tends to break down the rigidity of caste lines and to complicate the class structure, and thus induces a more ramified and differentiated framework of social stratification than is found in more integrated societies. The heightened mobility of the individual, which brings him within the range of stimulation by a great number of diverse individuals and subjects him to fluctuating status in the differentiated social groups that compose the social structure of the city, tends toward the acceptance of instability and insecurity in the world at large as a norm. This fact helps to account, too, for the sophistication and cosmopolitanism of the urbanite. No single group has the undivided allegiance of the individual. The groups with which he is affiliated do not lend themselves readily to a simple hierarchical arrangement. By virtue of his different interests arising out of different aspects of social life, the individual acquires membership in widely divergent groups, each of which functions only *with reference to a single segment of his personality*. Nor do these groups easily permit of a concentric arrangement so that the narrower ones fall within the circumference of the more inclusive ones, as is more likely to be the case in the rural community or in primitive societies. Rather, the groups with which the person typically is affiliated are tangential to each other or intersect in highly variable fashion.

Partly as a result of the physical foot-looseness of the population and partly as a result of their social mobility, the turnover in group membership generally is rapid. Place of residence, place and character of employment, income and interests fluctuate, and the task of holding organizations together and maintaining and promoting intimate and lasting acquaintanceship between the members is difficult. This applies strikingly to the local areas within the city into which persons become segregated more by virtue of differences in race, language, income, and social status than through choice or positive attraction to people like themselves. Overwhelmingly the city dweller is not a homeowner, and since a transitory habitat does not generate binding traditions and sentiments, only rarely is he truly a neighbor. There is little opportunity for the individual to obtain a conception of the city as a whole or to survey his place in the total scheme. Consequently he finds it difficult to determine what is to his own "best interests" and to decide between the issues and leaders presented to him by the agencies of mass suggestion. Individuals who are thus detached from the organized bodies which integrate society comprise the fluid masses that make collective behavior in the urban community so unpredictable and hence so problematical.

Although the city, through the recruitment of variant types to perform its diverse tasks and the accentuation of their uniqueness through competition and the premium upon eccentricity, novelty, efficient performance, and inventiveness, produces a highly differentiated population, it also exercises a leveling influence. Wherever large numbers of differently constituted individuals congregate, the process of depersonalization also enters. This leveling tendency inheres in part in the economic basis of the city. The development of large cities, at least in the modern age, was largely dependent upon the concentrative force of steam. The rise of the factory made possible mass production for an impersonal market. The fullest exploitation of the possibilities of the division of labor and mass production, however, is possible only with standardization of processes and products. A money economy goes hand in hand with such a system of production. Progressively as cities have developed upon a background of this system of production, the pecuniary nexus which implies the purchasability of services and things has displaced personal relations as the basis of association. Individuals under these circumstances must be replaced by categories. When large numbers have to make common use of facilities and institutions, an arrangement must be made to adjust the facilities and institutions to the needs of the average person rather than to those of particular individuals. The services of the public utilities, of the recreational, educational, and cultural institutions must be adjusted to mass requirements. Similarly, the cultural institutions, such as the schools, the movies, the radio, and the newspapers, by virtue of their mass clientele, must necessarily operate as leveling influences. The political process as it appears in urban life could not be understood without taking account of the mass appeals made through modern propaganda techniques. If the individual would participate at all in the social, political, and economic life of the city, he must subordinate some of his individuality to the demands of the larger community and in that measure immerse himself in mass movements.

THE RELATION BETWEEN A THEORY OF URBANISM AND SOCIOLOGICAL RESEARCH

Being reduced to a stage of virtual impotence as an individual, the urbanite is bound to exert himself by joining with others of similar interest into organized groups to obtain his ends. This results in the enormous multiplication of voluntary organizations directed toward as great a variety of objectives as there are human needs and interests. While on the one hand the traditional ties of human association are weakened, urban existence involves a much greater degree of interdependence between man and man and a more complicated, fragile, and volatile form of mutual interrelations over many phases of which the individual as such can exert scarcely any control. Frequently there is only the most tenuous relationship between the economic position or other basic factors that determine the individual's existence in the urban world and the voluntary groups with which he is affiliated. While in a primitive and in a rural society it is generally possible to predict on the basis of a few known factors who will belong to what and who will associate with whom in almost every rela-

tionship of life, in the city we can only project the general
pattern of group formation and affiliation, and this pattern
will display many incongruities and contradictions.

Urban Personality and Collective Behavior

It is largely through the activities of the voluntary
groups, be their objectives economic, political, educational,
religious, recreational, or cultural, that the urbanite expresses and develops his personality, acquires status, and is
able to carry on the round of activities that constitute his
life career. It may easily be inferred, however, that the organizational framework which these highly differentiated
functions call into being does not of itself ensure the con-
sistency and integrity of the personalities whose interests
it enlists. Personal disorganization, mental breakdown,
suicide, delinquency, crime, corruption, and disorder
might be expected under those circumstances to be more
prevalent in the urban than in the rural community. This
has been confirmed in so far as comparable indexes are
available; but the mechanisms underlying these phenomena require further analysis.

Since for most group purposes it is impossible in the city
to appeal individually to the large number of discrete and
differentiated individuals, and since it is only through the
organizations to which men belong that their interests and
resources can be enlisted for a collective cause, it may be
inferred that social control in the city should typically proceed through formally organized groups. It follows, too,
that masses of men in the city are subject to manipulation
by symbols and stereotypes managed by individuals working from afar or operating invisibly behind the scenes
through their control of the instruments of communication.
Self-government either in the economic, the political, or

the cultural realm is under these circumstances reduced to a mere figure of speech or, at best, is subject to the unstable equilibrium of pressure groups. In view of the ineffectiveness of actual kinship ties, we create fictional kinship groups. In the face of the disappearance of the territorial unit as a basis of social solidarity, we create interest units. Meanwhile the city as a community resolves itself into a series of tenuous segmental relationships superimposed upon a territorial base with a definite center but without a definite periphery and upon a division of labor which far transcends the immediate locality and is world wide in scope. The larger the number of persons in a state of interaction with one another the lower is the level of communication and the greater is the tendency for communication to proceed on an elementary level, i.e., on the basis of those things which are assumed to be common or to be of interest to all.

It is obviously, therefore, to the emerging trends in the communication system and to the production and distribution technology that has come into existence with modern civilization that we must look for the symptoms which will indicate the probable future development of urbanism as a mode of social life. The direction of the ongoing changes in urbanism will for good or ill transform not only the city but the world. Some of the more basic of these factors and processes and the possibilities of their direction and control invite further detailed study.

The Metropolis and Mental Life

Georg Simmel

The deepest problems of modern life derive from the claim of the individual to preserve the autonomy and individuality of his existence in the face of overwhelming social forces, of historical heritage, of external culture, and of the technique of life. The fight with nature which primitive man has to wage for his bodily existence attains in this modern form its latest transformation. The eighteenth century called upon man to free himself of all the historical bonds in the state and in religion, in morals and in economics. Man's nature, originally good and common to all, should develop unhampered. In addition to more liberty, the nineteenth century demanded the functional specialization of man and his work; this specialization makes one individual incomparable to another, and each of them indispensable to the highest possible extent. However, this specialization makes each man the more directly dependent upon the supplementary activities of all others. Nietzsche sees the full development of the individual conditioned by the most ruthless struggle of individuals; socialism believes in the suppression of all competition for the same reason. Be that as it may, in all these positions the same basic motive is at work: the person resists

Reprinted in abridged form from *The Sociology of Georg Simmel*, translated by Kurt Wolff (The Free Press of Glencoe, 1950), pp. 409–417. Used by permission of The Free Press.

being leveled down and worn out by a social-technological mechanism. An inquiry into the inner meaning of specifically modern life and its products, into the soul of the cultural body, so to speak, must seek to solve the equation which structures like the metropolis set up between the individual and the superindividual contents of life. Such an inquiry must answer the question of how the personality accommodates itself in the adjustments to external forces. This will be my task today.

The psychological basis of the metropolitan type of individuality consists in the intensification of nervous stimu-change of outer and inner stimuli. Man is a differentiating creature. His mind is stimulated by the difference between a momentary impression and the one which preceded it. Lasting impressions, impressions which differ only slightly from one another, impressions which take a regular and habitual course and show regular and habitual contrasts— all these use up, so to speak, less consciousness than does lation which results from the swift and uninterrupted the rapid crowding of changing images, the sharp discontinuity in the grasp of a single glance, and the unexpectedness of onrushing impressions. These are the psychological conditions which the metropolis creates. With each crossing of the street, with the tempo and multiplicity of economic, occupational, and social life, the city sets up a deep contrast with small town and rural life with reference to the sensory foundations of psychic life. The metropolis exacts from man as a discriminating creature a different amount of consciousness than does rural life. Here the rhythm of life and sensory mental imagery flows more slowly, more habitually, and more evenly. Precisely in this connection the sophisticated character of metropolitan psychic life becomes understandable—as over against small-town life, which rests more upon deeply felt and emotional relationships. These latter are rooted in the more unconscious layers of the psyche and grow most readily in the steady rhythm of uninterrupted habituations. The intellect, however, has its locus in the transparent, conscious, higher layers of the psyche; it is the most adaptable of our inner forces. In order to accommodate to change and to the contrast of phenomena, the intellect does not require any shocks and inner upheavals; it is only through such upheavals that the more conservative mind could accommodate to the metropolitan rhythm of events. Thus the metropolitan type of man—which, of course, exists in a thousand individual variants—develops an organ protecting him against the threatening currents and discrepancies of his external environment which would uproot him. He reacts with his head instead of his heart. In this an increased awareness assumes the psychic prerogative. Metropolitan life, thus, underlies a heightened awareness and a predominance of intelligence in metropolitan man. The reaction to metropolitan phenomena is shifted to that organ which is least sensitive and quite remote from the depth of the personality. Intellectuality is thus seen to preserve subjective life against the overwhelming power of metropolitan life, and intellectuality branches out in many directions and is integrated with numerous discrete phenomena.

The metropolis has always been the seat of the money economy. Here the multiplicity and concentration of economic exchange gives an importance to the means of exchange which the scantiness of rural commerce would not have allowed. Money economy and the dominance of the intellect are intrinsically connected. They share a matter-of-fact attitude in dealing with men and with things; and, in this attitude, a formal justice is often coupled with an inconsiderate hardness. The intellectually sophisticated person is indifferent to all genuine individuality, because relationships and reactions result from it which cannot be exhausted with logical operations. In the same manner, the individuality of phenomena is not commensurate with the pecuniary principle. Money is concerned only with what is common to all: it asks for the exchange value, it reduces all quality and individuality to the question: How much? All intimate emotional relations between persons are founded in their individuality, whereas in rational relations man is reckoned with like a number, like an element which is in itself indifferent. Only the objective measurable achievement is of interest. Thus metropolitan man reckons with his merchants and customers, his domestic servants and often even with persons with whom he is obliged to have social intercourse. These features of intellectuality contrast with the nature of the small circle in which the inevitable knowledge of individuality as inevitably produces a warmer tone of behavior, a behavior which is beyond a mere objective balancing of service and return. In the sphere of the economic psychology of the small group it is of importance that under primitive conditions production serves the customer who orders the goods, so that the producer and the consumer are acquainted. The modern metropolis, however, is supplied almost entirely by production for the market, that is, for entirely unknown purchasers who never personally enter the producer's actual field of vision. Through this anonymity the interests of each party acquire an unmerciful matter-of-factness, and the intellectually calculating economic egoisms of both parties need not fear any deflection because of the imponderables of personal relationships. The money economy dominates the metropolis; it has displaced the last survivals of domestic production and the direct barter of goods; it minimizes, from day to day, the amount of work ordered by customers. The matter-of-fact attitude is obviously so intimately interrelated with the money economy, which is dominant in the metropolis, that nobody can say whether the intellectualistic mentality first promoted the money economy or whether the latter determined the former. The metropolitan way of life is certainly the most fertile soil for this reciprocity, a point which I shall document merely by citing the dictum of the most eminent English constitutional historian: throughout the whole course of English history, London has never acted as England's heart but often as England's intellect and always as her moneybag!

In certain seemingly insignificant traits, which lie upon the surface of life, the same psychic currents characteristically unite. Modern mind has become more and more calculating. The calculative exactness of practical life which the money economy has brought about corresponds to the ideal of natural science: to transform the world into an arithmetic problem, to fix every part of the world by mathematical formulas. Only money economy has filled the days of so many people with weighing, calculating, with numerical determinations, with a reduction of qualitative values to quantitative ones. Through the calculative nature of money a new precision, a certainty in the definition of identities and differences, an unambiguousness in agreements and arrangements has been brought about in the relations of life elements—just as externally this precision has been effected by the universal diffusion of pocket watches. However, the conditions of metropolitan life are at once cause and effect of this trait. The relationships and affairs of the typical metropolitan usually are so varied and complex that without the strictest punctuality in promises and services the whole structure would break down into an inextricable chaos. Above all, this necessity is brought about by the aggregation of so many people with such differentiated interests, who must integrate their relations and activities into a highly complex organism. If all clocks and watches in Berlin would suddenly go wrong in different ways, even if only by one hour, all economic life and communication of the city would be disrupted for a long time. In addition an apparently mere external factor, long distances, would make all waiting and broken appointments result in an ill-afforded waste of time. Thus, the technique of metropolitan life is unimaginable without the most punctual integration of all activities and mutual relations into a stable and impersonal time schedule. Here again the general conclusions of this entire task of reflection become obvious, namely, that from each point on the surface of existence—however closely attached to the surface alone—one may drop a sounding into the depth of the psyche so that all the most banal externalities of life finally are connected with the ultimate decisions concerning the meaning and style of life. Punctuality, calculability, exactness, are forced upon life by the complexity and extension of metropolitan existence and are not only most intimately connected with its money economy and intellectualistic character. These traits must also color the contents of life and favor the exclusion of those irrational, instinctive, sovereign traits and impulses which aim at determining the mode of life from within, instead of receiving the general and precisely schematized form of life from without. Even though sovereign types of personality, characterized by irrational impulses, are by no means impossible in the city, they are, nevertheless, opposed to typical city life. The passionate hatred of men like Ruskin and Nietzsche for the metropolis is understandable in these terms. Their natures discovered the value of life alone in the unschematized existence which cannot be defined with precision for all alike. From the same source of this hatred of the metropolis surged their hatred of money economy and of the intellectualism of modern existence.

The same factors which have thus coalesced into the exactness and minute precision of the form of life have coalesced into a structure of the highest impersonality; on the other hand, they have promoted a highly personal subjectivity. There is perhaps no psychic phenomenon which has been so unconditionally reserved to the metropolis as has the blasé attitude. The blasé attitude results first from the rapidly changing and closely compressed contrasting stimulations of the nerves. From this, the enhancement of metropolitan intellectuality, also, seems originally to stem. Therefore, stupid people who are not intellectually alive in the first place usually are not exactly blasé. A life in boundless pursuit of pleasure makes one blasé because it agitates the nerves to their strongest reactivity for such a long time that they finally cease to react at all. In the same way, through the rapidity and contradictoriness of their changes, more harmless impressions force such violent responses, tearing the nerves so brutally hither and thither that their last reserves of strength are spent; and if one remains in the same milieu they have no time to gather new strength. An incapacity thus emerges to react to new sensations with the appropriate energy. This constitutes that blasé attitude which, in fact, every metropolitan child shows when compared with children of quieter and less changeable milieus.

This physiological source of the metropolitan blasé attitude is joined by another source which flows from the money economy. The essence of the blasé attitude consists in the blunting of discrimination. This does not mean that the objects are not perceived, as in the case with the half-wit, but rather that the meaning and differing values of things, and thereby the things themselves, are experienced as insubstantial. They appear to the blasé person in an evenly flat and gray tone; no one object deserves preference over any other. This mood is the faithful subjective reflection of the completely internalized money economy. By being the equivalent to all the manifold things in one and the same way, money becomes the most frightful leveler, for money expresses all qualitative differences of things in terms of "how much?" Money, with all its colorlessness and indifference, becomes the common denominator of all values; irreparably it hollows out the core of things, their individuality, their specific value, and their incomparability. All things float with equal specific gravity in the constantly moving stream of money. All things lie on the same level and differ from one another only in the size of the area which they cover. In the individual case this coloration, or rather discoloration, of things through their money equivalence may be unnoticeably minute. However, through the relations of the rich to the objects to be had for money, perhaps even through the total character which the mentality of the contemporary public everywhere imparts to these objects, the exclusively pecuniary evaluation of objects has become quite considerable. The large cities, the main seats of the money exchange, bring the purchasability of things to the fore much more impressively than do smaller localities. That is why cities are also the genuine locale of the blasé attitude. In the blasé attitude the concentration of men and things stimulates the nervous system of the individual to its highest achievement so that it attains its peak. Through the mere quantitative intensification of the same conditioning factors this achievement is transformed into its opposite and appears in the peculiar adjustment of the blasé attitude. In this phenomenon the nerves find in the refusal to react to their stimulation the last possibility of accommodating to the contents and forms of metropolitan life. The self-preservation of certain personalities is bought at the price of devaluating the whole objective world, a devaluation which in the end unavoidably drags one's own personality down into a feeling of the same worthlessness.

Whereas the subject of this form of existence has to come to terms with it entirely for himself, his self-preservation in the face of the large city demands from him a no less negative behavior of a social nature. This mental attitude of metropolitans toward one another we may designate, from a formal point of view, as reserve. If so many inner reactions were responses to the continuous external contacts with innumerable people as are those in the small town, where one knows almost everybody one meets and where one has a positive relation to almost everyone, one would be completely atomized internally and come to an unimaginable psychic state. Partly this psychological fact, partly the right to distrust which men have in the face of the touch-and-go elements of metropolitan life, necessitates our reserve. As a result of this reserve we frequently do not even know by sight those who have been our neighbors for years. And it is this reserve which in the eyes of the small-town people makes us appear to be cold and heartless. Indeed, if I do not deceive myself, the inner aspect of this outer reserve is not only indifference but, more often than we are aware, it is a slight aversion, a mutual strangeness and repulsion, which will break into hatred and fight at the moment of a closer contact, however caused. The whole inner organization of such an extensive communicative life rests upon an extremely varied hierarchy of sympathies, indifferences, and aversions of the briefest as well as of the most permanent nature. The sphere of indifference in this hierarchy is not as large as might appear on the surface. Our psychic activity still responds to almost every impression of somebody else with a somewhat distinct feeling. The unconscious, fluid, and changing character of this impression seems to result in a state of indifference. Actually this indifference would be just as unnatural as the diffusion of indiscriminate mutual suggestion would be unbearable. From both these typical dangers of the metropolis, indifference and indiscriminate suggestibility, antipathy protects us. A latent antipathy and the preparatory stage of practical antagonism effect the distance and aversions without which this mode of life could not at all be led. The extent and the mixture of this style of life, the rhythm of its emergence and disappearance, the forms in which it is satisfied—all these, with the unifying motives in the narrower sense, form the inseparable whole of the metropolitan style of life. What appears in the metropolitan style of life directly as dissociation is in reality only one of its elemental forms of socialization.

This reserve with its overtone of hidden aversion appears in turn as the form or the cloak of a more general mental phenomenon of the metropolis: it grants to the individual a kind and an amount of personal freedom which has no analogy whatsoever under other conditions. The metropolis goes back to one of the large developmental tendencies of social life as such, to one of the few tendencies for which an approximately universal formula can be discovered. The earliest phase of social formations found in historical as well as in contemporary social structures is this: a relatively small circle firmly closed against neighboring, strange, or in some way antagonistic circles. However, this circle is closely coherent and allows its individual members only a narrow field for the development of unique qualities and free, self-responsible movements. Political and kinship groups, parties and religious associations, begin in this way. The self-preservation of very young associations requires the establishment of strict boundaries and a centripetal unity. Therefore they cannot allow the individual freedom and unique inner and outer development. From this stage social development proceeds at once in two different, yet corresponding, directions. To the extent to which the group grows—numerically, spatially, in significance and in content of life—to the same degree the group's direct, inner unity loosens, and the rigidity of the original demarcation against others is softened through mutual relations and connections. At the same time, the individual gains freedom of movement, far beyond the first jealous delimitation. The individual also gains a specific individuality to which the division of labor in the enlarged group gives both occasion and necessity. The state and Christianity, guilds, and political parties, and innumerable other groups have developed according to this formula, however much, of course, the special conditions and forces of the respective groups have modified the general scheme. This scheme seems to me distinctly recognizable also in the evolution of individuality within urban life. The small-town life in antiquity and in the Middle Ages set barriers against movement and relations of the individual toward the outside, and it set up barriers against individual independence and differentiation within the individual self. These barriers were such that under them modern man could not have breathed. Even today a metropolitan man who is placed in a small town feels a restriction similar, at least, in kind. The smaller the circle which forms our milieu is, and the more restricted those relations to others are which dissolve the boundaries of the individual, the more anxiously the circle guards the achievements, the conduct of life, and the outlook of the individual, and the more readily a quantitative and qualitative specialization would break up the framework of the whole little circle.

The City

Robert E. Park

The city is something more than a congeries of individual men and of social conveniences—streets, buildings, electric lights, tramways, and telephones; something more, also, than a mere constellation of institutions and administrative devices—courts, hospitals, schools, police, and civil functionaries of various sorts. The city is, rather, a state of mind, a body of customs and traditions, and of the organized attitudes and sentiments that inhere in these customs and are transmitted with this tradition. The city is not, in other words, merely a physical mechanism and an artificial construction. It is involved in the vital processes of the people who compose it; it is a product of nature, and particularly of human nature.

The city has, as Oswald Spengler has pointed out, its own culture: "What his house is to the peasant, the city is to civilized man. As the house has its household gods, so has the city its protecting Deity, its local saint. The city also, like the peasant's hut, has its roots in the soil."[1]

The city has been studied, in recent times, from the point of view of its geography, and still more recently from the point of view of its ecology. There are forces at work

Reprinted from *The American Journal of Sociology* (March, 1916), pp. 577–612. Used by permission of The University of Chicago Press. Copyright, 1916, by the University of Chicago.

within the limits of the urban community—within the limits of any natural area of human habitation, in fact—which tend to bring about an orderly and typical grouping of its population and institutions. The science which seeks to isolate these factors and to describe the typical constellations of persons and institutions which the co-operation of these forces produces is what we call human, as distinguished from plant and animal, ecology.

Transportation and communication, tramways and telephones, newspapers and advertising, steel construction and elevators—all things, in fact, which tend to bring about at once a greater mobility and a greater concentration of the urban populations—are primary factors in the ecological organization of the city.

The city is not, however, merely a geographical and ecological unit; it is at the same time an economic unit. The economic organization of the city is based on the division of labor. The multiplication of occupations and professions within the limits of the urban population is one of the most striking and least understood aspects of modern city life. From this point of view, we may, if we choose, think of the city, that is to say, the place and the people, with all the machinery and administrative devices that go with them, as organically related; a kind of psychophysical mechanism in and through which private and political interests find not merely a collective but a corporate expression.

Much of what we ordinarily regard as the city—its charters, formal organization, buildings, street railways, and so forth—is, or seems to be, mere artifact. But these things in themselves are utilities, adventitious devices which become part of the living city only when, and in so far as, through use and wont they connect themselves,

like a tool in the hand of man, with the vital forces resident
in individuals and in the community.

The city is, finally, the natural habitat of civilized man.
It is for that reason a cultural area characterized by its
own peculiar cultural type: "It is a quite certain, but never
fully recognized, fact," says Spengler, "that all great cultures are city-born. The outstanding man of the second
generation is a city-building animal. This is the actual criterion of world history, as distinguished from the history
of mankind; world history is the history of city men. Nations, governments, politics, and religions—all rest on the
basic phenomenon of human existence, the city."[2]

Great cities have always been the melting pots of races
and of cultures. Out of the vivid and subtle interactions of
which they have been the centers, there have come the
newer breeds and the newer social types. The great cities
of the United States, for example, have drawn from the
isolation of their native villages great masses of the rural
populations of Europe and America. Under the shock of
the new contacts the latent energies of these primitive
peoples have been released, and the subtler processes of
interaction have brought into existence not merely vocational, but temperamental, types.

Transportation and communication have effected,
among many other silent but far-reaching changes, what
I have called the "mobilization of the individual man."
They have multiplied the opportunities of the individual
man for contact and for association with his fellows, but
they have made these contacts and associations more transitory and less stable. A very large part of the populations
of great cities, including those who make their homes in
tenements and apartment houses, live much as people do
in some great hotel, meeting but not knowing one another.

The effect of this is to substitute fortuitous and casual relationship for the more intimate and permanent associations of the smaller community.

Under these circumstances the individual's status is determined to a considerable degree by conventional signs—by fashion and "front"—and the art of life is largely reduced to skating on thin surfaces and a scrupulous study of style and manners.

Not only transportation and communication, but the segregation of the urban population, tend to facilitate the mobility of the individual man. The processes of segregation establish moral distances which make the city a mosaic of little worlds which touch but do not interpenetrate. This makes it possible for individuals to pass quickly and easily from one moral milieu to another, and encourages the fascinating but dangerous experiment of living at the same time in several different contiguous, but otherwise widely separated, worlds. All this tends to give to city life a superficial and adventitious character; it tends to complicate social relationships and to produce new and divergent individual types. It introduces, at the same time, an element of chance and adventure which adds to the stimulus of city life and gives it, for young and fresh nerves, a peculiar attractiveness. The lure of great cities is perhaps a consequence of stimulations which act directly upon the reflexes. As a type of human behavior it may be explained, like the attraction of the flame for the moth, as a sort of tropism.

The attraction of the metropolis is due in part, however, to the fact that in the long run every individual finds somewhere among the varied manifestations of city life the sort of environment in which he expands and feels at ease; finds, in short, the moral climate in which his peculiar nature obtains the stimulations that bring his innate dispositions to full and free expression. It is, I suspect, motives of this kind which have their basis, not in interest nor even in sentiment, but in something more fundamental and primitive which draw many, if not most, of the young men and young women from the security of their homes in the country into the big, booming confusion and excitement of city life. In a small community it is the normal man, the man without eccentricity or genius, who seems most likely to succeed. The small community often tolerates eccentricity. The city, on the contrary, rewards it. Neither the criminal, the defective, nor the genius has the same opportunity to develop his innate disposition in a small town that he invariably finds in a great city.

Fifty years ago every village had one or two eccentric characters who were treated ordinarily with a benevolent toleration, but who were regarded meanwhile as impracticable and queer. These exceptional individuals lived an isolated existence, cut off by their very eccentricities, whether of genius or of defect, from genuinely intimate intercourse with their fellows. If they had the making of criminals, the restraints and inhibitions of the small community rendered them harmless. If they had the stuff of genius in them, they remained sterile for lack of appreciation or opportunity. Mark Twain's story of Pudd'nhead Wilson is a description of one such obscure and unappreciated genius. It is not so true as it was that

> Full many a flower is born to blush unseen,
> And waste its fragrance on the desert air.

Gray wrote the "Elegy in a Country Churchyard" before the rise of the modern metropolis.

In the city many of these divergent types now find a

milieu in which, for good or for ill, their dispositions and talents parturiate and bear fruit.

Because of the opportunity it offers, particularly to the exceptional and abnormal types of man, a great city tends to spread out and lay bare to the public view in a massive manner all the human characters and traits which are ordinarily obscured and suppressed in smaller communities. The city, in short, shows the good and evil in human nature in excess. It is this fact, perhaps, more than any other, which justifies the view that would make of the city a laboratory or clinic in which human nature and social processes may be conveniently and profitably studied.

CHAPTER II

RELIGIOUS CONCEPTIONS
OF THE CITY

INTRODUCTION

*There are many approaches to an understanding of the
city. We can begin with a map and see it through the eyes
of a social planner or a sight-seer. We can get acquainted
with its slums and its derelicts and see the city as a story
of human tragedy. We can examine the life of a street gang
or the structure of a corporation and see the city as a series
of separate worlds, each with its own rules and its own in-
centives. We can chart the character of ethnic and religious groups, of institutions and political parties, and see a
mass of conflicting pressure groups.*

*This chapter adds still another approach. Here the at-
tempt is to see the city with essentially religious spectacles.
What is the place of religion in urban life? Is it one among
many social institutions? Does it have a unique place in the
social life and physical structure of a community? What
kind of influence does city life have upon man's spirituality?*

*The selections in this chapter focus on the religious con-
ceptions of the city. They argue that religion not merely
reflects urban culture, but should seek to shape and challenge it. Augustine's notion of the two cities and the transformation of the city of man into the City of God appears
as a dominant motif.*

*"The Children of God in the City of Man" is by J. V.
Langmead Casserley, formerly of General Theological
Seminary in New York City and now teaching theology at*

Seabury-Western Theological Seminary. This article explores the impact of such urban characteristics as mass apathy, class differences, and loneliness upon the urbanite's spiritual life. The ethical ambivalence of the city means that religion has a prophetic task to interpret the city of man and the City of God.

Peter L. Berger, Associate Professor of Social Ethics at Hartford Theological Seminary, discusses the problem of "Community in Modern Urban Society." Pointing to the anti-urban animus and illusions of ruralistic nostalgia shared so widely in Protestant circles, he argues that the city is the locale of freedom. Indeed, urban society provides new and significant opportunities for community. Protestantism's failure to relate to the city stems from its agrarian understanding of community in an urban setting. Since a community of eros *pervades all forms of social life, it is a mistake to identify* agapé *with rural society and* eros *with urban life.*

John Osman, Vice-President of The Fund for Adult Education, states that "A City Is a Civilization" if it possesses a complete cultural system and has a concern for the realms of the mind and spirit. Great cities often express this concern in their architectural form and visual image. The cultural functions performed by a city and its capacity for regeneration and spiritual growth make it a civilization. Religion's task is to transform urban culture into a civilization.

Roger Lloyd, Canon of Winchester, England, contributes a provocative article in "The City as a Christian Symbol." He suggests that the idea of the holy city is one of man's most profound literary images. This idea yearns for physical embodiment, for the City to become a city of stone and bricks. The church whose members are related in a transformed and enriching relationship to one another in Christ is an expression of the City as a Christian symbol.

The Children of God
in the City of Man

J. V. Langmead Casserley

In inspecting any particular form of human culture, we may legitimately ask these questions: What kind of influence does it have upon man's spirituality? Toward what types of spiritual behavior does it ordinarily constrain him? In discussing such questions, certain aspects of city life will be considered from the viewpoint of their impact upon the spirituality of the citizens: the apathy of metropolitical man, the clash of the classes, loneliness, and the ethical ambivalence of the great city.

The forces operative in city life are so numerous that no single one can exercise an absolutely determining influence upon the conduct of any particular person. The fundamental error of all forms of philosophical determinism is the failure to perceive that in a world which includes so many possible sources of determinism, no single one of them can ever be expected to succeed. This fact indicates the possibility and defines the area of our limited freedom.

THE CHARACTERISTIC APATHY OF METROPOLITICAL MAN

Apathy refers to a certain inability to do justice to the depth and subtlety of experience. It pertains to an erosion

Reprinted in abridged form from *The Metropolis in Modern Life*, edited by Robert M. Fisher (Doubleday & Co., Inc., 1955), pp. 334–343. Used by permission of The Trustees of Columbia University in the City of New York.

of the inward capacity for response which may cause men to become indifferent to many aspects of their existence. The great city's most obvious way of dealing with this lethargy is to administer heavy doses of stimulants. Hence the tendency toward the sensational in entertainment and even in the reporting of news.

This tendency does not necessarily imply that city life is itself dramatic or vivid. The vogue of sensationally advertised sexuality, for instance, does not mean that the citizens themselves are oversexed. Nor does the popularity of freak religious sects or sensational preachers indicate that city dwellers are overreligious. In fact, they point in the opposite direction. Only the jaded appetite and the worn-out mechanism of response require repeated doses of artificial stimulation.

Widespread apathy is closely connected with the impersonality of city life. Although large numbers of persons crowd together in cities, the relationships which bind them together are mostly impersonal. City life emphasizes the so-called secondary associations which require and evoke no recognition of personality and individuality in the other man. Normally, we neither see nor know the people who supply our food, manufacture our clothes, or heat our apartments. To us, most of them are functional agents— almost things—rather than known and trusted persons.

The depersonalizing of the personal is the essence of apathy. City life compels us to do it every day, and we are unaware of its implications because we hardly notice what we are doing. Yet of all kinds of experience, personal intercourse is the most profound and exacting. It calls for subtle and discriminating powers of response. In a technological civilization, we are apt to discover that it is easier to manipulate things than to deal with other human beings.

This is perhaps the source of the impatience of so many popular political judgments. If only men were things, we tell ourselves, we could deal with these problems much more adequately than we do. So we become impatient with people because their personality seems to obstruct our own ends. It is little wonder that techniques of social administration which treat people as things constantly break down.

Under such circumstances our philosophical, religious, and ethical systems tend to concentrate upon serene and indifferent patterns of cosmic and spiritual processes rather than upon substantial personal being. Materialism and scientific humanism stress the self-sufficient, the admirable and adorable, the indifference of a remote and self-enclosed reality to human needs and aspirations. Reality is too perfect or complete to concern itself with people like us.

Nevertheless, reality's indifference may be venerated as the hallmark of its self-sufficiency and perfection. Many nineteenth-century materialists characteristically held a profoundly religious attitude toward the material universe. The contemplation of its serene processes evoked an admiration akin to the spirit of worship.

Nor is this attitude by any means dead. It is easy to understand that a mode of life which tempts us to become indifferent to the personality of each other will also make us indifferent to personality in our religious and philosophical thinking. This indifference to personality in life, religion, and philosophy is the quintessence of apathy.

The Clash of the Classes in the Great City

What differences exist among the typical spiritual attitudes of the different classes within a city? To answer this question we must first consider how the various classes are composed.

Important Classes in a Modern City

The important classes in a modern city include the bourgeoisie, the working class, the new middle class, the professional class, and the intelligentsia.

The *old middle class* or *bourgeoisie* comprehends all persons engaged in commerce and finance on a more or less independent and responsible basis.

The *working class* includes the great mass of wage earners, manual laborers, factory employees, and others engaged on a wage basis in distribution and retail trade. The individual members of this class are the weakest and poorest members of the community. But the class itself is usually better organized than the others, and normally consists of the majority of the voters. Where trade unionism is widespread, the working class is usually a well-disciplined, cohesive group. Thus the organization of the least powerful people tends to be the most powerful class. In many great cities, it is the politically dominant class. Yet its mentality is profoundly influenced by the resentments and inferiority complexes characteristic of people who know themselves to be weak.

The *new middle class, salaried bureaucracy* is becoming rapidly more numerous. In the most highly developed cities, it may eventually outnumber the working class. It consists of white-collar wage earners engaged in administrative occupations in government, banking, insurance, industry, commerce, and many other bureaucratic enterprises. In the great city of the twentieth century, everything becomes more and more bureaucratic, even the church. Where a working class succeeds in imposing socialist institutions on the great city, bureaucracy develops even more rapidly and the working class is quickly extinguished.

This new middle class is affiliated economically to the working class, because its members derive their living from the sale of their labor at more or less fixed rates. But in conscious aspiration, it tends to affiliate itself to the old middle class, a social phenomenon which Marx failed to foresee. Although the city may create socialistic institutions for itself, the powerful bureaucracy which results from urban socialism is the supreme bulwark against any subsequent transition to communism. This bureaucracy is best understood and defined as the new middle class of the twentieth century.

The *professional class* consists of lawyers, doctors, teachers, clergymen, and so on. It is closely related to the old and new middle classes. But it is distinguished from them by its different mode of livelihood and generally by a more specialized education and higher intelligence. Culturally speaking, this is perhaps the most important group in contemporary urban society and its influence is out of proportion to its numbers.

The *intelligentsia* to some extent overlaps with the professions, but its members are found in all social situations. It is characterized by a certain detachment from class feeling and class loyalty—except perhaps when it occurs in the working classes—and by a prevailingly critical attitude toward existing institutions.

Among the various classes, the greatest contrast prevails between the outlook of the old middle class and that of the working class. Originally, the old middle class created our cities which are monuments to its achievement and relics of its enterprise. Today the old middle class is not numerous; more and more of its members reside outside the city whose activities are the source of their wealth. Their place has been taken by the working class which now tends to dominate the cities established by the old middle class.

The Spirituality of the Various Classes

Formerly an enterprising revolutionary force, the old middle class has become predominantly conservative and even reactionary. Its ideal is the self-sufficient man who creates his own fortune, shoulders his own burdens, pays his own way, and minds his own business. At its best, the bourgeois ethic was essentially a system of personal responsibility. It sometimes added a laudable stress on philanthropy—a conception of *richesse oblige* which echoed the older aristocratic idea of *noblesse oblige*. Our country is full of imposing monuments testifying to the extent to which this kind of obligation was fulfilled.

The prevailing spirituality of the old middle class was individualistic and ethical in tone. On the whole, it was not a churchly spirituality, because this group had only a relatively superficial sense of human solidarity. For it, the human race was simply a large number of separate men and women holding more or less contractual and ethical relationships with each other. Humanity was not a real entity in its own right with profound metaphysical significance. The most characteristic forms of such a spirituality are an ethical and dutiful agnosticism or an evangelical Christianity which seeks individual salvation.

The spirituality of the working class is very different. Its experience teaches that man is weak and powerless to help himself. The historic struggle of the working class emphasized the importance of mutual loyalty and mass solidarity. Hence the tendency for mass political movements of the working class emphasized the importance of mutual loyalty and mass solidarity. Hence the tendency for mass political movements of the working class to take an anti-democratic direction if political leadership is not wise.

Working-class life provides all the requisites for a strong and highly unified church life. In most places, however, the working class has long been remote from the kind of presentation of Christianity so well suited to the needs of the old middle class. As a result, the working class is often detached from any kind of church life whatever. One of the tragic accidents of history is that the working class appears so often to be comparatively irreligious. Perhaps this attitude is due to the fact that much of the leadership of the early working-class movements was provided by middle-class intelligentsia in revolt against its own origins. On the whole, the more churchly forms of Christianity make the most appeal to the religious instincts of the working class.

But the new middle class is most characteristic of our own time. More than any other group, it probably provides the existentialist philosophers with their theme and the psychoanalysts with their patients. It is the class which experiences individualism as loneliness and spiritual dereliction; the class for which freedom too often becomes a dreadful burden of responsibility; the class which tends to live "inauthentically" and in "bad faith" because its social aspirations consort so poorly with the social and economic basis of its existence. Perched precariously between old middle-class and contemporary working-class attitudes, it has a tremendous opportunity to work out a great synthesis of the precious elements which are to be found in both of these forms of spirituality. At the moment, it has achieved no more than an uneasy and unintegrated compromise between the two.

The new middle class presents the churches with their most formidable challenge. If the churches can give this new class the necessary leadership and illumination, it can reconcile the individualistic spirituality of the old middle class with the collective spirituality of the working class. Then the churches will not only reintegrate the new middle class and the city life of the future, they will also reintegrate themselves.

Any truly authentic Christian spirituality must necessarily overcome the tension between an individualist spirituality and a collectivist spirituality in a mighty synthesis which reconciles them both in a religion which is personal and at the same time churchly. Only in the context of this spirituality can the new middle class discover the principle of its own integrity and the foundation of its own solidarity.

Loneliness in the Great City

Urban loneliness is quite distinct from the solitude of the rural worker. It is a loneliness which a man experiences only among a large number of his fellow men in the knowledge that he is not related to any of them on a genuinely personal level. In fact, urban loneliness is not really solitude at all. It is the experience of being outside of rather than away from a group. As such, it is the by-product of the city's tendency to substitute propinquity for community and to expand the range of its associations only on the secondary level.

Many secular and religious urban activities are devoted to alleviating this sense of loneliness. Churches and religious organizations are often valued as community centers where people can become acquainted. Yet the primary purpose of an urban spirituality, and the work of the church in urban areas, cannot be to give back to men what urban life takes away from them. For the replacement of what is lost is not sufficient to consecrate what we have. The real task of spirituality and religion is to consecrate and exalt the values of city life. Spirituality and religion must find some way of giving ultimate meaning to city life by transforming its activities so that they can be dedicated to the greater glory of God.

The Ethical Ambivalence of the Great City

The best and the worst things happen in cities. The metropolis is a center of culture as well as a home of uncultivated masses whose debased standards present a constant threat to our culture. It is the source of law and order and the headquarters of crime; a religious and ecclesiastical center and a place of indifference and impiety. The great city lives in a perpetual state of paradox. In the Bible, side by side we find images like Sodom, Gomorrah, and Babylon on the one hand and Zion and the New Jerusalem on the other.

All great cultural and spiritual achievement finds its center and focus in the city. Christianity established its first hold among urban populations in the great cities of the Roman Empire. The word "pagan"—originally meaning "rustic"— bears witness to the difficulty which Christianity experienced in subsequently establishing itself in the countryside.

The city, therefore, offers the most vivid contrast between good and evil, truth and falsehood, beauty and ugliness, and religion and superstition. The city is Armageddon and its denizens are they upon whom the ends of the world are come. To live in a great city is to stand on the edge of the world and participate in the ultimate combat.

In such a context, some people are subjected to the basic antinomies of human experience more sharply than elsewhere. For this reason, the characteristic urban form of religious leadership is prophetic. The gentle pastor, caring for his people, seems to belong naturally to a rural rather than an urban setting. Only the prophetic witness shows the response of vigorous religious forces to the challenge of urbanism. "It cannot be that a prophet should perish out of Jerusalem." The Word of God must be spoken in the great city even though the activity and its consequences may destroy the man who speaks it. The Curé d'Ars for the village; Jeremiah for the city.

The first task of the prophetic form of spirituality is to explain to the people the mystery of where they are and what is happening to them in terms which give these things an ultimate significance. The prophet must interpret city life as epic drama. For him, there are always two cities: the City of God and the city of man. The responsibility of choosing repeatedly between them means that city life is in perpetual spiritual crisis.

But if the prophet sharpens the antagonisms of the city by defining and interpreting them more clearly, he also softens them. He declares war with one breath and then speaks peace with the next. For this prophetic spirituality knows that the conflict within the city is actually the conflict within each citizen. It realizes that any permissible hatred and rejection of what we find in others is at the same time a hatred and rejection of something that we find in ourselves. Thus the great ringing affirmation of the providence of God and his imperative call for personal and social righteousness prepares men for the battle. Then the great healing and wounding concept of original sin reminds us that the victory to be won if the city of man becomes the City of God is the victory of God over all the citizens and not the ephemeral triumph of one particular group of citizens over another.

In the city, whenever men's consciousness of the distinction between good and evil is more lucid than profound, the citizens rise up against each other in wrath and denunciation. This is so because we first learn to recognize sin by discovering it in other people. But once we learn, through the response which our spirituality makes to the ministry of our prophets, to apprehend the distinction between good and evil so profoundly that lucidity itself is inadequate, then we repent together in dust and ashes. For we do not properly recognize the reality of sin and experience its tragedy until we have discovered it in ourselves.

Community
in Modern Urban Society

Peter L. Berger

The term "community" conjures up specific associations. The most common association will be identification of the term with Ferdinand Toennies' *Gemeinschaft*, that is, a social structure in which, by contrast with *Gesellschaft*, people relate to each other in profound, "holistic" ways. This association can easily be translated into terms more common to American sociology by saying that in a *Gemeinschaft* social relationships occur mainly in "primary groups," while in a *Gesellschaft* they occur mainly in "secondary groups." Thus the typical family in Western civilization represents *Gemeinschaft*, while the typical business office represents *Gesellschaft*.

Toennies' concepts have been very useful in a great variety of sociological investigations, such as studies of socialization, of bureaucracy, of the social processes of industry, and many others. All these studies tend toward the general conclusion that, following the industrial revolution, our Western civilization has enormously enlarged its *Gesellschaft* sector, while *Gemeinschaft* has shrunk correspondingly. At the same time, in response to what are undoubtedly deep drives of human nature, new forms of *Gemeinschaft* continually spring up in the midst of the *Gesellschaft* structures. This has been most dramatically

Reprinted in abridged form from *Lutheran World* (Summer, 1960). Used by permission of the author and the publisher.

illustrated in the famous Western Electric experiments as expounded by Elton Mayo and as incorporated into the ideology of "human relations." The contemporary "family renascence" is another important expression of the drive for *Gemeinschaft* in an age that forces people to live most of their lives in large, impersonal, bureaucratically organized structures.

It is these sociological complexes which underlie the popular slogan of "mass society," a slogan which began as an attempt to grasp conceptually what is happening, but which today has taken on an almost demonic connotation. Even in very sober discussions the term and its application is shot through with the implication that modern urban society is like Gomorrah to a Jerusalem of pre-industrial *Gemeinschaft*. This is true of Ortega y Gasset and of David Riesman, though less so of the latter. It is even true at least of the early studies of urbanization in America, the work of the so-called "Chicago School" of urban sociology. In a recent address Truman Douglass aptly quoted a short poem of Ogden Nash as expressing beautifully the attitude especially of Protestant Americans to the modern metropolis. The poem, referring to the Bronx in New York City, states succinctly:

> The Bronx?
> No Thonx!

It is quite possible to approach modern urban society with a different animus. The work of Georg Simmel can serve as a healthy corrective to this kind of bucolic nostalgia, especially Simmel's discussion of the metropolis as the social habitat of freedom. It is interesting in this connection that the anti-urban animus is mainly an attitude of the city dwellers themselves. Rural people continue to view the city and its mass society as the place of freedom, opportunity, and personal expansiveness. This, of course, is why the exodus from the countryside into the city continues throughout Western civilization. From the viewpoint of sociological analysis it is not difficult to decide which of the two attitudes, that of the city dwellers dreaming of the country and that of the country dwellers dreaming of the city, is closer to reality. Certainly there are many illusions about "urbanity" glittering into the Podunks of our nation. But the illusions of the ruralistic nostalgia are by far the greater ones. Simmel put his finger on the crucial point. The city is the locale of freedom. And it is precisely because of its "mass" character that this is so. It might be added that this is not a peculiarity of modern times, but was even true in classical and preclassical times. Only within a *Gesellschaft* can personal freedom develop to its fullest potentialities. The *Gemeinschaft* is, indeed, the locale of deep roots, belonging, and loyalties. At the same time it is the locale of thwarted development, of pervasive conservatism, of gossip as a potent mechanism of social control over all parts of the individual's life. Needless to say, this is not to deny the novel threats to personal freedom brought about by mass organization and mass communications. However, these problems cannot even be faced realistically as long as we continue to view urban society as an incarnation of evil.

We would contend that, contrary to prevailing prejudices, modern urban society provides quite new and highly significant opportunities for community. In this setting the individual is freed from many of the traditional bondages. He can find his own community, a community that will express his freedom, his individual interests, even his eccentricities. We would suggest that the viewpoint that "community" and "mass society" are contradictory terms ought to be rejected.

This sociological analysis impinges on the churches as much as on other social institutions. Not least because in the churches there exists a particularly strong anti-urban animus, both in Europe and in America. In view of the singular inability of the churches, especially the Protestant ones, to adapt themselves intellectually and practically to the changes brought about by the industrial revolution, this is quite understandable. The animus here is easily evocative of pictures. We see before us a peaceful village, the houses grouped around the church spire, evening calm, farmers returning from the fields in friendly conversation, greeted eagerly by wife and children. The counterimage to this pastoral idyll would be a picture of the New York subway in the afternoon rush hour. The implication then is again that the village scene is somehow more Christian than that of the counterimage.

We need not here dig into the theological implications of these conceptions. May it suffice again to quote Truman Douglass, who aptly points out that the notion that one is closer to God on the hills than in the city goes back in a straight line to the Baalim, the venerable rustic enemies of the God of Israel. What is more important at the moment is that the concepts of community which our churches attempt to preserve in modern society are frequently agrarian concepts totally out of place in the urban situation. As a result, the real problems are not perceived and the churches fail to face up to the immense challenges of the city. The American church sociologist, H. Paul Douglass, has analyzed this throughout his lifework. The over-all sociological category to describe the process is that of "cultural lag." It is well expressed by the guilt feelings of the urban housewife, guilty because she does not have "neighborly" relations with the people living next door in her huge apartment house, but who not only feels no guilt about, but is quite unaware of, the desperate problems of the slum down the block. Perhaps the epitome of this naïveté was expressed by Billy Graham, shocked to the core of his charismatic self by the amorous goings-on in the public parks of London, commenting on the "moral purity" he found by comparison in the cities of the Soviet Union. Evidently such an attitude completely distorts the real question as to what Christian community ought to be in modern society. Whatever answer we may come up with, Christian community is certainly *not* the establishment of agrarian enclaves within urban culture. There is no reason, other than that of personal taste, why Christians cannot welcome the possibilities of highly individuated community that modern society has to offer.

A very different train of thought can be started in our minds if we associate the term "community" with its cognates in the Bible and in church history—*kahal, koinōnia, ekklēsia, communio sanctorum*—or even *ecclesiola, collegium pietatis, Gemeinschaft* not in the sense of Toennies but of, say, the Swabian Pietists. We can, of course, easily veer off at this point into ecclesiological doctrine. But we can also stop short of this and attempt to relate this perspective to the sociological analysis just left behind. We might say quite simply that "community" in this perspective is concerned with finding social forms in which *agapē* can express itself. We can then ask whether "community," in the sociological sense outlined above, is likely to do this. At this point our uneasiness as Christians becomes acute. For we come to the realization that "community" in all its possible social manifestations will be a community of *eros*, as much in modern society as in the closely knit, traditionally integrated village of the past. Our Christian concern, however, is not to offset one type of "erotic" community against another one. The community we seek is the community of *agapē*. It can be seen in passing here that the ruralistic image of community, in so far as it understands itself as Christian, can be theologically criticized as confusing *erōs* and *agapē*.

Let it be said quickly that this is not a peculiarly modern problem. It sets in as soon as there begins the process which Max Weber called "routinization" in a religious movement. The ideal-typical situation in terms of the sociology of religion is the transition from sect to church. The close community of believers, visible in the nascent stage of the movement, now becomes dissipated in the large structures of ecclesiastical organization. In the development of the Christian religion the uneasiness becomes all the sharper because *agapē*, in any empirically meaningful sense, appears an impossibility within the "catholicity" of ecclesiastical organization. The appearance, again and again in church history, of various forms of an *ecclesiola in ecclesia*, not to mention a variety of sectarian schisms, can partially be interpreted as the effort to rediscover social forms in which *agapē* could be empirically expressed.

With this we come to an important sociological insight. If we can imagine *agapē* as a principle underlying empirical communities, we will have to imagine these communities as radically different from the normal social forms, not only in modern but in any society. We could even formulate this insight more sharply. *Agapē* as a principle is destructive of community as empirically available. Nor, indeed, should this surprise us theologically. We are, of course, dealing here with what Reinhold Niebuhr calls the "impossible possibility" of realizing Christian ethics in the world.

A City Is a Civilization

John Osman

A city is a civilization.

Such a civilization need not be ideal. A city cannot be perfect. Probably it will be a mature city. Necessarily it must be a complete city.

It is not sufficient for a city to provide services for its people. Mere largeness does not count. Business and industry with consequent economic prosperity are not enough. Even good government cannot build a civilization alone. It needs the works of many hands. But the complete city is concerned with the realms of the mind and spirit. People, by nature, tend to gather into urban communities. But these communities do not naturally become cities.

A true city is a civilization in itself.

Ancient Athens stands for something beyond itself. It signifies the very concept of excellence. Its history proclaims a unique achievement in civic affairs. From the time of the Romans until today men have been united in their admiration of this ancient city.

Why has so much of the world for so long a time looked upon Athens as the perfect city? Is it not because of the image that Athens evokes in the mind? Many of the ideas and the institutions which are regnant in our lives today

Reprinted in abridged form from *The City Church* (January-February, 1958), pp. 2–5. Used by permission of the author and the Department of the Urban Church, National Council of Churches.

had their genesis in the theater of Athenian life and thought. Amenities must have been meager indeed for many Athenians. But it is the visual image of the Acropolis crowned by the Parthenon presiding in such majesty and serenity over the city that makes its marks on the minds of men.

Dominant yet not dominating, Athena, the civic deity signified in the Parthenon, suffused the life of Athens with a quality of things spiritual. The plays of Aeschylus reveal how Athena provided a civic conscience. All of life was lived under the aspect of civic theology. Religion was built into the culture. It transformed the culture into a civilization.

Athens is perfect as the Parthenon is perfection and all life is related to it and draws from it. Religion is in the culture. Religion is not outside the culture. Religion is not set against the culture.

Is Athens the portrait of a city as it should be? Clearly it is a city ruled by the mind and spirit. It is a civilization. Athens is a city ordered by the highest reaches of its civilization—its civic theology.

But Fustel de Coulanges in the classic study of *The Ancient City* demonstrates how Christianity destroyed this city. And, as Christianity broke up the idols and wrecked the shrines of the civic deities of the ancient cities, it shattered the civic institutions which had been built upon this theology.

Christianity destroyed Athens. Paul of Tarsus in his address to the Athenians on Mars Hill dramatizes the manner in which Christianity destroyed civic deities. Indeed the journeys of Paul among the ancient cities of the Mediterranean were directed toward this end.

Yet civic theology was restored for a time in the cities

which emerged in western Europe after the advent of Christianity. The cityscape was again dominated by the manifestation of man's spiritual quest. The Cathedrals of Orvieto and of Chartres and of Canterbury, like the Parthenon, signify the rule of theology in civic affairs. The social structure of the medieval city was simple. It was divided into either Dominican or Franciscan. The church was the community. The community was a church. Religion saturated life. All behavior became acts of piety. All vocations were in service of religion. Religion was in the culture. The culture was transmuted into a civilization.

This is as it should be. Athens and the Parthenon. Chartres and its Cathedral. Here are represented the highest aspects of man's civic life. Here are symbolized his spiritual aspirations. Here are the places which provide for his spiritual growth. It is proper that the Temple and the Cathedral should be the prevailing forms against the skylines of man's towns and cities. Old Trinity Church at the entrance to Wall Street and Saint Patrick's Cathedral set against Rockefeller Plaza are parables of the ways of men in cities. It is desirable that these sacramentals of his religion should be the background against which he lives and plays and works and thinks and prays day by day.

We admire the perfection of Athens. We wonder at the unity of the medieval city. We have a nostalgia for the serenity of the New England village. Perhaps it is because the visual and the conceptual images of these cities and towns are, in our minds, ordered by these signs of the spirit. There is no such order in the modern city. All coherence is gone. Relentless forces have brought about a change.

The spiritual is no longer sovereign in the cityscape. Neither is the spiritual paramount in the life of the people.

A civic culture is emerging in America. It is not a civilization. The task of religion is to transform this culture into a civilization.

The logic of America is relentless. The logic of the pre-industrial eighteenth century was the rural agrarian society of Thomas Jefferson. The logic of Victorian England's industrialization, railroads, and steamships was Birmingham and Manchester. The logic of nineteenth-century United States was Pittsburgh and Chicago. The logic of twentieth-century United States is not only the Detroit that produces the automobile but the Los Angeles and the Dallas that are, in turn, the products of it. The logic of America is the city.

Urbanization is changing our character, modifying our culture, and transforming our institutions. Among these institutions are the church and the synagogue. *Religion today is challenged to create an urban civilization.* It is a task for religion. The task should not be abdicated. Religion has abandoned the city and left its redemption to business and industry. Only religion can redeem. Only religion can regenerate our cities by making them a place for spiritual growth. Business and industry are finding a way to replace the *market.* But how is the *altar* restored to a whole urban region—to the new city? Surely, the same forces that had a part in the formation of the city must play their part in its transformation, but the tasks are different and make insistent demands upon corporation and church alike.

Urban life today represents a break with the past. It is distinct. It has a new orientation. Urban life today takes place in the large city. We need to think in larger concepts. We cannot restore an ancient tradition. We cannot use a civic tradition out of the nineteenth century. We cannot use the urban ways of even the first half of the twentieth century. The shift from rural to urban America today engages new forces with new functions.

We are moving into a new phase of civic culture. A vast civic system of tentacular bodies is sprawling over this continent with the urban concentrations pushing toward the edges of it—along the Atlantic seaboard—around the Great Lakes—following the Gulf of Mexico—having a rebirth in the Mississippi Valley—appearing in the Southwest and dramatically transforming California.

Nothing would be more unfortunate than to see in the total urbanization of the United States today a simple continuation of the process of preceding years. New forces are giving shape to the cities that are performing new functions. New concepts will have to be created to work with them.

The logic of America is one vast city. How do we avoid this ruthless logic of urbanization? One way is to transform our large urban communities into a system of civic civilizations. Each urban region could possess its own civilization. How do we make a civilization out of an urban region? How do we transform it from an *urbs* to a *civitas?* The logic of America is the city, but we do not have good cities. The reason urban life is so unsatisfactory is because cities are incomplete. Urban centers are undefined. They have no limits. They leave life incomplete, frustrated, and fragmented.

The ancient city was complete. It had a visual wholeness. It had a total set of institutions. It was a simple city but it provided a total experience of life.

What is a city? What makes for the difference between an *urbs* and a *civitas?* What distinguishes between an urban agglomeration and a true city? What is the nature of the city?

The city possesses a complete cultural system. It is a total cultural entity. But cities can have a culture without being a civilization. New York is a civilization. San Francisco is a civilization. Hartford is a civilization. Charleston, South Carolina, is a civilization. There are few true cities in the United States. Cities that are complete civilizations.

But what is the *measure?* What makes for the total cultural system that creates a city? Pausanias, a Greek traveler of the second century A.D. and a commentator on the cities of his time, described the *polis* as having as its essential units a *temple* to the civic deity, a *gymnasium* where the young men gathered to talk philosophy, a *theater* where the people learned of the civic tradition, an *agora* where civic debates took place and destinies were determined, and an *aqueduct with fountains* which provided the city with its supply of water. Any community which had these five elements was, according to Pausanias, a city. These parts were adequate to provide a complete experience in civic life.

What are some of the criteria by which we measure cityness? What are the elements that give character to the city? Since, by its nature, *a city* "educates" we expect it to have a total program of education to provide for the continuing intellectual growth of its citizens. *A city* will have inspired creative activities in the arts which embody the unique aspects of its own personality. Perhaps we can expect an individualized style of architecture to give character to *a city*. Some *cities* have their own language. The complete *city* reflects a diversified financial, commercial, and industrial spectrum. *A city* thinks enough of its history to build a town hall worthy of it. *A city* is expected to have a symbol which reflects its heritage such as Mount Vernon Place in Baltimore or Monument Avenue in Richmond, Virginia. *The complete city* will furnish itself for gracious

domestic living, for to live in the city means interior living. A *city* sustains a variety of vocations that enables
every man to fulfill his aspirations. Again, *the city* must
have "a place" for the cultivation of the mind and the
spirit.

City living has become a ritual. There are many roles for
men and women in its theater of life. It is a highly differentiated society. This urban and industrial society tends
to treat men as interchangeable parts.

Man is a part. He is an electrician, an engineer, an executive. Whether he lives in Albuquerque, Los Angeles, or
Pittsburgh, he plays the same role in the same manner.
Modern mobility makes this an easy thing. But there is
danger in such interchangeableness. The interchangeable
man becomes the standardized man. The civic system tends
to standardize. Cities appear to be interchangeable too.

So the city needs a complete rationale of culture, for the
complete city will be a unique city and create a unique
personality—integrated and civilized—the complete man.
This is the new urbanity. The urbane man. Not suburbane.
Not exurbane.

The city is not a jungle stalked by terror although cities
have jungles. The city is not a laboratory for social research
although much can be learned from it. The city is not a
prison filled with hatred although it can be indifferent.
The city is not a place of dehumanization although parts
of it are inhumane. Cities are not uncivilized although
there are barbarians who live in cities. Some of the barbarians did not come from cities. Some are emigrants from
town and country.

There is evil in the city, but the city is not inherently
bad. Men make the city. It will be just as imperfect as men
are imperfect. To be a complete city does not mean to be

a perfect city. It does not need to be an ideal city. But the complete city will approximate the ideal city, and its citizens will be complete to the extent that the city is complete.

It is not that the city has an intrinsic value. Neither does the downtown. Nor the suburbs. It is the civic function that is important. It is the function that the city performs that makes it a civilization.

What is the function of the city? It is through the city that the individual realizes his citizenship. The city provides the civilization that enables man to be a complete human being. By means of the city a man can realize himself in community with other men. There is a division of responsibilities. The city has a responsibility to be a city. The people of a place have the responsibility to make it a civilization. The city is not only a creator—it is a creation.

If it is complete and whole, it is generating or creating a civilization. A great city is capable of a renaissance. It has the capacity to renew itself from generation to generation. Cities pass through cycles. There is a law of obsolescence. Slums, disease, delinquency, and ugliness have to go. They are symptoms of civic immorality. You redeem a city from these sins because of a sense of humanity.

Every so often it becomes socially necessary, functionally desirable, politically possible, and economically feasible to renew parts of cities.

We seek the regeneration of cities for no other reason than to civilize. Our purpose is to restore its humanity. You make a city humane by saturating it with the humanities. There is no other way. It is according to the nature of the city "to civilize."

Now to make a complete city there must be a place to inspire spiritual growth. There are two ways of seeing a city. Two ways of living in it. Two scales for it. One is the town-scale. Here many parish churches serve their neighborhood communities. The other is the city-scale. The whole city needs one place for spiritual growth that is commensurate with the size of the city.

It should be a place where the religious life which is now lying around in pieces is unified and brought together—a religious center. There are civic centers, medical centers, educational centers, and shopping centers. Why not a center for religion? Such a center is a sanctuary for a whole city. Yet it stands in judgment over the city. It is *prophetic* as well as *sacramental*.

Social welfare, recreation, episodic revivals are not enough. The city needs "a meeting place" which provides for the sustained cultivation of the spirit. An architecture of religion would incarnate the visible arts and be both a refuge from, and a rebuttal to, the *market place*. Performances in the action arts would, through radio and television, reach into a whole urban region. Such a center could help to restore a sense of community to the large city. Such a center would be the focus of the thrust for civic individuality. For it is in the realms of the spirit that our greatest differences appear. It is in the reaches of the spirit that our truest freedom lies. Such a center should reflect the "genius" of the city.

Look at Manhattan. There is the Rockefeller Plaza for business and industry, the Lincoln Square Center for the Performing Arts, the United Nations Plaza for the ecumenical movement in world affairs, and the Columbia University-city for academic activities. A center for religion would help to give proportion to the city. Like the Parthenon it would be the spiritual symbol of the city. As the Cathedral, it would embody the aspirations of the people. An architecture of theology would once more mark the cityscape. Architectural visibility gives definition to the purposes of these "places."

The American city is a place of cultural and, particularly, religious pluralism. Perhaps the *Three Chapels* of the Roman Catholic, Protestant, and Jewish traditions on the campus of Brandeis University are an archetype of what might be raised up on a grand scale to dramatize the place of religion in the life of our cities. Differentiation would be preserved. Traditions would be continued. But the consequent center would be large enough to have meaning against the scale of the city. The city is not and never will be again a center of religion but religion can be given a central place in the city. Through such a center the Hebraic tradition and the Christian tradition can be restored to their places in the life and thought of the people and made the essence of the city.

Such a religious center might be the repository of the spirit of a city and its people. It would serve the function of creating a humane community. It will stand in protest against the ugly, the degrading, and the mean. And the spiritual growth which it nurtures will work a transformation in the city's ways. Religion once served a civic function. Perhaps religion again can set up the higher rules for citizenship in a city—as it restores the civic virtues to their proper place.

The City as a Christian Symbol

Roger Lloyd

If the effectiveness of an image can be estimated by the weight and variety of literary comment which it excites through the ages, then one of the most effective texts in all the Bible must be the triumphant phrase in the Apocalypse of St. John: "I saw the holy city, new Jerusalem, coming down from God out of heaven, prepared as a bride adorned for her husband." Ever since that was first said, comment upon it, analysis of its meaning, and the provision of a host of subsidiary images has been almost ceaseless. Thus, the idea of the City (with a capital C) has been and is one which is capable of provoking a tremendous emotional response. Clearly, then, it is likely still to be one of the most powerful symbols under which the Christian religion can be presented.

This ideal City on earth, which St. John announced, and which men so different as Marcus Aurelius, Walt Whitman, and Wordsworth, and so many others have all passionately hailed—what exactly is it? To this question, of all modern writers, Charles Williams has done most to provide an answer. He returned to it again and again, and suggested many answers (the texts are in his posthumous book, *The Image of the City*), but they all seem to boil down to one. The City is an orderly arrangement of puri-

Reprinted from *The Manchester Guardian Weekly* (May 14, 1959), p. 6. Used by permission of the author and the publisher.

fied relationships between persons, and it exists, and is there to be verified, wherever the relationships of nature have paid the price of becoming relationships in Christ. On that single and profound clue he hung a host of rich commentary on the nature of these relationships, on the process which brings them to become relationships in Christ, on the character of the "Infamy" which always opposes the process. Altogether, he has greatly helped all our thought about this richest of symbols.

Yet, perhaps as a consequence of his early death, he left his explorations of the City at the point where all his disciples were eagerly hungering for more. For the sacramental principle which runs through all life seems to demand that there should be a City of bricks to be a field of verification of the City of human and divine relationships. All history witnesses to the potency of ideas in their own right, and the idea of the City has an endless power to stir imagination. But no idea achieves the fullness of its power until it can be seen, here and there, in action; and the City requires a city. Williams once said that the single line in English poetry which gave the best picture of the City on its human side came at the beginning of Shakespeare's *Henry V,* and was "Singing masons building roofs of gold." He was feeling after the need to verify ideas in bricks.

The symbol of the City, then, becomes the great church which broods over the whole life of the community it serves, and offers it to God to be stamped with the seal of the changed and enriched relationships in Christ. The great church need not be the large church. For many reasons, cathedrals seem to have the best chance of symbolizing the City, even of actually becoming it, but any church in town or village where worship is enriching relationships is an effective symbol of the City, and a field for the verification of its beauty and its power. Such a church must be filled by "high and low, rich and poor, one with another." It must exhibit the outward signs of being lovingly cared for and tended. Through its worship and its teaching, it must so bring the best out of all its people that they become "members one of another," and grow to be so precious to one another that no one ever lacks help when needed or is left to rejoice miserly and alone. The hurt of one is the hurt of all, and the joy of one is the joy of all. Such are relationships in Christ, and they are the first business and the deepest function of the church which tries to be the City. Where that beatitude is won and obtains, all the rest of evangelism can be left to look after itself, for it will then find its own channels, and these will always be the most effective channels. The City is so great a thing that it can never be easy for parish church or cathedral to serve it, but the characteristic service lies in this field of transformed and enriched relationships. We can always try, provided that we know what our aims and purposes are.

CHAPTER III

THE CHURCH
FACES THE CHANGING CITY

INTRODUCTION

The growth of the metropolis to its dominant place in American culture has ushered in radical changes—in the face of the landscape, in the pace of life, in the mobility of population, in the ordering of society. In the midst of these changes stand urban churches.

What happens to the church when its familiar environment begins to shift? Is it true that "As goes the neighborhood, so goes the church"? Are churches in transitional areas faced with the alternative of death or adaptation and renewal? Churches that have fled from changing neighborhoods have been aptly described as drowning in an ocean of humanity while hunting for men.

The articles in this chapter trace the patterns of institutional response as the church faces the changing city. In "The Job the Protestants Shirk," Truman B. Douglass provides a provocative analysis of the reasons for Protestantism's failure to penetrate the culture of modern cities. The author, who is Executive Vice-President of the Board of Home Missions of the Congregational Christian Churches, traces the sources of alienation to Protestantism's anti-urban bias, its rural origins, and its middle-class moralistic orientation. The city is a mirror of the "mingled splendor and tragedy of man's existence."

H. Paul Douglass was one of the pioneer leaders of religious research in America and Director of the Institute of Social and Religious Research from 1921 until it ended operations in 1934. "Ways of Meeting Urban Change" succinctly outlines the alternative ways in which churches respond to the changing city. Douglass identifies nine modes of response, ranging from avoidance methods to compromise and readaptation.

Samuel C. Kincheloe, now Professor Emeritus of Sociology of Religion at Chicago Theological Seminary, has profoundly influenced scores of contemporary urban church researchers. "Major Reactions of City Churches" is one of several suggestive articles Kincheloe has written on the behavior patterns of urban churches. Church reactions are couched in terms of an institutional struggle for survival.

The H. Paul Douglass and Kincheloe articles, although written in the 1920's, still bear a familiar ring. They offer background working materials that contemporary students of the urban church cannot overlook when they come to devise a typology of city churches, or when they consider the interaction of the church as a social institution with its urban environment.

As Kincheloe observed, "Few people seem to know how to administer religion in the apartment and hotel areas of the city." Protestantism can scarcely succeed in urban areas without an effective ministry to apartment dwellers. Hence the importance of "Church Work in Apartment Areas," by Frederick A. Shippey. The author is Professor of Sociology of Religion at Drew Theological School. Apartment living is a pervasive aspect of urban residency. Ten characteristics of apartment dwellers are depicted to provide a framework for understanding the requirements and challenges of church work in apartment areas.

The Job the Protestants Shirk

Truman B. Douglass

The typical attitude of America's Protestant churches toward cities is neatly summarized in Ogden Nash's poem:

> The Bronx?
> No Thonx!

In almost direct proportion to the increasing importance of the city in American culture has been the withdrawal—both physical and spiritual—of the Protestant Church.

Today one out of every eight people in the United States lives in a city of more than a million inhabitants; four out of every ten, in cities of at least 25,000; and another four, within twenty-five miles of such cities. And from these cities spring the ideas, tastes, standards, folkways, and value judgments which—through radio, television, and the mass-circulation magazines—become those of the whole nation. If Protestantism gives up the city, it virtually gives , up America. Yet that is precisely what it has been doing.

In Cleveland, from 1920 to 1950 the membership of five Protestant denominations (American Baptists, Congregational Christian, Methodist, Presbyterian U.S.A., and Protestant Episcopal) declined by more than 13 per cent. In Detroit, fifty-three churches deserted the heart of the city

Reprinted in abridged form from "The Job the Protestants Shirk," *Harper's Magazine* (November, 1958), pp. 45–49. Used by permission of the author.

within a fifteen-year period. The statistics of one denomination's history in New York City shows that during
the past century in Manhattan and the Bronx it has dis-
solved fifty-four churches and merged forty-two with other
congregations. The record of one of the oldest and most
consistently middle-of-the-road Protestant bodies is probably typical: during the quarter century from 1930 to
1955, while the nation's population was increasing by 19
per cent and its own membership by 41 per cent, the
number of churches affiliated with it in sixteen of the
major cities of the United States declined by 20 per cent.

One of the documents published in preparation for the
First Assembly of the World Council of Churches held in
Amsterdam in 1948 declared: "There are three great areas
of our world which the churches have not really penetrated. They are: Hinduism, Islam, and the culture of
modern cities." In the ten years since this statement was
made, no reasons for amending it have appeared. Not only
has the church continued to give evidence of a radical inability to penetrate the culture of modern cities, it has
largely failed to take that culture seriously.

The underlying cause, I believe, is an anti-urban bias
which has become almost a point of dogma in American
Protestantism. Many leading Protestants genuinely feel
that a permanent and deadly hostility exists between urban
man and those who are loyal to the Christian faith and
ethic; that village ways of life are somehow more ac-
ceptable to God than city ways.

Biblical scholars have long appreciated the difficulty of
translating the pastoral language and symbolism of the
Bible—the shepherd figure of the Twenty-third Psalm and
the tenth chapter of St. John's Gospel, for example—into
terms that are relevant for modern town and city dwellers.
But difficult does not mean impossible. Yet although there

are large and ecclesiastically influential congregations of almost all the major denominations in all our principal cities, Protestantism's viewpoint remains stubbornly that of the village. As such it has often become entangled in the suburbs' and exurbs' desperate attempts to reclaim synthetically the virtues of village and small-town life. The effort to modernize a pastoral religion by providing it with a split-level, ranch-house façade is one of the more depressing Protestant ventures of our time.

PROTESTANT PROVINCIALISM

For myself, I hope I have attended the last of a long succession of convocations of the "holy earth" cult, where I have listened to endless sermons on the incident of Jesus weeping over Jerusalem—all with the implication that it was the city and its ways that caused him to weep. I trust I may be spared additional expositions of the text: "For the place where Jesus was crucified was nigh to the city." (I am always tempted to point out that it reads *nigh* to the city." This undoubtedly means a suburb, and I think there is a neglected parable here that is worth expounding.)

I don't want to hear any more addresses on the theme: "God made the country, man the city." The cold fact is that man has made many of the most conspicuous features of the country too. He has made them by chopping down forests, plowing earth which ought never to have been broken, exhausting soil, and bringing in migrant workers. For monuments of sheer avarice, the country can provide exhibits the city cannot hope to surpass.

The church is, of course, by nature a pilgrim community that can never be entirely at home in any settled society— the community that has "no continuing city but seeks one to come." However, it is not this which has caused the present tension between it and the metropolis. The tension has arisen because Protestantism has succumbed to a peculiar form of provincialism, which it seeks to equate in a general way with "a Christian society."

The society thus defined is the rural type in which American Protestantism won its most conspicuous success —and which it therefore regards as being peculiarly favorable to the preservation of "religious values." Will Herberg in his acute study of the sociology of religion in America, *Protestant—Catholic—Jew*, reminds us that in the nineteenth century, as a result of the revivalist movement, American Protestantism outside of the older settlements was essentially a church of the lower classes, especially on the frontier. With the subsequent economic development of the country it became "established, respectable, self-satisfied, preoccupied with itself as an institution of standing in middle-class America." As such, it tended to regard with suspicion and hostility the later immigrants who increasingly shaped the nation's urban life.

In more recent years its alienation from the life of the city has been accentuated by the rural origins and outlook of its ministry. Protestant ministers are disproportionately drawn from the smaller communities, disproportionately trained in the small colleges of the South and Midwest. A recent study of the sources of the Protestant ministry revealed that in a sampling of 1,709 ministerial students only 36 per cent came from cities of more than 250,000 population. Because of their rural and small-town origins, many ministers bring to their work in a city church a distaste for city ways—a distaste which is the more disabling because it is largely unconscious.

Facing the life of the city, the average Protestant minister's dominant emotion seems to be not the "love that casteth out fear," but the fear that excludes love. He is terrified by this vast agglomeration of human beings, by its monstrous vitality, myriad forms, restless energies, and by the impudent way in which the city, in its thrust into the future, deals with the proprieties which a polite, middle-class Protestantism identifies with a "Christian culture."

Even the ministers of outwardly successful metropolitan churches may lack any real understanding of the interior character of their community and be fundamentally hostile to its ways and values. I know eminent New York ministers who seldom touch the city in any of its most sensitive areas, where the shape and promise of the future are taking form. Their associations are mainly with people who *use* the city, vocationally and economically, but whose vital concerns are for the most part outside its life. These people collect the financial rewards the metropolis offers but detach themselves from its real life and problems. So do many ministers. They make their pastoral calls by chauffeur-driven car or taxi—never by subway, assuredly one of our most remarkable cultural institutions.

There is more serious reading on the subways of New York than in many colleges. In a twenty-minute journey one may see people reading the editorial page of *The New York Times* (a not inconsiderable curricular resource in itself); books on a wide variety of technical subjects; the classics of most of the great living literatures of the world; discussions of political and international affairs; and serious contemporary novels and plays. From the electric effect of this intellectual voltage, some of the most prominent Protestant ministers seem to be completely insulated.

MEECHING MORALISM

In its dealings with the city Protestantism also suffers from its chronic moralism. This is derived not from the

Christian ethic, but from its own rural past. For more than a thousand years the characteristic form of the church was the village church; the typical unit of church organization, the parish in the small rural community. American Protestantism's moral code still testifies more to its rural upbringing than to any profound understanding of the gospel of love and forgiveness.

This is evident in the relative gravity it assigns to particular lapses and sins. Drinking and carelessness in the observance of sexual conventions—moral divergences which, rightly or not, are considered characteristic of city life—are judged far more harshly than small-town snooping, gossip, Philistinism, and cruelty toward the nonconformist.

The most serious consequence of this moralism is that it makes church people unable to see the real nature of city life clearly and to share in its triumphs. One would expect every Christian to rejoice in the transition of a one-class city neighborhood to a multiracial, multicultural community. Instead city churches usually regard such a development as a serious setback to the Christian enterprise— by which they mean simply that it has made it harder to hew to old ways. They fail completely to appreciate the stunning accomplishment the change represents. It is only in cities that man has begun to cast off the ages-old primitive superstition that the "different" is, of necessity, something to be hated and feared. To be able to walk along Fourteenth Street in New York City or lower Market Street in San Francisco and experience an exultation of spirit at the variety of human features and tongues—and the measure of mutual acceptance evident in the passing crowd—requires a degree of Christian insight and thankfulness not often cultivated in country parishes.

It is the same with the city's other accomplishments.

Churchmen often speak disparagingly of the "anonymity" of city life. They do not recognize that this confers, when it is needed, the precious gift of privacy, without which creative work is seldom possible. There is a better chance at productive privacy in the city than in any of the well-advertised bucolic hideaways—and more genuine individuality among city dwellers than among any of the carefully labeled, self-consciously picturesque "characters" in the country.

Church people also like to attack the city as a "monument to materialism." Actually it is a protest against it. The modern metropolis demands a special kind of asceticism. The city dweller must prize some things of the spirit —art museums, music, lectures, theaters, first-hand encounters with people who are doing exciting intellectual and artistic work—enough to endure real physical hardships—crowding, dirt, noise, overburdened and inefficient transportation, scarcity of fresh air and sunlight.

Even the brash, vulgar, overaggressive manifestations of city life have a kind of beauty, if one's perceptions have not been dulled by the moralizers. Often they are expressions of the vitality of people on the way up—celebrating release from grinding want and hopelessness; tasting the freedom of making choices, even bad choices; experiencing, perhaps for the first time, the insurgent joy of doing something wasteful. This may be offensive to Calvinist presuppositions, but I think it must be beautiful to God.

To the anti-urban man the metropolis is the supreme manifestation of human pride, and many churchmen still like to refer to it as such. But in the modern city, far more vividly than anywhere else, one can see the absurdity of the sin which St. Augustine called *superbia*—the claim of man to be ultimately autonomous and self-sufficient as against the virtue of *humilitas,* the recognition of man's "creatureliness" and the final precariousness of all existence. By a curious reversal of traditional roles, the rural community now provides the only place where illusions of prideful self-sufficiency can survive.

For we know now that all cities are destructible. E. B. White concludes his prose love song, "Here Is New York," with this reminder:

All dwellers in cities must live with the stubborn fact of annihilation. . . . The city at last perfectly illustrates both the universal dilemma and the general solution, this riddle in steel and stone is at once the perfect target and the perfect demonstration of nonviolence, of racial brotherhood, this lofty target scraping the skies and meeting the destroying planes halfway, home of all people and all nations, capital of everything, housing the deliberations by which the planes are to be stayed and their errand forestalled.

And just as the city exemplifies "the universal dilemma and the general solution," so it also enunciates with greater clarity than any other social artifact that understanding of man's life which is set forth in the Christian faith. In its buildings which seem so mighty but are actually so vulnerable; in the decisiveness of the issues it deals with; in the thin line between blessing and curse it offers—between, for example, the benison of privacy and the despair of loneliness—we are permitted to see, more clearly than anywhere else, the mingled splendor and tragedy of man's existence.

The Bible tells the story of many cities. There are Sodom, Gomorrah, Babylon—symbols of dissolution and disaster. But there are also Jerusalem, Zion, the New Jerusalem—affirmations of the indefeasible hope that the city of man may yet become the City of our God.

Ways of Meeting Urban Change

H. Paul Douglass

The control of an institution by its environment, either immediate or remote is, of course, not absolute. Between successful devices for avoiding the natural consequences of adverse environmental change and the complete acceptance of the changed situation as furnishing the clue to what the church ought to be and do institutionally, there intervenes a considerable series of compromises and transitional stages. Some of the typical patterns of behavior in which these principal ways of meeting the situation work out are the following:

AVOIDANCE METHODS

(1) The most radical means of avoiding the consequence of adverse environmental changes is for a church to break away from them and remove to another location where the environment is favorable.

(2) Short of the radical solution of removal, the most common means of escape from adverse environmental pressure is through the selective operation of the church in the original vicinity; that is to say, by its appeal to a limited number of people of a given sort. Under conditions

Reprinted in abridged form from *The Church in the Changing City*, by H. Paul Douglass (George H. Doran Company, 1927), pp. xvii-xxii. Used by permission of Harper & Brothers.

of average density of population in large cities, the constituency of a church, even the largest, is scarcely more than a drop in the bucket. Cities in their most characteristic areas present extreme contrasts in social fortunes on the part of people living within a short distance of one another. Very wealthy people, for example, may inhabit little patches of territory, like islands in a sea of less favored society. Mixed areas do not go entirely bad, nor do bad areas go bad all at once. Hence, in many cases, at least for a time, a church can get along fairly well in its original location in spite of extreme environmental change, if it confines itself to its own kind of people and avoids the particular areas of extremest disadvantage where its own kind is not present.

(3) Another method of avoiding the consequences of environmental change is to retain the church site but to substitute a new and distinctly urban basis of human association for that of the original church group based on proximity. The church plant continues to stand where it was, but the church as identified by the residences of its members almost entirely removes itself from the locality of the church building. It then proceeds to draw a new following from a distance. This means that the mobility of urban population and the accessibility of central institutions have been adopted as the principles of religious fellowship. The dominance of this principle in cities is such that, in the most extreme cases, a church with almost no constituents living anywhere near it becomes so related to the city as a whole that its site continues to be as good as or even better than before, from the standpoint of prestige and general institutional advantage. The centralizing forces of the city, the habitual use of its downtown focus by all its inhabitants, irrespective of their place of resi-

dence, and a certain downtown-mindedness in city populations, all find religious expression in the vogue and popularity of the great central church. Such churches have become virtually independent of environment as defined by the character of population and by the social conditions prevailing in the immediate vicinity of their plants.

METHODS OF COMPROMISE

Very often a city affords no room for a church to move and still retain its former prestige and advantage. Yet changed local conditions may be too acute for the selective cultivation of its old field to be fully successful. A church may cherish a strong conviction of its mission on its historic site or possess a particularly sensitive conscience as to its duty to the people of its locality—yet without seeing how to make either the main clue to policy or to connect them with practical resources of church support. Such a church naturally seeks some method of compromise.

(4) The most obvious method is to go a step or two in the direction of adaptation, continuing to work selectively along old lines and developing distant constituencies which urban mobility and the prestige of central locations make available. Such churches also add to the old program distinct though generally limited ministries designed expressly to meet the needs of the dominant populations now living in the vicinity. The methods through which compromising churches seek to serve such populations are varied. But almost always they are obviously in the nature of appendages to their established activities and they not infrequently appear somewhat foreign and incongruous.

Churches thus develop separate programs for dual and
even for triple constituencies.

TRANSITIONAL CASES

(5) At any given moment churches whose circumstances are not unduly exigent and whose tentative adaptations are taking several directions at once will be hard to
characterize. They retain a selective hold on the locality,
while, at the same time, they are building up a city-wide
prestige and drawing on widely scattered constitutents
which they hope to continue to hold as the local supply
diminishes. They may also maintain limited ministries to
distinct populations. Such transitional situations are naturally more numerous than "pure" cases.

READAPTATION

Coming down now to that stratum of churches whose
institutional characters unmistakably bear the marks of the
effort to fit themselves consciously to environment and
which proclaim the purpose of their ministries in terms
of adaptation, one still finds striking variation of method.

(6) New activities and elements of program, which
begin as few and loosely attached additions to the old
institution, may become so numerous, well established, and
successful that they end in characterizing the church in
the public mind and ultimately in dominating its own
thought and purpose. Thus, without intending to be
changed, the church gets profoundly changed. This fact
being accomplished, it ultimately makes a conscious policy
of what had already become a habit.

(7) Again, there may be a revolutionary shift in the

emphasis of the church's life, but one that is not primarily localized in expression, that does not completely register itself in the reshaping of method, and that does not reflect the special needs of any particular neighborhood. This is to say that a church's adaptation may be to certain broad aspects of urban life as a whole.

The typical situations that reveal the urban spirit in its most characteristic experiences are often nonlocalized. Thus, industrial struggle as it goes on continuously for the control of public opinion, the generalized issues between organized labor and organized employers; or, equally, the struggle for racial equities shown in the multiform issues of assimilation and adjustment, find organized expression on a city-wide and nation-wide scale and virtually divide civilization into opposing camps. Highly developed group interests create their central forums for generalized utterance. This identifies them quite as definitely as they are revealed in specific controversies. They evolve general movements, appoint official leaders, maintain organs of agitation, and follow recognized voices. A church may adapt itself to urban civilization by concerning itself with such aspects of organized group interests centering in cities and without concerning itself exclusively with the social needs of any territorial neighborhood. The church, while doing distinctive community work as defined by the needs of the local neighborhood, is characterized by the fact that, on the one hand, it is making a city-wide appeal to a somewhat select supporting constituency, while, on the other, it is advocating, facilitating, and fostering the objectives and self-expression of organized labor groups. It is by these alliances that its work gets peculiar flavor, outreach, and interest.

The successful use of the foregoing methods of avoid-

ance, of compromise, or of readaptation is virtually reserved for the centrally located church. To the church in
the deteriorating residential district it is generally not open
to escape the consequences of adverse environmental
change by any of these means.

(8) What, then, can the residential church do in similar
circumstances? Unless it moves, it can die or become
negligible (continuing for a time to live but at a "poor
dying" rate); or it can adapt itself radically to the immediate environment. This acceptance of the situation involves, on the whole, the complete inner transformation
and modification of program and method, a characteristic
widening of program in the community-serving church to
meet the needs of a changed and often handicapped
population.

Such churches obviously must generally solve their financial problems by getting support from outside their
own fields and constituencies; and they rarely escape a
serious warping and unbalance of institutional structure.

(9) Finally, a church may have successfully grown up
with, or it may deliberately from its foundation have
chosen to enter upon and be identified with, a hard situation. These situations also almost inevitably imply that
from the first and continuously thereafter the church will
be more or less dependent upon outside financial support.
But the fact that its adaptation was complete from the
beginning frequently saves it from the one-sidedness of the
hastily readapted types.

The more highly developed of these latter types of institution have so little the character of churches and are so
much those of something besides churches that the name
"church" ceases to fit them. They consequently supplement
it with a secondary name like that of "institute." This case

17384

marks the limits of adaptation within the ecclesiastical form.

The present series of cases thus illustrates a wide range of distinct logical possibilities and probably covers most of the major directions of actual adaptation to environment exhibited by churches in large city communities. Future environmental change may make the situation of some of the cases studied still more exigent. Multitudes of other churches are still to be caught in the currents which unmake as well as remake cities. The church at least has "not here an abiding city." Its hands ought to be strengthened against adverse change by the somewhat systematic knowledge of some of the successful ways in which similar experiences have been met and by glimpses of the principles underlying them.

Major Reactions of City Churches

Samuel C. Kincheloe

The traditional church of the Protestant denominations is in the grip of changing circumstances and is struggling to make the adjustments which will permit it to live. Conditions are changing more rapidly in our great cosmopolitan cities than they are in our more stable rural communities, but circumstances are changing more rapidly at the centers of great cities than on the circumferences.

The conscious changes which churches are making are closely related to the changes which are taking place in other city institutions, including business. There is the use of the telephone, the radio, the motion picture, printed materials, and increased advertising. Churches build staffs of specialists to meet the particular demands of their situations. Techniques for securing the attention and interest of the apartment house dweller are devised. Much time and attention are given to religious education. We are beginning to hear of church clinics for those in trouble. Churches devise ways and means for their people to become acquainted. Some are daring to enter the competitive market of human fellowships. They resort to the practice of eating together. Some seek to keep their young people

Reprinted from *Religious Education*, Vol. 23 (November, 1928), pp. 868–874. Used by permission of the author and The Religious Education Association.

by the introduction of dances and other forms of recreation in an effort to demonstrate that the church is willing by all means to seek the good life here and now.

The reactions of Protestant churches in the city environment may be stated in terms of efforts on the part of the churches to survive. In Chicago these major reactions are those of downtown churches, the churches which move, federate, or die, rescue and church missions, institutional churches, Christian centers and neighborhood houses, and primitive Christian churches. Out toward the circumference of the city the historical churches still prosper. It may be said that churches do what they must do. The reactions are all the more interesting because of the fact that the church is an institution which has goals and ideals.

In the marginal areas of invasion by new groups the conditions are less favorable, the struggle is more severe, and the adaptations greater. Churches which are located either in the midst of populations favorably inclined or where the incoming population is favorably disposed toward them are able to depend upon existing religious attitudes and habits. They may then proceed according to their customs and are able to preserve their ancient traditions. In areas where the incoming immigrants are unfavorably disposed toward Protestantism the adaptations which churches are willing to make are of such nature that the institutions may even cease to be called churches. Competition may reach the stage where the adherents choose between different institutions on the basis of "physical blessing" which they receive.

Churches in the suburbs are responding to the general stress of city life, but the struggle for self-preservation does not seem so imminent. The changes which take place in a suburban church are made to suit a constituency which the church already has. The church in an area in which the population movements are unfavorable must make changes to meet the demands of a group which is outside the Protestant Church.

Among the factors which cause the reactions of struggling churches to vary are the following:

The Nature of the Incoming Groups. Similar or dissimilar racial and cultural groups make a big difference in the process of assimilation and in the way in which the churches react. Where the deteriorating community remains native American by residue or invasion of lower economic classes, the church is more likely to die a slow death or to secularize its activities. It is more likely to move if the incoming group is very different from itself, as is seen in the case of the Negroes on the south side of Chicago.

The Nature of the Church Itself. Among the factors are its liberality of attitudes or ideas of social service; its missionary spirit and world outlook; its type of physical equipment; its moneys or endowments; its membership distribution; its solidarity; its ecclesiastical organization and the willingness of the denomination to subsidize it; its location with reference to other churches and settlements, and especially with reference to transportation and visibility.

Personality Factors. Often a pastor of unusual ability may prolong the life of a church or even change its trend. The changes which a pastor advocates are, however, often in a way forced upon him by the larger situations in which he finds himself. There are members in these churches who, because of their great devotion, may hold a small group together for a long period of time, or may prevent any radical changes from being made.

The earliest churches which were founded in Chicago were located in what is now downtown. When there were only the "first churches" in the young community they reached out to its limits. As the city grew, these first churches sought to reach the entire city until other local communities came to be formed. There were then established branch or sister churches of these principal denominations to care for neighborhood groups. These neighborhood churches began to take both members and means, and there was set up a struggle between the first churches and their offspring. In some instances the offspring have grown faster than the mother church, which has had a struggle for life, or has been compelled to move and to join with churches of its own group.

There was the tendency to remain in the center and to represent the denomination in the heart of the city, and also the effort of each significant group of members to pull the church in its own direction. The consequence is that churches in such situations have difficulty in deciding where to locate when they must move. A few organizations have been able to survive in the downtown.

DOWNTOWN CHURCHES

As the city has grown, the downtown churches have been compelled to adjust themselves and to take on the characteristics of the area to which they are making adjustments. Only one congregation in the Loop owns its own church building, and this it has been able to do because it has entered the real estate business. Other religious organizations of the Loop rent the space they occupy. Undoubtedly there are different attitudes toward rented halls and theaters than to a building for which a people have made sacrifices. The church building itself becomes a symbol of the church body. The structure and furnishings of the church help to pass on the traditions and sentiments of the group.

While the three principal downtown groups are similar in emphasizing voices they do so in the same way. The Sunday Evening Club has emphasized great speakers but, like the movies, they advertise a different star every week. The club, without respect to creed, employs men and women of international reputation. "The prophetic messages of their speakers are not," says Dr. A. E. Holt, "indigenous to Chicago." The leaders of the group do not attempt to tie people to one local man and to have a Gunsaulus or a Shannon church. The club is sponsored by certain prominent Chicago business firms and individuals. The Bible talks and prayers are usually given by different local celebrities.

The First Methodist Church has a Methodist preacher. The Central Church has a liberal interdenominational Protestant Evangelical preacher, but still he is "a regular preacher" to whom people become attached. This church is in a way the elongation of his personality. It is a Gunsaulus church or a Shannon church.

There are other religious and semireligious groups which meet in the Loop, such as cults of various sorts and an occasional mission or "night church." This is not the natural habitat for the mission as is seen by a study of their distribution in Chicago. They are found in greater numbers along West Madison Street, the homeless man area. Cults which have their meeting places in the Loop usually pull their clienteles from over the city. The cult is not a neighborhood affair. National societies of healing may establish in the downtown their headquarters from which to work. Small groups which are well distributed over the city may rent halls there to advantage. Lecturers in spiritualism, numerology, and other esoteric cults who go from city to city may advertise in the Saturday and Sunday papers and use halls which are centrally located. They speak of their entrance fees as "admission donations." Many of these groups are people who have failed to get satisfaction out of Protestantism and out of life.

Religion in the downtown of Chicago has taken on the protective coloring of its area. These churches either minister to the transient or to those whom the city has made free from the bonds of the local community and the local congregation. They have become metropolitan. Plant ecologists speak of a "climax vegetation," by which they mean the vegetation which comes at the end of a series of changes and does not give way to some other form of plant life. In the great voices in the heart of the city the church seems to have the "climax religious vegetation" for that area.

The churches of the great "inner-city area" which are outside the central downtown area have a different problem of survival than do the downtown churches. Dr. Ernest Graham Guthrie, General Director of the Chicago Congregational Missionary and Extension Society, has recognized this special problem by the appointment of a committee to deal with it. For these churches he uses the descriptive phrase "the inner-city churches." Their fate often varies with the movements of racial and cultural groups, the invasion of business or manufacture, or the shifting from single homes to apartments. They may upon occasion entertain with great musical performances people from all over the city. The ministers may be well-known men. In these ways, they are behaving as a metropolitan church would behave. A spotting of their membership and even of the contacts reveals, however, that each of these churches has a definite relationship to the side of the city in which it is located. This is true even in those cases where the church is near the center of the city. While these churches have endeavored to draw from distances such as a metropolitan church would do, each one is attempting some work at least with people who have their places of residence in the immediate vicinity of the church. The downtown churches of Chicago attempt to do something for people who come into the Loop, but they recognize that the Loop is not their dwelling place.

Moving Churches

The historical churches often seek to preserve the integrity of their congregations by escaping from community changes which are unfavorable to them. Some historical American churches show a scattered distribution of membership and therefore frequently find it impossible to change location, even though the membership shifts in the same general direction. Strong racial and denominational ties often enable a congregation to relocate its building.

The historical American churches in these areas may become so weakened and disorganized that when they do move, it is only a movement of death. These churches are sometimes groups of older people whose children have grown up and moved to the suburbs. These people have become tolerant of other denominations in the city environment and have often lost their pioneering spirit. As the group becomes smaller the financial burdens for the relocation of the church become greater. Often the churches in these areas are able to sell their property to good advantage only on quite long-term payments, and this means that they do not have ready cash for a relocation. A further problem of these moving churches is the preservation of their solidarity in the face of so many occasions for disagreement. The divisions of a moving church may become so acute as to threaten its unity. Often there is a group of people in the vicinity of the church who, for financial reasons or because of sentiment, prefer to have the church remain at its old location.

FEDERATING CHURCHES

In areas of transition where once there was a prosperous Protestant community, churches may federate. These areas may have been overchurched in the beginning. Just as soon as a number of the attendants and supporters of these churches move away it becomes patent that there are too many churches in the community. It is natural, therefore, for these Protestant churches in their efforts to live, to federate. Federation may make for the preservation of the old relationship and the preservation of a membership which, unless bound by these old relationships, might drift from the church.

If they make no other adaptations, however, they may merely delay the day of death, since the same problems remain which the individual churches found in the beginning. They have not only their changing community to deal with, but also the problems of unifying the several congregations. Federation is possible because of the toleration which denominations develop toward each other. This toleration is increased because of the need of increasing the size of the congregation and of easing the financial burden. The size of other city institutions and the great mobility of urban populations demand that a church be a going concern, demand what Prof. William L. Bailey has called "a city-sized church." In areas where the population is largely Catholic or Lutheran the only hope for the old-line Protestant churches is that they be spaced with reference to their possible constituencies.

DYING CHURCHES

The church which dies in the changing community is often the historical church, the church which emphasizes the Sunday services, including preaching and church schools, young people's societies, and the mid-week service. These churches have socials, ladies' aids, men's clubs, missionary societies, organized Sunday school classes. The work is carried on by their own members for their own sake. They are "denominational" churches which gradually take an attitude of toleration of other groups. They tend to lose their zeal for their particular denomination, and therefore cease to fight back when attacked. If these churches persist in being conventional churches in changing communities, and make no adaptations, they will die as their membership dwindles.

The first observation which we have to make on these churches is in regard to the areas in which the historical American churches are dying. They have, as the maps of dead churches indicate, a socially characteristic location. The mortality is greatest in the great inner-city area. Graphs of the total Protestant membership by natural areas arranged from the downtown out to and including the suburbs on the west indicate that the graveyard of white American Protestant churches has pushed farther out as the city has grown. Even though there are factors which cause the behavior to vary from church to church, intensive case studies over a period of years reveal great similarity in the processes of decline of these institutions and give us what might be called the behavior sequence of dying churches.

INSTITUTIONAL CHURCHES

The successors of the historical church are either institutional churches, religious settlements, or missions. I shall pass over the discussions of missions and mention briefly the institutional church as the secularization or as some would prefer to say, the "socialization," of the historical church.

Maps which we have made of churches which died over a period of twenty years and of institutional churches indicate that institutional churches exist in the graveyard of the historical churches. This does not mean, however, that they get their support from the area in which they live. A plotting of the people who are served by institutional churches shows what we already know, that the people who are served live near the churches, the church members farther away, and the members of the boards of control still farther away. These churches are characterized by the emphasis upon the ministry to the social, educational, and physical needs of the people, especially the children. They go in for activities and discussion. They place an emphasis upon the equipment and paid staff. They may secure volunteer help but also employ specialists in different fields. Their activities comprise such things as gymnastics, competitive athletics, dramatics, debates, household sciences, manual training, clubs for men and women, medical clinics, or the services of visiting nurses. In general they hold the viewpoint that they are doing religious work by secular means.

A change in technique, however, does not always mean a change in attitude. The terms proselytism, evangelization, Christianization, and Americanization are terms which indicate important distinctions in the attitudes of institutional church workers. There would seem to be within the institutional church itself a great range of attitudes. This should not, however, divert our attention from the fact that in the main the institutional church tends toward the secularization of the church by the substitution of the teaching of English or the giving of instruction for citizenship, or the directing of recreation or the conducting of classes in cooking and dressmaking, for the more definite teaching of the religious life. These institutions might be arranged in the following series with reference to their attitudes toward evangelization.

1. The institutional church mission which uses all the devices of the settlement in an effort to evangelize the people to whom it ministers. These often develop a passion to convert a particular race. Their successes are measured in terms of the number of "converts" which they win.

2. The institutional church which does not think of itself as a proselyting church but rather a Christianizing and Americanizing agency. It seeks to Christianize by educational social service. There are many subtypes within this general group. The workers in these institutions speak of their results in terms of contacts and members and the building of character. They do not emphasize the preaching of the gospel. It often happens that in these institutions where it is impossible to hold preaching services, Sunday schools are conducted for the children of the neighborhood. In many instances the children are from homes whose religion is not that of their teachers, or they may come from homes where little or no interest is taken in religion.

3. A third group takes a name which indicates that it is not a church. These institutions are known as neighborhood houses, Christian centers, and religious settlements. They do not seek converts or members but to "serve the community." They work on the assumption that it is possible to live their Christianity where it is not good policy to teach it.

One of the few things left for a church to do if it wishes to maintain an organization in a region in which the traditional Protestant church cannot survive is to become an institutional church. There are in Chicago a few striking illustrations of this type.

PRIMITIVE CHRISTIAN CHURCHES

Some of the most successful churches of the city are what might be called primitive Christian churches. (The term "primitive" is used as a descriptive phrase and has no implications regarding the value of the instructions thus described.) A preliminary classification of primitive Christian churches is that of the doctrinally primitive, the emotionally primitive, and the socially primitive. The doctrinally primitive are the sects which have come in from the country. As their members have moved into the city the country people have contributed money to secure leaders and equipment for them. This is true at least of the Church of the Brethren (Dunkards). Others of these groups are the Mennonites and the Adventist groups. These have sought to preserve the pure practice and doctrine of the church. The little sectarian church can live at least for a generation because its interest is not in the "world." It does not will to have the things that certain other churches have. Its standard of living is low; its standards for the spiritual life, if not high, are strict. It may even despise the things of the world and rejoice in its weakness as a sign that it is of God. It comforts itself in the thought that God will use its weakness to show forth his power. Its present humble condition is taken as proof that someday it will be exalted. Much emphasis is placed upon the Scriptures. A leader in one of these churches said to a newcomer on Sunday morning: "No study I know is as gratifying as the study of the Bible. The study of the Bible entails effort, but it is worth it. We are a small Bible group. We need you so much. I know we can help you. You should come to our church since it is the only church founded on the Scriptures."

The emotionally primitive group is represented by the Pentecostal groups which emphasize conversion, tongue speaking, healing, and a definite knowledge of salvation. These are often highly emotional in their services. They emphasize dependence upon the Scriptures as do the doctrinally primitive. Their doctrine is authoritative and absolute. They preach and sing in a vigorous manner and attract to them people who have become tired of lukewarm churches. These churches have goals and what is called collective action. There is contagion in their enthusiasm. Some of these groups emphasize personal work and believe in "convincing" people that they should become Christians. So far as formal doctrine is concerned, the difference is very great between these groups and the radical church groups which arise in the city, but psychologically speaking they are very similar. Both have the enthusiasm of youth and the conviction that they are right and that they have something for which to live. The attitude is that of the sect as against that of the denomination.

These may be divided into two groups on the basis of whether or not they emphasize preaching or praying.

Those who preach are the extroverts who seek to take the kingdom by arguments; and those who pray, the introverts who withdraw from the world and pray that they may not become contaminated by it.

The socially primitive groups are best represented by the Salvation Army, which seeks to minister to human physical need and thus gain an entrance for the soul's salvation. Dr. Robert E. Park suggests that the adherents of these groups represent the city proletariat—those who are detached and lost and without a culture.

A spot map of the primitive Christian groups reveals the fact that they are found in greatest numbers in about a three- to six-mile area out from the heart of the city—in the area in which the old-line churches have been failing.

The adaptations vary in the different areas of the city. The "climax vegetation" for the Loop seems to be that of great voices; of the homeless man areas it is at present the rescue mission; in immigrant communities it is the institutional church, the neighborhood house, and the church mission; and in the great area on the outer margin of the immigrant groups it is, in some cases, the vigorous preaching of a gospel. In the apartment house region some outstanding personality who has something different or startling may have great success. Christian Science churches seem to do well in these areas. Few people seem to know how to administer religion in the apartment and hotel areas of the city. We need more intensive studies and experimentation in the special groups which are developing in our cities. Few people are satisfied with the reaction of Protestantism in any of these city areas.

Church Work
in Apartment Areas

Frederick A. Shippey

Protestantism can scarcely succeed in the urban environment today without an effective ministry to residents of the apartment areas. Already American cities have evolved to the point where multiple structures are an accepted and probably permanent form of housing, and however disconcerting this development may be, it thrusts itself upon religious leaders as an urgent problem which cannot be circumvented. The tremendous accumulation of population in a small area overwhelms some denominational executives and leads the naïve and inexperienced clergyman to assume that church work among apartment dwellers is easy. The exact opposite is frequently true. Obviously a ministry to the apartment area is primarily an urban church opportunity.

CHARACTERISTICS OF APARTMENT RESIDENTS

Apartment dwellers are human beings living under apartment conditions. The annoyances, disappointments, frustrations, tragedies, hopes, ambitions, and successes which characterize common humanity likewise constitute the diurnal texture of apartment life. Perhaps the most

Reprinted from *Church Work in the City*, by Frederick A. Shippey (Abingdon Press, 1952), pp. 137, 142–148. Copyright, 1952, by Pierce and Smith. Used by permission of Abingdon Press.

striking fact about this segment of urban population is residence in a multistoried building. Protestant leaders frequently overlook the fact that here are people who yearn for and require the regular ministries of the church.

However, apartment residents do possess characteristics which set them apart as a distinct urban public. Sorting processes which function in other phases of city life operate in this connection also. As a result people with common traits and viewpoints are "piled up" or grouped together. Individuals possessed of common domicile needs are attracted to a multiple type of housing. A cumulative outcome consists in the emergence of a segment of urban population which contrasts clearly with the remaining residents of the community. The city sorts its people into relatively homogeneous groups.

To be effective the Protestant clergyman must achieve an understanding of the apartment resident. Experienced leaders emphasize the importance of the ten traits briefly described below, recognizing of course that all characteristics would not necessarily be found in every apartment district. However, it is doubtful if there exists a multiple-housing area in an American city which does not possess several of the traits named. Perhaps the discussion will shed some light upon the difficult problem of ministering to apartment residents. Understanding may provide an important preliminary step toward effective action on the part of the conscientious pastor.

Economic Status. Persons of varying income and from many walks of life may take up residence in multiple-housing structures. Indeed the apartment buildings themselves represent a wide range in average rentals and in quality of accommodations. Suites rent for more than two thousand dollars per annum in some cities. Other apartments are so modestly priced that persons of subsistence income may live there. Geographical location in the urban community and size and quality of quarters are important factors related to the amount of rent paid. This would indicate a range of rentals which corresponds with the full gamut of urban incomes. One gets what he pays for in housing. Thus low rental apartments are principally located in the deteriorated sections of the city, medium rental facilities in more desirable neighborhoods, and expensive suites in exclusive territory where prestige elements and restrictions are conspicuously present. For this reason a study of the multiple-housing structures in a particular neighborhood of the urban community can reveal the approximate economic status of the residents. Such information may enable Protestant leaders to be realistic in local church work. In the field of religion all persons regardless of income level may avail themselves of the ministries of the church. The economics of Christianity are the economics of spiritual need.

Inaccessibility. Pastoral calls cannot be made with facility upon persons who live in multiple-housing structures. This is especially true of the larger apartment buildings. Not only is it difficult to gain entrance to the building, but frequently residents are not at home. The common complaint made by clergymen and laymen who do church visitation work in apartment areas is that much time is lost in trying to make contact with residents. This is a new problem in American Protestantism, for ministers are used to finding someone at home, though it may be only a child. The church's awareness of the situation has been stubbornly slow in development. Additional years will be required to hammer out a solution, and therefore local church leaders should be encouraged to make experiments.

In general the apartment resident rather enjoys the fact that he cannot be contacted too readily. The bother of solicitors and the nuisance of salesmen have thus been obviated. No one is more inaccessible in the urban community than the resident of an exclusive apartment house. However, the application is even broader, for most multiple-housing populations are hard to contact. The annoyance of not finding persons at home is a conspicuous difficulty for pastors serving any type of apartment. Urban people utilize the residence less as a place to live than do suburban and rural dwellers. Thus the minister cannot just happen by and expect to find someone in. If people cannot be contacted, they cannot be won to God.

"Come and Get Me." Although studies reveal that apartment residents are interested in religion and will respond to pastoral calls and cultivation, yet only 2 per cent of the multiple-housing residents voluntarily take the initiative in finding a church. This is a prominent characteristic of the apartment dweller. The local church is compelled to go to the residents via a program of cultivation and personal visitation. Initiative should be taken and held in providing participation opportunities in the life of the local congregation. The institution should let the apartment resident know he is wanted, needed, and will be used. In spite of the fact that findings accumulated from religious censuses reveal that most residents are interested in the church and religion, fellowship cultivation is needed to galvanize people into participation action. The church is expected to come and get them. Residents expect to be found and asked to participate, yet they will do little to hasten or facilitate the process. A city church gets the people it persistently cultivates.

Small Families. Several types of small families reside in

apartments. Here is an elderly couple whose children have
reached maturity and have established homes elsewhere.
Here is a childless older couple who choose to pass the
declining years with a maximum of comfort and a minimum of homemaking and property responsibility. Sometimes chronic illness makes apartment life a more convenient pattern of living. Here are a young husband and
wife who possess little furniture and have a limited income. For them a temporary solution of the problem is
provided by the furnished apartment. Residence in modest
quarters becomes an ad interim instrument of economy
until savings are accumulated in an amount which will
permit the purchase of a home or the rental of larger
quarters. When children are born to the couple, the com-
pactness of the apartment is further emphasized. The
growing family size compels a search for more adequate
housing elsewhere. Thus a dominant characteristic of the
apartment area is small families. Religious needs vary
according to the domicile under consideration, but all
individuals should be placed under the aegis of the Christian church.

Nonfamily Households. There are various types of nonfamily households in apartment areas. Most common is
that of bachelor girls. In rarer instances one finds bachelor
men living together. Two or more individuals will rent a
suite for light housekeeping. Such persons commonly are
found in cities where ample opportunity is afforded for employment
in the white-collar occupations. Cities which are
political capitals or which house the main offices of the
large insurance companies and kindred business enterprises attract many unmarried individuals to the community. Divorced persons and widows often take residence in
apartments. There also quasi families, that is, a
daughter or son residing with an aged parent, or sisters

sharing an apartment. Often the nonfamily household is but a temporary or transitional status.

Compact quarters and convenient facilities require a minimum of housework and furnish the added advantage of anonymity so often cherished by unmarried adults. Older persons covet the quietness and absence of confusion which are largely impossible in accommodations where many children are growing up. The relevance of religious ideals to persons living in nonfamily households must not be overlooked. Often moral standards loosen under such dwelling conditions. For this reason Protestantism should maintain a vigorous ministry in multiple-housing areas.

Preponderance of Adults. The predominant population of the apartment is adult. Approximately 80 per cent of the residents are over twenty-one years of age, and this includes persons varying widely in marital status and chronological age. Young single adults are present, especially females. Widowed and divorced persons constitute another important segment. Further, older and younger married couples reside in apartments in great numbers. Few teen-age and younger children are present except in low-cost redevelopment projects and "garden-type" facilities. Therefore a local church's fundamental relationship to apartment residents is a relationship with adults, and its ministry should be so conceived if reasonable effectiveness is to be achieved. Employment conditions, state of health, and psychological emancipation are among the factors which condition church work with adults in apartment territory. Few institutions are more competent in this field than the Christian church. Mainly it needs to mobilize its resources and experience to bear upon this unsolved urban problem.

Anonymity. Many apartment residents cherish the anonymity which is made possible under such living conditions. The person may come and go as he pleases with minimum concern for those who live about him. He may secrete himself from relatives and from unpleasant public contacts. He may live in isolation, or he may cultivate a small coterie of acquaintances. The size and personnel of his friendship circle is his own business. No one is much concerned about the next-door neighbor, who also goes and comes in his own insular way. The privilege of not being intruded upon by other people is a protection coveted by some apartment dwellers. Many have lost the art of being friendly and the skills of approaching a stranger. Privacy is wanted at almost any price. The advantages of anonymity are sought not with a conscious intent to eliminate religion from life, but rather with a desire to avoid the annoyances of gossip, of persistent salesmen, of inquisitive neighbors, and of unsavory human contacts.

Habitation in such close physical contiguity, however, provides a number of opportunities to make casual contact with other residents. In some apartment situations the women meet in the basement laundry, in walks with the dog, or as the baby is wheeled out for an airing. Confrontations occur in hallways, in elevators, in the manager's office. Where individuals find themselves *en rapport*, the relation is likely to develop into a permanent friendship. However, where a desire for isolation continues, one may reduce personal contacts to a minimum. Anonymity is secured by delimiting one's contacts with humanity. Such is the antithesis of Christianity, for the church emphasizes personal worth and social interaction. Thus a basic principle of the Christian fellowship is challenged in the apartment situation. Residents should be encouraged to explore the sanative possibilities of personal growth in religious group life. This is a task of the church.

Density of Population. No other territory in the city is more densely populated than the apartment area. Often several hundred families live in a single city block. By contrast blocks of one-family residences may average as few as twenty households. Population is often ten times more numerous in multiple-housing territory. Obviously the Protestant church adjacent to apartments is situated in a densely populated area. People in great numbers thus may reside within easy access of a neighborhood church.

Mobility. In some cities one fourth to one third of the families change residence every several years. I know a family who moved eleven times in fourteen years. Though this illustration may appear exceptional, it emphasizes the fact that population shifts do occur in the city. Mobility is particularly noticeable among apartment residents where the housing accommodations are overpriced and/or unsatisfactory in location. When buildings are substandard as is often the case in low and medium rental territory, turnover of population is a foregone conclusion. In high-grade and exclusive apartments duration of residence is much longer. This is a result, in part, of the more satisfactory pricing of accommodations in terms of value received by the tenants. Additional sources of mobility include changes in marital status, in family life, in economic circumstances, in vocation, and in domicile preference. The search for a desirable neighborhood underlies mobility.

Since population shifts are endemic to the urban environment, the church does not have an interminable period in which to cultivate apartment residents. Time is short, and cultivation should start almost immediately upon receiving the prospect's name and address. Because of the possible brevity of residence the apartment dweller should be encouraged to commence participation in the local church program before another change of residence occurs. Mobility emphasizes the importance of prompt and relevant local church action.

Port of Entry. Apartments situated in medium-priced and low rental areas frequently afford a port of entry for newcomers to the community. Strangers tend to locate in or near the central business district. Until well established economically, newcomers often procure housing which is inferior to that which they are accustomed to and thus make a temporary home while becoming acquainted with the city. Prior to the war port-of-entry areas had a relatively complete turnover of population every five years. Many families moved within a year.

Apartment areas which come under this description afford short-term housing for bachelor girls, newly married persons, and couples who have started their families. Such residents do not look upon the present housing facilities as permanent. Eventually acquaintanceship with the city and improvement of economic status prepare the erstwhile newcomers for home ownership or a change of residence to better rental property.

One would expect that in many cities because of extreme shortage of housing the rate of mobility has greatly declined. However, pastors who are serving port-of-entry territory report that they are confronted currently with problems of mobility which match prewar conditions. Effective religious work with transient apartment residents or shifting population groups may strengthen the work of the denomination in other parts of the city as well as render significant service to the persons involved. A major denomination should furnish a vigorous religious ministry to the entire urban community.

CHAPTER IV

RENEWAL
IN INNER-CITY CHURCHES

INTRODUCTION

One of the most significant developments in twentieth-century Protestantism is the renewal of inner-city churches. Traditionally known as the "graveyard of Protestant churches," the inner city is today's new frontier where there are stirrings of new life. Lessons learned here are having their repercussions in church life elsewhere.

The articles in this chapter present several case studies of renewal in the inner city.[1] These experiences are unique, as every creative response is unique, but they are not without parallels in nearly every large city in America. Above all else, they represent an attitude toward the mission of the church, a burning concern for people in the city, and a willingness to struggle in the midst of situations so unstable and variable that evaluations of present success or future survival are well-nigh impossible.

Each of the articles touches on the thorny question of whether success and failure can be evaluated in inner-city situations. This debate is indicative of the radical rethinking which engages the minds of sensitive inner-city church leaders. It is no academic question, but one that reveals something of the creative ferment that the city demands and arouses.

"Renewal in the Inner City," by Martin E. Marty, is a case study of two vital churches in Chicago's west side. This article by the Associate Editor of The Christian Century *is of particular interest because it deals with two*

125

inner-city churches that are strikingly different in background and approach. Yet each makes a significant impact upon the same neighborhood in distinctive but complementary ways.

"The Task of the Church in the Inner City" is a provocative article by David W. Barry, Executive Director of the New York City Mission Society. Reacting against a "theology of failure," Barry argues that the task of the inner-city church is to be a successful church in sociological terms. It should be a church that is indigenous to its community, and it will necessarily be a subsidized church. Rather than celebrate its failures, the inner city desperately needs churches that are "visible symbols of success."

In "'Success' and 'Failure' in Inner-City Churches," George D. Younger, minister of the Mariner's Temple Baptist Church in New York's lower East Side, takes issue with David W. Barry's thesis. Younger is highly critical of an undue emphasis on numerical success. The promise that awaits a church true to its calling is a cross rather than a crown. The church's task in the inner city, as elsewhere, involves risk and exposure.

George W. Webber, Associate Professor of Practical Theology at Union Theological Seminary and one of the founders of the East Harlem Protestant Parish, gives an appraisal of this trail-blazing venture in "EHPP: Emerging Issues." Written after a decade of experience, Webber cites these crucial issues: involvement and identification in the life of the community, the role of the professional clergy in relation to the laity, the search for new and vital forms of church life, and the question of success or failure. In the final analysis these issues confront the church not merely in the inner city but also in every community.

Renewal in the Inner City

Martin E. Marty

The exodus to the suburbs that disrupts urban church life today began on Chicago's near west side before the turn of the century. After the World's Fair of 1893, the "elite" flocked to Garfield Park, Hyde Park, Oak Park, the north shore. New people moved in. By 1895 a map of the area prepared by the Hull House staff needed sixteen colors to show the different national and racial population blocs. Each wave of immigration left its mark. Today Negroes and Latin Americans predominate in the melting-pot area from which "respectable" people long ago fled, leaving behind them churches which tower above the slums like the skyscraper façade that hides the rows of shacks in a Steinberg cartoon. Now new towers rise, marking Chicago's largest public housing projects and the world's largest medical center—developments that further confuse this microcosm of population problems.

Among the slums and towers, near the intersection of Roosevelt Road and Ashland Avenue, two institutions illustrate complementary ways in which churches are trying to serve this inner city. They offer startling contrasts. First Immanuel Lutheran Church (Missouri Synod) operates from an old, still stately edifice; it represents a conservative theological and liturgical tradition, holds close

Reprinted from *The Christian Century*, 73 (December 5, 1956), pp. 1417–1420. Used by permission of the author and the publisher.

denominational ties. Near by, West Side Christian Parish works in store-front centers and garages; it ministers in experimental fashion to the patent needs of the moment, is undenominational. The one is a paradigm of agonizing adjustment on the part of a long-established congregation; the other typifies the frontier experience of beginning all over again. Both are worth watching, and watching together, despite the meagerness of their achievement when measured against the vastness of human need around them.

Three signs grace the old church's face. "Ev. Luth. Emanuels Kirche," chipped into the sandstone exterior, indicates the linguistic intent of the builders. "First Immanuel Lutheran Church," in less durable painted metal, witnesses to the enduring mission daringly inaugurated in 1901 with a monthly evening English service after a half century of German church life. "Iglesia del Emanuel," lettered on a cardboard tacked to the door, completes the parable of transience. After decades of decline, the congregation has begun to pour fresh, creative energies into an effort to integrate seemingly disparate elements. It uses a churchly approach.

Perhaps Immanuel's ministers cast envious glances at times at the unencumbered parish around the corner. To raze the structure, demolish its traditions, make a new start—such alternatives must have seemed tempting. To create a parish for the heirs of a German tradition, for engineering apprentices, for medical personnel, for Negro and Puerto Rican neighbors, for students—that is a project with improbability written all over it.

When Pastor Ralph Moellering came from a campus pastorate to Immanuel in 1953, he was aware that the congregation five years before had voted not to "vacate." Having experienced more rapid and devastating change than any of the more than 400 other Missouri Synod churches in Chicago, it looked to the day when "undesirables" in the neighborhood would be replaced by its "own kind of people." Only a dozen of that kind remained near by; the other hundred members lived far out from the area. All hoped that the medical center and the urban renewal projects would serve as a *deus ex machina* to bring back the good old days. The old church that with its horseshoe balcony seated 1,400 people and once had 3,100 members had reached its numerical nadir. A German-language constitution, adopted in 1870, provided little guidance for 1953. Gloom for the present, nostalgia for the past, were all that were left.

AN AGING PARISH REVIVED

Today, three years later, returnees who sign the guest register ("old-time member"; "baptized here in 1895") find that the change which once swirled around the congregation now moves within it. The good old days are not returning. The medical center is indeed huge—eventually one out of four doctors throughout the world will have received at least part of his training there—but its staff is transient, or has chosen not to live in the immediate neighborhood. Urban renewal has not brought stability. Immanuel now ministers not to a dream of a future community but to the community it finds at its door.

To accomplish that ministry, severe adjustments were necessary, and considerable inventiveness has had to be used within the context of circumscribed possibilities.

The first adjustment was racial. This turned out to be not the most difficult. No wholesale transferring-out oc-

curred when the doors were opened. Still, the opening had
to be accomplished with care. Nelson Algren has described
the "soft and protean awareness of white superiority" that
characterizes the attitude toward the Negro in Chicago
as being psychologically worse than stand-up, head-on
hatred. An interracial pastorate has been helpful at Immanuel. As vicar (theological intern), Korean Takuri Tei
this year succeeded the Samuel Hoards, a Negro couple.
William Puder, the assistant pastor, has a Mexican wife—
no small asset in relations with the Spanish-speaking neighbors. Pastor Moellering's wife, who is in charge of music,
and a deaconess, Rita Sadosky, round out the full-time
staff.

Full integration of the disparate elements of the community has been the more difficult adjustment. Chicago's
west side is accustomed to speaking of "blocs," but "bloc"
does not well describe the shared fellowship of those
called in love of Christ. To achieve true communion First
Immanuel is trying to make a strong point of what would
seem to be its weakness in a changing community. The
tradition, confession, liturgy, and even institution which
could be barriers are becoming assets. Instruction, initia-
tion, and nurture in the Christian context have given members roots and strength for outreach.

The process is not complete. On a typical Sunday morning Pastor Moellering recognizes among the 200 or so worshipers a goodly number of heirs of a congregational life
that as long ago as 1857 and again in 1864 had moved before
the influx of "undesirable elements." By 1888 the church
had moved for a fourth time. If some of the heirs have remained for reasons that are inadequate, others have stayed
to share the vision which made transition possible. If some
have grumbled that the pastor does not spend enough time

with them, others have lent support. Several have trans-
ferred *into* the congregation to help out.

IN THE SUNDAY SCHOOL

Negroes predominate in the Sunday school; they represent Immanuel's fastest growing element. Many Puerto
Ricans and Mexicans, disillusioned by the cold gray environment of their new life in Chicago, have found their
way to the church to become its newest component. Assistant Pastor Puder has them as his special charge. He says he
is less involved in a counter-counter-Reformation experience than in trying to help people undergo the Reformation experience for the first time. He leads these Spanish-
speaking parishioners to see God not as fearsome but as
loving, not as judge but as Savior. Meanwhile, he maintains continuities with the ethos of the newcomers' familiar
past: he stresses liturgical worship, wears clerical garb.
All this is designed to prevent crises arising at the wrong
psychological point. Most of the Spanish-speaking worshipers are "first generation"; they cling to their old cultures. But the direction of the Spanish work is away from
separate worship toward full integration. The second generation, resenting "foreign" identification, is already prepared for that step.

Beyond all these are the unclassifiables, for the near
west side is a patchwork of diversity. Out of it all a new
life is beginning. Immanuel's Sunday school has grown
from 25 to 250; last year there were 88 baptisms—more
than in any year since 1923. Communicants number 200.
In addition to the full "normal" parish program sponsored
by the church, a social concern is manifest in Puder's "no
strings attached" English classes, in the health courses

taught by parishioners from the medical center, in the personalized clothing distributions, in the Scouting and teen-age recreation program. Moellering feels that this is but a beginning. The church is already accepted by its community; no longer is it among the "don't cares."

DISCOURAGEMENT FROM OUTSIDE

Pastor Moellering and his assistants have met more apathy and antipathy than encouragement from other pastors and from denominational boards. Dismissed as an idealist, Moellering has relied for financial support partly on interested individuals and congregations, though he engages in little formal solicitation. Lutheran Concordia Teachers College has been of great help in providing part-time staff personnel. A suburban church extends help to the Sunday school. But most of the battles have been lonely, and financial support of the multiple pastorate hangs by a thread. It has been hard for Moellering to have his racial policies discouraged. But his greatest discouragement arises from his inability to point to a date at which Immanuel can become self-supporting. Under congregational polity a possibly perpetual subsidy is unheard of, and the near west side offers little hope that the congregation in its midst can soon pull its own weight—though it somehow manages to raise two thirds of its own budget.

The creative energy poured into Immanuel has its parallels and effects beyond its own borders. Moellering's Reformation Day letter to his mission board sounds like a ninety-sixth Lutheran thesis: "The time has come that we cease to deplore the changes taking place and recognize them rather as extraordinary opportunities placed before us by God as a test of the sincerity of our Christian confession." He has begun to make a dent on the social quiet-ism once so conventional in American Lutheranism. In an article in the official Missouri Synod theological journal he has pleaded for new perspectives on the social gospel, even on Walter Rauschenbusch, the synod's old whipping boy. Though critical of Rauschenbusch's theological pre-suppositions, Moellering in his article adds perhaps auto-biographically from his own Hell's Kitchen: "Those who have encountered in an existential way most of the social evils which aroused Rauschenbusch's ire, as some Lutheran ministers have in recent years, cannot help admiring [his] heroic stand."

No Departure from Doctrine

Such insight has not led this Missouri Synod pastor to basic discontent with Lutheran theology; he would be poor game for Lutheran heresy hunters. He has criticized in Luther's terms the social gospel's practical expression, its failure to make "faith active in love." Challenging the assumption that all will go well in the inner city if only the Word is preached, he criticizes the narrow conception of "preaching the Word" which would bring about a "neat division between the physical and spiritual."

Immanuel's staff lays no claim to a blueprint for success; success is hardly dramatic in the transitional community. But the strength of its churchly approach—its historic liturgy, its confessional and theological vigor, its relatively high standards of church membership—has helped it pro-vide religious and theological roots for twentieth-century nomads. Residents of housing projects, slums, and crowded apartments share the instability and transience of the students and medical residents. Seeds blown by a wind which can hardly be of God, they are finding lodgment and germination in the church come to find them.

But in this strength is also Immanuel's admitted weakness. The diversity, dissimilarity, and disparity of the people who make up the fellowship impresses the casual visitor more than it does the pastors. That diversity, Moellering claims, is not so great as one would imagine. But the very existence of so imposing a building and institution, the "literate" standards of membership, the forms of worship which contribute to Immanuel's health also limit its effectiveness in the near west side "jungle." While he tries to remedy his own church's weakness, Moellering for the moment points to the West Side Christian Parish as an effort which at least in one respect meets a need Immanuel has not yet filled.

"If I thought that instead of being complementary we were competitive with Immanuel, I would close up and go elsewhere," says Rev. David Wright at the West Side Christian Parish's little store-front headquarters around the corner. As awed by the dimensions of human misery, loneliness, poverty, and the need for the Christian good news as is his Lutheran colleague, Wright cannot conceive of either approach to the community overlapping or limiting the other. They are in contrast in almost all respects. Immanuel was almost a century old when, in 1950, J. Archie Hargraves, a young Negro minister, brought his experience at New York's East Harlem Protestant Parish to Chicago. He did not try to find a church building; he rented a vacant furniture store on Roosevelt Road. Across the front he painted in large black letters on a red background: "West Side Christian Parish." Soon the parish had worked its way into the community more firmly than most of the historic churches roundabout, including Immanuel before its transition.

Hargraves convinced the Chicago Congregational Union that the most neglected, least desired, least promising area was the place where the churches should do their mission work. Inner Chicago offered many opportunities, but few were so dismal (and therefore so bright) as this Ashland-Roosevelt corner. Though he persuaded his sponsors that denominational ties would hamper him, the Congregational Union supported the work exclusively for its first eight months. Now it is an undenominational venture. Hargraves told the union he wanted no central temple; within his parish there could be several congregations. For that matter, within it could be almost anything, for aside from the lessons of the East Harlem precedent the new project would be guided only by free experimentation on Christian motives. The parish had no past to overcome, no traditions to guide. The intent, as Wright puts it, was to "confront people with Jesus Christ as Lord and seek to gain commitment of life to him"—on the level where they lived.

THE KEY: A GROUP MINISTRY

Hargraves has now returned to New York . . . , leaving behind a group ministry. As his successor defines it, this creative center of the parish differs from Immanuel's multiple ministry as it does from other "team" ministries. It does not stress differences of status (pastor, associate, assistant) or distinction of function (minister of music, minister of education). The heart of this technically defined group ministry is in the character of the commitment its members must make.

The nature of the work of the parish makes high commitment necessary, partly because denominational ties are weak. Members of the group ministry have argued that particular denominations are irrelevant to residents of the west side jungle, where the *esprit* that can go with denominational ties is absent. Demoralizing when undertaken alone, the work becomes meaningful when it is shared. Any prima donnaism, any riding off in conflicting directions on the part of some, could jeopardize the group's work. Without stifling personal initiative or energy, the group ministry has tried to redirect individuality into a common channel.

Those committed to the group ministry stress their common staff worship. More significantly, no one makes vocational plans or policy decisions or changes his role in the ministry without direction and guidance from his colleagues. In theory and in accidental practice this may play a part in many a multiple pastorate, but the group ministry demands it. Economic matters are pegged to the limitations or possibilities of the group. Even political action is taken in common. When all agree, the ministry speaks; dissenters who cannot conscientiously follow must sit on their hands and not wave them to distract from the effectiveness of action.

The ministry assumes its importance from the role it must play in the parish life. The degree of dependence on the staff by some parish members at first is almost embarrassing. The demoralization and deterioration that go with life in a blighted neighborhood make leadership potential a rarity. Yet the intent of the parish is to help create as soon as possible an "indigenous" church, a valid expression of the religion of its members. It should be one of the younger churches in its own right with no "canned" superimposition of mainstream American Protestantism on non-understanding adherents. Guidebooks and denominational planning boards have been of little use at East Harlem or West Side Chicago; on-the-spot dialogue between problem and possibility has been vastly more significant.

"ON THE MOVE, BUT NOT MOVING ON"

The store front which has served as center of the parish is not imposing. To attempt to make it look like a church would be absurd and would, in the eyes of the group ministry, reduce its effectiveness. A prominent cross, a Bible open on a table, a lectern, and a piano confront a room filled with folding chairs. The floors slope a bit, the plaster looks insecure, the area is dim. Adjoining the main hall is a large room in which the social and educational projects are carried out. Behind these are two crowded offices.

Expansion at present looks in two directions: to a garage several blocks south and to a store front to the east. The parish has not renewed the Roosevelt church's lease, leaving initiative with the congregation. What will happen neither ministry nor congregation can predict. But a recent Sunday morning announcement reassured: "Please understand: *The parish is on the move,* but it is not '*moving on.*' Its *office* may be here or there, but its *work* is in this community."

Whereas at Immanuel worship follows historic Lutheran patterns, at the Roosevelt church patterns of worship emerge that stress whatever ties they can to classic worship but which also include "lower" forms that are, in their own ways, continuous with the worshipers' religious pasts. Thus "Call Him Up" may be sandwiched between "Come Thou Almighty King" and "The Church's One Founda-

tion." Sermons have moved from simple social justice
themes, past false simplifications of the Christian gospel,
to illuminating narratives. Validity on the level where the
parishioner finds himself is determinative. Instead of a
liturgical sacramental worship, the parish conducts a table
fellowship that consciously relates to the *agapē* meals of
the early church. It may be observed at the worship center
or in parishioners' homes. This does not mean that the
rite is moved to the edge of the parish's existence; the
chalice and loaf with the cross constitute the letterhead
and symbol of all its activities.

Finances are of course a problem for the parish. It has
been partly dependent on suburban churches, and in particular, on outlay from Congregational and Baptist mission
boards. A parish council meets with an advisory board
from beyond, but the ties are informal. Though a certain
precariousness makes membership in the group ministry a
financial hazard, no alternatives seem to present themselves. Closer affiliation with a particular denomination or
institution would tend to restrict the virtuosity the parish
now possesses both on the theological and practical levels.

The Roosevelt church will disappoint those who look
for statistics in an era of denominational muscle flexing. A
brief prepared by the ministry enlarges on this. "We seek
to save our life as a church as we seek to be 'successful' as
measured by statistics; we lose our life as a church as we
seek to give of ourselves always to those who live about
us. . . . The parish seeks to so lose itself and identify
itself with its community that God's transforming power
might be known and experienced in every avenue of life."

Perhaps as few as 50 of the 400 served monthly by the
parish will be in church on a Sunday. Wishing does not
make it otherwise. In the city jungle, people know Christ

first through the actions of Christians. Distributing rat poison, climbing slum steps to argue with a rent-gouging landlord, appearing in court for someone caught in a crossfire of justice and injustice—these may be the only means of ministry valid at certain moments. A youth who has a way with broken-down autos may be enlisted to attract others to the garage youth center. A leader in a street corner gang may be induced to begin rehabilitating his friends. Each of these situations provides an entree to the life of others who through disinterest or fear or the sheer mass of population have built walls around themselves that no pious wishing will remove.

The east side of Chicago's west side, as all around the inner town, has need for more religious activity. In this it shares the situation of most urban areas. Pastoral directors of these creative parishes are reluctant to prescribe their patterns. "It takes five years to assimilate and ten years to project some of the things we're doing," says Wright. "And we're not yet five years along." It is easy to ask from a distance why Immanuel has not yet had full impact on the jungle, or why the parish is less successful than a conventional church at providing roots.

The inadequacies of the separate approaches have not escaped the ministers. Experimentation abounds. A British visitor once remarked that he would not be surprised if a Chicagoan tried to build an S-shaped bridge out of a wedding cake; he was sure that if a Chicagoan tried it the experiment would succeed. At Roosevelt and Ashland, Chicagoans are trying more realistic but hardly less difficult ventures. One senses that they are "playing by ear," alert to the startling cadences and strange improvisations of the Spirit.

The Task of the Church
in the Inner City

David W. Barry

The inner-city church should be a church. I don't think today many people will argue this point: there was a time when some felt it should be a neighborhood house, and sometimes today I find people who think it is a kind of work camp or service project. I have social work friends who see no function for the church other than as a social service center; but we who are within the church, I think, understand pretty well that the inner-city church, like the church anywhere else, is a place where the Word is preached and the sacraments are administered, where children and adults receive education in the Christian faith, where professing Christians come together as a witnessing community, and that these are its primary functions, before all others. That these functions must be adapted to the inner-city situation should be obvious, although I am sorry to say it not always is; that the Christian witness almost inevitably demands the performances of services to individuals and families seems equally obvious, but the services are a believing fellowship in action; they are not a substitute for the fellowship itself.

Our churches *have* tended to be cultural forms, some of

An address delivered at the Princeton Inner-City Seminar, sponsored by the Board of National Missions of The United Presbyterian Church U.S.A., June, 1958. Reprinted by permission of the author and the Department of City and Industrial Work, Board of National Missions, The United Presbyterian Church U.S.A.

them *have* been less than honest about their motives for social service—but having confessed our sins, we still confront one big and basic fact: the sicknesses that infect our cities today are sicknesses of the soul. The families that fall apart because they have no spiritual center and no picture of how a loving God intended his children should live together, the youth without moral standards or purpose or goals, the drab conformity of an urban culture which deals with humanity as masses and not as individuals, the conflict between groups based on language or color, the clamoring voices telling urban man that satisfaction is to be sought and found only in material possessions, the denial not only of opportunity but even of human acceptance and human relationships to large groups—all these, whose fruits are delinquency and divorce and mental illness and narcotics addiction and alcoholism—all these illnesses are fundamentally spiritual problems, problems of values and understanding, and ideals and morals, and they will never even be diagnosed, much less cured, if the church is not at work in the inner-city communities where these problems are piled up.

A Successful Church

The task of the inner-city church is to be a successful church. I won't be evasive on definition of terms. I am talking about institutional success in terms of standards we all understand, and the criteria I would offer would be something like these: it ought to have somewhere around 350 to 700 members; in communities of newcomers, Negro or Puerto Rican communities or public housing project areas, the Sunday school ought to be the same size; the members should be contributing or raising something like

$55 to $60 per member per year; it should have an active program at all age levels; it should have a full complement of volunteer Sunday school teachers and other leaders; and there should be some evidence that it is deepening the spiritual life of those who participate, and making a difference in the community around it.

Now none of these are very startling criteria or very Christian, for that matter; they are a sociologist's idea of a successful voluntary institution; in what is called a high-potential church extension field they would actually be rather low. But it is remarkable how different our criteria for success have often been in the crowded areas of the inner city. One of our standard criteria has been simply survival. If a church manages just to exist under unfavorable circumstances, this seems to satisfy our sense of mission. We have a history; we parcel out our mission funds to pulpits that year after year preach to a faithful fifty in the midst of masses of untouched humanity, and have the audacity to say we are "maintaining a Protestant witness." We know these situations are often a result of a kind of systematic starvation by National Mission Committees and Boards.

Much more exasperating to me personally are the men—sometimes quite recently out of seminary (it seems to be connected with the new look in theology)—who make a special virtue of failure. "We are learning," they say, "to wait upon the Lord. We are learning that we might work six years and nothing will happen. It teaches us meekness and humility and patience." My reaction to this is very un-Christian; it is that if the purpose of missions is the spiritual education of the missionary, we can get the same results by setting him to work chopping down a hickory tree with a stone ax; he will certainly learn humility and patience. The purpose of missions, it seems to me, is to win people to Christ; when a man or a method does not succeed, I cannot see that perseverance is a virtue; maybe the Lord is telling us to try something radically different, or that we're in the wrong business. When clergymen want to take Job as their model of the Christian life, I am always inclined to remind them that Job was first of all a highly successful man before God chose to test him, a model of prosperity in his worldly life and of uprightness in his spiritual and moral life; it is spiritually presumptuous to compare ourselves to him unless we can start from similar premises.

I don't mean by this that there is not a great deal of hard and routine work in the inner-city church. It is as true here as someone said about Washington that there are a lot of grindstones around waiting for noses. There are hundreds of thousands of doorbells to be pushed, leaders to be recruited, sermons to be preached. But a grindstone is supposed to make you sharper, not duller; if you want to be used by the Lord, each day's work should make you a little sharper, a little more effective. When a church loses its cutting edge, it's time for a good long look at both its concepts and its practice of the ministry.

Since the depression of the 1930's began, if not before, we have tended to set our sights too low in inner-city work and to expect too little in the way of results. We know by heart all the reasons why we cannot succeed in these areas, and it is time to stop reciting them, to stop offering to God our complaints and begin offering him accomplishments. I am well aware of all caveats here; that judgment is the Lord's, not ours; that we mustn't apply worldly standards to the measurement of Christian success. But if we cannot judge, we can at least evaluate. Surely we will fail, and many times over, but let's not throw ourselves on the mercy of the Lord until we have bruised ourselves trying, and used every ounce of creative imagination to find methods that work; and let's not accept anything less than success, the thriving living church and the redeemed community, as our goal. To quote Arnold Toynbee: "It is a paradoxical but profoundly true and important principle of life that the most likely way to reach a goal is to be aiming not at the goal itself, but at some more ambitious goal beyond it."

Sometimes we aim at an easily accessible goal and actually hit another beyond it, with disastrous results. The church that aims its program at the in-group, the insiders, in the contemporary city will in the long run not only fail with them, but destroy itself. The fundamental fact about today's urban civilization is change, and the church not only must learn to live with it, but to deal with it creatively, to align itself with and not against the dynamics of changing community life, if it really expects to be a redemptive force.

In a changing community the constant job of the church is recruitment, and it is not only possible but probable that the families the church has to recruit from will be different from those within the church, and the older the families within, the more different they will be from the families from without. Kenneth Miller likes to quote what he saw on a church bulletin board: "This church exists for those outside it," and this is the attitude the inner-city church must have if it is going to be a living force for the Kingdom. And the first thing it has to do is recognize that the outsiders *are* different, in all probability, from those who built the church—different sometimes in such obvious characteristics as skin color or language, but different almost always in less immediately apparent ways as social and cultural values, education, background, economic status, and life style. And given this situation, it takes a conscious effort of the will, the mind, and the imagination to devise a program of evangelism and recruitment that will speak effectively to the outsider.

An Indigenous Church

The inner-city church, if it is to have any real meaning to a community, must be indigenous. It must be a voluntary expression of the religious concern and religious striving of the people of the community, and not something imposed from outside, however lofty the motivation of those who maintain it.

This means, bluntly, that it must be Negro in a Negro community and working class in a working-class community, and to carry the logic further, composed of disorganized seekers after truth in a community where all families are disorganized, and most difficult of all, mixed in a mixed community. Of course, a church is not a community cross section; it is selective; its members are called out of the world, but they should be called out of the community that is, and not the community that was ten years ago. And I am further ready to suggest that a church should make a special effort to reach certain groups in the community; the gospel is offered to all, but the minister might well concentrate especially on potential leaders—the ablest and most vigorous men and women around him—for we are Protestants, and are committed to working through the laity. But this selectivity must be in terms of the dynamics of the community that exists today, or in a changing community, the one that is coming into being; we cannot afford to waste too much time frantically hanging on to the residue of population groups moving out.

This has some serious implications for you and me as clergymen. The overwhelming odds, even in a conference of inner-city ministers, are that we are white in color and middle class in background. Can we *be* the spiritual leaders in communities that are neither white nor middle class? I have to say the odds are against it, even though for an unusual man it is possible. The class bias, with much effort, can be overcome, for a man who is objective enough to look at his own values and behavior patterns and assess them against his Christian standards—ask yourself such questions as—Do you rate a businessman higher than a bricklayer on any of your value scales? What is the connection between Christian virtue and a college education? Do you prefer associating with professional and white-collar workers to associating with manual laborers?—and when you have answered these and similar questions you can decide whether you have the attitudes of a leader for these communities.

To be a leader across such major social barriers as that of race is an even tougher problem. The minister needs to be able to identify easily with his parishioners; we white folk are plagued with deeply seated attitudes of both guilt and condescension; we both overestimate and underestimate the Negroes we work with, because our emotions get in the way of our understanding; we have notoriously poor judgment as to what Negroes as a group consider important. But these things can be ultimately dealt with, like social class attitudes, if we are willing to be humble and objective about ourselves; the real millstone that hangs around our necks when we try to provide spiritual leadership to a Negro constituency is, ironically enough, the color of our skin, which we can never escape from. When we

ring the doorbell of a new Negro family, and the door is
opened, our color immediately raises a multitude of questions which must be answered, at least implicitly, before
we can get on with our work, questions the Negro minister
need not be bothered with. And forever arise questions
of whether we understand, and whether we can be trusted
—because our life experience has been on the other side
of the fence, and because the Negro has so often found
that his friends can do him as much damage as his enemies.

None of these, either, are obstacles that cannot ultimately be surmounted by the dedicated man, like some
who are sitting among you today, but they are obstacles,
and serious ones. In the New York City Mission Society,
we recognize this through a simple formula of policy; the
man at the lead of a church staff, the minister in the position of both real and symbolic leadership, should, except
in very unusual cases, be a leader indigenous to the major
ethnic group we are trying to reach. In Puerto Rican communities he should be Puerto Rican; in Negro communities,
he should be Negro. This does not mean a segregated staff;
for we will add as many white or English-speaking assistants as we can afford and as can work effectively. But
leadership must be visibly indigenous and we will turn
away many highly qualified, well-motivated candidates to
wait for one who has this crucially important qualification.

This again is not a Christian criterion, but a practical
one. Ideally Christian can speak to Christian in fundamental enough terms so that these racial and cultural
barriers melt away. Practically we have found this just
isn't the case; there is a spiritual issue involved; the ego
will not permit them to take second place in a hierarchy of
leadership, even for Christ's church. For others, the satisfactions of accomplishment are enough.

If this is not a workable strategy and often it is not, for

many reasons, chief among which has been our failure to produce enough qualified ministers from minority ethnic groups—then, the inner-city church must place a great deal of emphasis on recruiting and training indigenous lay leaders and giving them as rapidly as possible positions of influence and control.

Indeed, we have come to place a very high priority on leadership training, and we have begun to learn that we must broaden our concepts, both of what it is and over what length of time it must be planned for and leadership developed. Training should start at high school age—don't cry about lack of leaders—train them.

A SUBSIDIZED CHURCH

You may have noticed that I said nothing in my criteria of a successful inner-city church about self-support. Support, yes—one valid test of the health of a church is whether or not its members are contributing up to their capacity to give. But the financial capacities of the people of the inner city are not those of the more privileged communities; the most important single social fact which defines the inner city is the low income level of those who live there. The families of the inner city as a group must be subsidized in all aspects of life—health, housing, education, welfare, even subsistence—and there is no reason for us in the church to assume we will not need to subsidize their religious life as well, if it is to be kept up to reasonable standards.

Our City Mission Society has five churches that would qualify as successful by the standards I suggested; our direct subsidy averages $25,000 per church and ranges from $13,000 to $50,000, the latter figure involving the support also of a neighborhood house program. Churches raise $12,000 to $23,000. The experimental projects you read about run even higher in cost. You know something about East Harlem Protestant Parish; the annual cost is $130,000. You have certainly read about the work of Father C. K. Myers in his lower East Side and have seen his book *Light the Dark Streets;* the annual cost of his parish is $144,000. Money won't buy success, any more than it will buy intelligence and imagination and commitment, but it will buy a lot of things that are very important in this work—space and staff and equipment and specialized service and such essential personnel as secretaries and janitors that permit a minister to get about his real business.

So one aspect of the mission of the inner-city church is to convince the Board of National Missions, and other echelons of the denomination, that *more funds are mandatory* for inner-city church work. The churches with financial resources and the men of wealth should be shown the terrible plight of our inner-city churches. The future impact of a "soulless generation" in the inner city needs to be made plain. How can we be true to the mission Christ has laid before us without speaking in truly prophetic words about what will happen to the church in inner-city areas unless a dynamic program is instituted immediately?

Now I don't know whether I have provoked you; I would guess that for some of you who are most sensitive to the spiritual demands of our faith, to the silent and devastating judgment of our Lord upon the things we do in his name, the emphasis I have placed on success and numbers is, to put it kindly, limited, and, to put it more severely, scarcely in the spirit of the Master. I plead guilty and confess that often we have done all we can to make a church successful as the world counts success, we still

150   CITIES AND CHURCHES

wait upon the grace of God to give this church his blessing, to redeem his people and make them an instrument of his redemptive work. It is possibly because I am a sociologist as well as a missionary that I am preoccupied with numbers; I am impelled always to look beyond the inner-city churches to the vast multitudes outside these churches, and ask: "What about these others?" I have seen study after study, which shows the heavy concentration of church members in the more stable, more prosperous sections of our cities, and only a sparse sprinkling of members in the congested neighborhoods of the inner city, and the sheer size of the need, the volume of the unchurched, is something that gives rise to a sense of desperation. I keep looking for ideas and men who can reach people in the hundreds rather than in the tens, even though I know God saves us one by one. It is one of the big dilemmas and one of the major tensions of this kind of ministry.

And I keep encountering another kind of paradox: the message which is soporific and even sinful in the suburbs may be just the message to preach in the inner city. Where people are smug and complacent and self-satisfied, sermons on love and success are spiritual soothing syrup; the preacher must convict his people of sin and failure which they have not even recognized; but what is soothing syrup in the suburbs may often be the meat of the gospel in the inner city where sin and failure and frustration are the stark realities of life; here people must learn of God's love and compassion and must be convinced that with God's help some measure of success *is* possible—and to some degree this must mean worldly success in terms of education and a job and a decent home. And where in stable communities the so-called simple gospel may be simply an evasion of the moral complexities of our age, among people not trained to think in abstractions or experienced in the power structures of urban life, a simple gospel is often just the rock they need, and the preacher who presents moral and theological subtleties may be indulging himself rather than speaking to need.

And on the institutional level, where too much success in numbers in a suburban situation ought to cause a church to think hard about whether it is genuinely a church and not a popular social club, the inner city desperately needs churches that are visible symbols of success, churches that say: the gospel has relevance here, it meets your neighbor's needs and can meet yours; here is the place where men and women of good will come together in this community, and there are many of them; here is understanding and compassion; and this is an important group; it is strong enough to make a real impact on this community, on this big impersonal city that rejects you, that puts up cold, hard barriers everywhere else you try to go.

Come in and taste the excitement of a Christian fellowship where something is happening. For if we are not to be written out of history as the church that failed, we must have the kind of churches that make things happen, and not the kind that let things happen to them.

"Success" and "Failure" in Inner-City Churches

George D. Younger

Church workers in the inner city these days find they must seek to carry out their ministry while a continuing debate whistles past their heads. The major terms of the debate are the words "success" and "failure"—an unhappy antinomy that freights the discussion with all the emotional overtones of our economic system's attempt to measure achievement by what it calls "success."

David W. Barry, Executive Secretary of the New York City Mission Society, must be given responsibility for having introduced the word "success" into the picture, when he told a group of Presbyterians, "The task of the inner-city church is to be a successful church. . . ."

I am talking about institutional success in terms of standards we all understand, and the criteria I would offer would be something like these: it ought to have somewhere around 350 to 700 members; in communities of newcomers, Negro or Puerto Rican communities of public housing project areas, the Sunday school ought to be the same size; the members should be contributing or raising something like $55 to $60 per member per year; it should have an active program at all levels; it should have a full complement of volunteer Sunday school

Reprinted from *Christianity and Crisis* (November 28, 1960), pp. 171–175. Used by permission of the author and the publisher. For David W. Barry's reply to this article, cf. "Correspondence," *Christianity and Crisis* (December 26, 1960).

teachers and other leaders; and there should be some evidence that it is deepening the spiritual life of those who participate, and making a difference in the community around it. [See the preceding article.]

Barry also struck out at "the men—sometimes quite recently out of seminary (it seems to be connected with the new look in theology)—who make a special virtue of failure."

Barry's central intention in these remarks was to point to the changing composition of the inner-city population since the 1930's. With a majority of the people now occupying the low-income residential areas of our major cities already Protestant by heritage or, negatively, not Roman Catholic or Jewish, it is no longer necessary to be satisfied with small, feeble, perpetually struggling congregations. However, he went beyond this intention when he tried to identify his "failure" group as being clergymen who "want to take Job as their model of the Christian life," using their ministry in an urban area as an occasion for their own spiritual growth rather than for the redemption of others.

EXPOSURE AND RISK

Reaction was not slow in coming. Many responded with statements like this: "God does not require of us success, but rather a faithful and obedient ministry." George E. Todd, then with the East Harlem Protestant Parish, went farther in his challenge to Barry's argument:

I really believe that evangelism takes place most significantly when the church is led into situations of danger and when members of that church are made to feel that they are threatened. It is in this context that Bible study really begins to take on meaning. It is in this kind of tension between study of the Scripture and exposure to the world that a church begins to find its meaning as given by God and it is there that the world begins to hear something about what the gospel really is. The church, when it is the church, is, in the eyes of the world, a failure. Evangelism is not measured by success patterns, but by the church's capacity to absorb hostility.[2]

Believing that the church will be looked on as a failure even as people looked upon Jesus as a failure on the cross, Todd summed up this understanding of the work of the church in two words "exposure" and "risk." By exposure, he meant that the church must share in the life of the world and be exposed to its problems and sins; by risk, he meant that when the church acts it cannot be sure that this will result in building up the life of the church.

At this point the discussion became really confused when some, having heard of Barry's call for success with its *obiter dictum* concerning the prophets of failure and of Todd's defense of failure, began to speak of the debate as being between a "theology of success" and a "theology of failure." In fact, the tension is between no theology and a part-theology. All that Barry had been giving was "a sociologist's idea of a successful voluntary institution." Such institutional criteria might—or might not—be describing a church of Jesus Christ. However, taken by themselves, they could not possibly provide the basis for a theology of the church, whether in the inner city or anywhere else; they were no theology at all, although some of Barry's other statements did have definitely theological implications.

As for Todd's propositions, we can see that they speak of the incarnation and the atonement but not of the glad assurance of Christ's victory. In his eagerness to offset the emphasis on a formula for success, his reply emphasized failure in a way that is in danger of forgetting that the way of the cross leads to victory, thus denying the present Lordship of Christ. This, then, is a part-theology and not a whole one, although it is a valuable corrective to any attempt to construct the church as an institution without first taking into account what God is doing both inside and outside its fellowship. However, we must be sure to affirm that redemption can occur and that salvation is real. The cross is a constant factor in the church's experience, but Barry is quite right in pointing out that those who go expecting failure usually end by finding it.

So much for the so-called "theology of success" and "theology of failure." The entire discussion would become a great deal simpler if both phrases were quickly buried and forgotten. Yet, it is evidently not going to be so easy to bury Barry's assertion that the task of the inner-city church is to be a "successful" church, for he has compounded his felony by publishing an article that leaves little room for misunderstanding his earlier statement.

What do numbers give us? Well, in general, possibilities of these kinds: a good physical plant; staff and lay leadership with a variety of talents; the chance for a greater variety of human associations and more varied approaches to Christian living and understanding; open doors to avenues of ministry that would be frustrated without available leadership and funds; visibility in the community as a group to be reckoned with; the intangible sense of excitement when anything—no matter what —attracts a number of people, making others curious to know what it is. . . .

I think our churches in the inner city should be as strong— numerically, financially, physically, professionally—as we can possibly make them. Redemption is God's work; our areas of competence seem to be buildings and budgets, training in skills, imagination in recruiting people and exposing them to the work of God, responsiveness to needs we can meet—and building good, strong local churches.[3]

Success, then, means numbers, and let's not bother about trying to understand God's work.

THE ADMINISTRATIVE PERSPECTIVE

Some of this emphasis on success and numbers seems to stem from the difference between where David W. Barry sits as "a missions administrator, an entrepreneur in inner-city work" (and what a world of meaning is in that word "entrepreneur") and where many of us labor from day to day in inner-city parishes. The executive can look at the monthly statistical reports and say, as Barry does, "When a man or a method does not succeed, I cannot see that perseverance is a virtue; maybe the Lord is telling us to try something radically different, or that we're in the wrong business." Exercising stewardship over a limited budget of mission funds, he must constantly ask the question, Where will they produce the most church members or touch the lives of the most people?

But the inner-city pastor who lives close to his people knows that the answer cannot be given that easily. He knows the way in which the very figures in those reports lie. They cannot show that the Spirit of the Lord was performing a mightier work when the members of a house Bible study group ministered to one of their members recently discharged from a mental hospital than when a sunny Sunday in May brought out a large congregation. They cannot show the innumerable hours spent with people who will not—and seemingly cannot—unite with the church or send their children to church school, yet who deeply need the comfort and encouragement given by a church fellowship in the bleak box created for them by a host of impersonal authorities and powers. The figures lie, but these are what the administrator must constantly use for his evaluations.

More serious still, the faithful presentation of the scandal of the Christian gospel does not always win a ready acceptance, particularly among those who associate it with a remote institution, the church, that has never really drawn near their own lives. This resistance is not only noted by professional workers who have been spawned in comfortable middle-class backgrounds and educated in seminaries specializing in the "new look in theology."

One of the first signs that a lay worker in the church has really begun to grasp the magnitude of the church's mission today comes when he complains to the minister: "I don't see how you can keep it up. These people just don't want to listen. How are we ever going to get through to them? For every one who cares, there are a thousand who don't give a damn." If the preaching and teaching and living of the gospel are being rejected, it may not mean our methods are wrong; it may be indicating that people are rejecting God. Can the church and its members expect to be accepted, to be a numerical success, when God himself is being rejected?

However, more of this emphasis on success comes, as Barry himself admitted in the address in which he introduced the term, from the sociologist's preoccupation with numbers. The practice of sociological analysis as an ex post facto operation to study what has already occurred in the life of a human institution is a necessary enterprise.

As one who has already spent a good deal of his life poring over the findings of social scientists about our urban society and particularly their research concerning the role of the churches in that society, I would be one of the last to deny this necessity. But I would also like to point out that a serious distortion enters the life of a local church or its clergy when, using the results of such analysis as guideposts, they set out to reach particular numerical goals or to produce a pattern that conforms to the accepted criteria.

CRITERIA FOR EFFECTIVENESS

In this connection, it has been interesting to watch the progress of the Effective Church Study carried on by the Department of the Urban Church of the National Council of Churches since 1955. Aimed at discovering what is an "effective" (not "successful") urban church, these studies have ranged far and wide, examining both the local church and the church member. But when it comes to the question of criteria for "effectiveness," they have found that these are not given with the situation, for "any criterion of effectiveness implies a doctrine of the church." (Cf. summary of present status of this research in *The City Church*, Vol. XI, No. 3, May-June, 1960, pp. 9-16.) We are thus led by the sociological researchers themselves back from the numbers on which Barry would have us rely to the work of God— and man's response to that work—which theology alone can give.

It is at the theological level, then, that our most basic discussion and evaluation of the work of the inner-city church must take place. And it is here that those who, for Barry, "seem to make a special virtue of failure" have the greatest contribution to make. Those of us who work in inner-city parishes know only too well that our successes are far outweighed by the imposing structures of human authority and power with which we and our people must wrestle; by the sheer numbers of children, youth, and adults who swarm outside our doors; by the massive weight of sin, collective and personal, that presses down on their lives. You do not embroider silk cabbage roses on the surface of a cesspool; neither do you construct ingeniously "successful" local churches in the life of a modern community that has denied commandments and rejected the love of God.

George E. Todd's categories of risk and exposure are the way of affirming that the inner-city church—or any other church, for that matter, which takes seriously its mission in the twentieth century—must share both the incarnation and the atonement of its Lord. If "the Word became flesh" in the middle of the world of sin and woe, then he can take form in the impersonal life of the factory or the urban jungle. If the cross stands for the supreme sacrifice of God before the terrible forces of sin and death, then this sacrifice can have meaning in those places where death seems the final liberation from the bondage of dark powers that never let go. And—to go beyond Todd's statement—if Christ's victory has freed men to life eternal, then this victory should be most triumphantly proclaimed to those who are most defeated.

The whole work of our churches in the inner city is predicated on the belief that God's redeeming work can be known here and now. Yet, as those of us who work in the cities would be the first to admit, this is not an easy, self-evident assertion. To proclaim the victory of God's redeeming work in the very jaws of hell and at the edge

of death's oblivion is to enter into the same stringencies
known by Jesus in his earthly life. God incarnate could
say, "I have a baptism to be baptized with; and how I
am constrained until it is accomplished!" (Luke 12:50).
A church that is true to the incarnation finds itself bound
over and over again by the fact that it seeks to do God's
work in this place and at this time.

Further, the cross of Christ reminds us that victory on
God's terms is never purchased without cost. When his
Messiahship became known to the disciples, Jesus com-
manded them to tell no one, saying, "The Son of man must
suffer many things, and be rejected by the elders and chief
priests and scribes, and be killed, and on the third day
be raised." Then he went on and said to all, "If any man
would come after me, let him deny himself and take up
his cross daily and follow me" (Luke 9:21–23). A church
that is true to the suffering Savior finds over and over that
its call to the world's side promises a cross rather than a
crown.

THE CONFIDENCE OF THE CROSS

Let us, then, have no more talk of success and failure.
The real test is whether a community of faith, hope, and
love can survive in the midst of the life of a dehumanizing, technical, urbanized industrial society. If we are
going to seek to know that we have made an achievement
through statistical measurement or personal feelings of
success, then we shall be disappointed, for the ends of all
that we do lie not with ourselves but with God. How can
we know all the fruits of our labors? And how can we
expect that, if God is to be rejected by his creatures, the
church will be accepted and given a place of honor and
acceptance?

Our mission, therefore, *does* involve exposure and risk; it also involves dialogue with those to whom we speak and with whom we share the trials of life in the inner city. But we can work with a sure confidence that the suffering and the cross were not the end for our Lord Jesus Christ, and they are not the end for those in the church who seek to be his faithful disciples. We labor today with the same hope that was able to sustain the Christian martyrs in the midst of a hostile culture, the hope expressed in the vision to John on the island of Patmos:

After this I looked, and behold, a great multitude which no man could number, from every nation, from all tribes and peoples and tongues, standing before the throne and before the Lamb, clothed in white robes, with palm branches in their hands, crying out with a loud voice, "Salvation belongs to our God who sits upon the throne, and to the Lamb!" And all the angels stood round the throne and round the elders and the four living creatures, and they fell on their faces before the throne and worshiped God, saying, "Amen! Blessing and glory and wisdom and thanksgiving and honor and power and might be to our God for ever and ever! Amen!" (Rev. 7:9–12).

Here is the only success we need to desire—or can expect.

EHPP: Emerging Issues

George W. Webber

On the last Sunday in October, 1948, the first worship service of the East Harlem Protestant Parish was held in what had been an abandoned store on the corner of 102d Street and Third Avenue in New York City. The experience of that Sunday was symbolic of the attitude of the community toward the new Protestant venture. So many children arrived for Sunday school that the little room could not begin to accommodate them. But at the hour for church, in spite of the weeks of calling that had preceded, only one worshiper from the community appeared. In this needy but indifferent community, the white, middle-class, theologically educated clergy and their wives (for all their good intentions and enthusiasm) found no welcome.

During the early years of the Parish, the needs of the community seemed to the ministers to be beyond imagination. The tenement buildings of East Harlem had been built at the close of the nineteenth century in an effort to provide housing cheaply and quickly for the wave of immigrants then flooding New York. Almost at its beginning, this part of the city had become a slum. Now, in an area slightly larger than one square mile lived a population of

Reprinted from *Union Seminary Quarterly Review*, XIV (May, 1959), pp. 9–17. Used by permission of the author and the publisher.

Italians, Puerto Ricans, and American Negroes numbering nearly a quarter million. The problems they faced were those characteristic of modern urban culture: racial discrimination, inadequate housing, broken homes, overcrowded schools, juvenile delinquency, alienation from meaning in work, problems in the use of leisure time, and all the issues of which one reads in *Harper's Magazine* or in the Sunday magazine of *The New York Times*. Hoping to find New York a port of entry into rich, free America, these people had found in East Harlem only a place of misery and frustration.

It would be a mistake to suppose that East Harlem represents an area of this country's social and economic life which remains simply to be cleared up as America moves toward the solution of its domestic problems. Rather is the troubled life of this community a stark forecast of the issues which are emerging in our urbanized culture and which overshadow the future. Dr. Paul Tillich suggests that in modern art and literature one sees in sharp delineation the brokenness of modern life. East Harlem presents something of the same ominous portent.

With all its great and obvious needs, East Harlem, like numerous similar communities, had baffled Protestant efforts to maintain a vital Christian witness in the inner city. The Protestant settlement house made a genuinely selfless attempt to serve the newer immigrants when attempts at proselytism were all but hopeless. But as tides of immigration brought Jewish and Catholic families into the community many churches closed or managed only to retain enough of former Protestant membership to enable them to keep their doors open.

By 1948 the religious situation in the inner city had changed again. In East Harlem the church now faced a mission situation in which less than 25 per cent of the residents retained an active affiliation with any church. American Negro families, traditionally strongly Protestant, and Puerto Ricans, supposedly Roman Catholic, seemed neither to maintain their religious heritage nor to develop any new religious affiliation amid the pressures of urban life. Evangelistic efforts encountered many misconceptions of the Christian faith, and provided the basic insight that in the inner city, in spite of the fact that the pseudo-Christian patterns of American life still prevail, the missionary cannot assume that he works among people sympathetic to "religion."

The pagan character of this community, the previous withdrawal of Protestant forces from the area, and the consequent need for depth and variety of missionary resources made a united approach on the part of the Protestant Church necessary from the beginning. Hence, almost from its inception, the Parish has been supported by American Baptists, Congregational Christians, Methodists, Presbyterians (U.S.A.), the Reformed Church in America, the Evangelical United Brethren, and the Evangelical and Reformed Church. A valuable witness to the unity of the church, this support has also ensured for the staff of the Parish freedom and openness in the attempt to find patterns of obedience and witness. The staff has not sought primarily to develop new techniques, not even "a storefront, group ministry approach"; it has sought to be responsive to the leading of the Holy Spirit. It has not been under pressure to maintain any particular home mission pattern or emphasis. Rather has it been led again and again back to the experience of the Reformers and of the early church, which seems to be strikingly relevant to the Parish situation. The staff has been grateful for the forbearance of the denominational executives responsible for the Parish. They have been patient when the line between foolishness for Christ and just plain foolishness seems to have been transgressed.

The ministry of the Parish has been directed toward one area—the lower eastern quadrant of East Harlem, roughly from 96th to 112th Streets, between Lexington Avenue and the East River. Within these boundaries 25,000 people live both in the old, deteriorated tenements and in the newer, high-rising public housing projects. The Parish employs the following facilities: three store-front churches, begun in the early years of our ministry; a Presbyterian Church, formerly a mission to the Italian Community; two rented clubrooms used for work with two street clubs; two apartments on 100th Street that serve as the base for a fine medical clinic; a store-front headquarters for work with drug addicts; a large office in a former furniture store on Second Avenue, where there is also a Federal credit union, legal aid clinic, and library; and a retreat center fifty miles from the city used extensively for weekend retreats and, in the summer, for family camping.

I

Over the past ten years there have been certain persistent issues with which the staff of the Parish has had to deal. Of these more can be said in the way of diagnosis than in the way of solution. The problems discussed here are those which remain on the critical list.

The first issue, symbolized in that first worship service on 102d Street, arose from the fact that as strangers we, the staff, were intruders into the world of East Harlem.

In spite of our enthusiasm and concern to be of help, the community cared little about our new church on the corner. Protestantism had not been there for a long time. The arrival of some young, eager clergy was hardly enough to convince anyone that something new and important was happening. Only later did we learn that people thought this might be a racket of some kind, or a new angle employed by the fellow traveling Congressman from East Harlem, or worse, since seminarians had to learn somewhere, a place for students to practice being ministers. For the most part the attitude of the community toward the church was one of indifference or distrust, though often it found expression in open hostility. We were intruders. We were "white of face," and so fell heir to the opprobrium usually reserved for landlords, plainclothes cops, or racketeers.

On our part, we were *middle class* to the core. We were shocked at the appalling living conditions in the tenements, at the incidence of narcotics addiction, at all the social problems that beset the inner city and confounded our middle-class ideas of what America was like. When the staff families moved into the community to live, they found that simply *who they were* created barriers which had to be recognized in order to be surmounted. So much of what churches do in their activities and worship services depends upon cultural homogeneity rather than upon oneness in Christ. Obviously the subculture of East Harlem had little in common with the world in which most of us had been raised. We soon realized that we could not expect the people of this community to become like us; we would have to build the bridges. If it has taken a while for East Harlem to accept the staff, the reason has been our own inability to cross the barriers which *we* created, to become one with our neighbors, to go "native in all things save faith and morals."

Of course, we were *theologically trained,* and we found it disconcerting to spend our time with people who did not appreciate our nice distinctions or relish our discussion of best sellers or Broadway plays. Sermons preached in homiletics classes did not sound relevant in the pulpits in East Harlem. And we were all caught in the dilemma of being able to talk a good game theologically but unable to live by what we preached. Some of us found it easy to talk about the struggle for social justice. We affirmed that in Christ all men are one. But we found that it is another matter to be empowered by the Holy Spirit with real compassion, to feel in one's heart real love for one's parish, to have patience with the ugliness of life, to hope in the face of tragedy and pain when one discerns no hope. Even now it remains difficult to face the realities of our community, to stop our theologically sophisticated romanticizing, and come to honest identification with a full participation in the life of the community.

II

The second issue encountered by the Parish to be mentioned here involves the nature of the ministry and the role of the laity. In a mission situation, the church begins with the clergy as the visible sign that the gospel is being preached. To the mind of the community, the church is thus identical with the minister. In this situation it is often easy for a minister to gather around himself weak and dependent Christians who become far more deeply related to himself as minister than to Jesus Christ. The minister is often *used* by those who find some fulfillment in relating to him or in participating in the life of the growing congregation without coming to the recognition of their dependence upon the grace of God.

Another aspect of the same problem is the tendency of the minister to become like Mickey Mantle—the star of the team. The secular press, not to mention the denominational periodicals, does not hesitate to publish glowing articles about personalities in the Parish ministry. Ministers themselves are often tempted to assume that the Parish hardly needs the people to continue its work quite satisfactorily. Perhaps it is this very temptation which has brought home the fact that the integrity of our ministry depends directly upon our becoming the servants of our congregations, faithful to them and to God. Yet only recently have the policy decisions for the whole Parish begun to be determined by the principle of genuine lay participation. The ministers of the Parish have become convinced that as ministers they must work *within* or as actual members of their congregations rather than as dominant community figures. The power of the Christian witness in the world, both in terms of service and proclamation, depends not upon the clergy but upon the laity who already live in the world. Perhaps the role of Casey Stengel, the manager of the team, is a more suggestive metaphor for the situation. The task is to preach the Word, administer the sacraments, and thus to prepare the saints for their ministry in the world. This may seem to be a limiting and confining task for those who are used to dominating the church. But as true servants of the congregation, the clergy must be willing to stand aside and let Jesus Christ be Lord.

Related to this point about the task of the ordained clergy is an idea contained in an article in *Laity*, a publication of the World Council of Churches. In this article,

Ephesians 4:11 is translated: "And his gifts were that some should be apostles, some prophets, some evangelists, some pastors and teachers, *in order to* equip the saints for the work of ministry. . . ." In fact, most clergy are expected to possess all of these gifts together, even though some of them might be mutually contradictory in one human being. At best in the church of today laymen are considered only as *assistants* to the clergy, and such presumption may well represent a blocking of the Holy Spirit. Does this passage from Ephesians not rightly imply that these various gifts of the Holy Spirit are in fact poured out upon different members of a congregation? There are a variety of gifts of ministry necessary within the church to prepare the saints for their ministry in the world. These are valid and important, and not to be confused with nor restricted to the office of the ordained clergy.

The current stress on the minister as pastoral counselor is a good example. In any congregation most of the members turn automatically to the clergyman for help in personal crises and problems. He is the "paid specialist" in this area. But if we in East Harlem were to take on all the problems of our congregations, we would find our resources both of time and spirit simply overwhelmed. Christian men and women are called to bear one another's burdens and therefore ought to be pastors to one another, able in times of stress and trial to stand with each other in strength and comfort. In every congregation there are men and women gifted with compassion and sensitivity by the Holy Spirit who would be superb pastors and burden bearers. It is the minister of the church who ought to release, direct, and train those who have been thus gifted, and not himself remain the focus of the counseling of the congregation.

III

This leads directly to the third issue, which has to do
with the form of congregational life. In the Reformation
tradition, we have placed central emphasis upon the corporate worship of the church. In regular Sunday services
the Word is read and preached in language men can understand, and the sacrament of Holy Communion is offered in
the hope that the people of the Parish may discover the
meaning of Christian faith and freedom. At the time of
the Reformation, this was wonderful and exciting. Word
and Sacrament came alive in men's hearts. It is this sense
of vitality in Christian worship that we have been fighting
to recover.

But to the author of this paper, this return to the em-
phases of the Reformation does not seem to be all that is
needed to meet the challenge of vital religious life in our
day. The teachings of the Reformers are true and important in the life of the church. But single, weekly services
are simply not enough to enable the members of a congregation usually scattered widely in the world to know
the reality of life as members of the body of Christ. In
our depersonalized, urban culture, the powerful, cutting
thrust of the gospel must be manifest in the *koinōnia* of
God's people. The world must see the miracle of a fellowship in which men have found oneness in Christ. And
this can only be achieved if possibilities for its realization
are structured into the life of the church in such a way
that life together may become a reality for Christians.
Examples of such group or "cell" life within the total life
of the congregation are the house church, the Methodist
class meeting, the Bible study group, the prayer fellowship, and the vocational interest group.

Whatever the form taken by the small-group life of the congregation, one crucial point must never be forgotten. The orientation of Christians when they gather together as the church, the *ekklēsia,* for worship and study, must always be toward their return to their life in dispersion in the world as salt or leaven. For the life of the church must be made aware of the concrete problems of obedience and witness in the world. Many of these can be dealt with adequately only in the context of a small group of trusted fellow soldiers of the Lord.

Acts 2:42 suggests that the agenda for group meetings might include the apostles' teaching and fellowship, the breaking of bread, and prayers. Here is forged the discipline of the life of Christ. In the process, one may dare hope that Christians will find what it means to transcend every kind of cultural difference and to achieve real unity in Christ. Here mutual understanding achieved in freedom in Christ may make bearing one another's burdens possible. Possibly too, an incredulous world might be again astonished by the miracle of the gospel when in the church it sees "how Christians love one another."

Within these "enabling groups" we have suggested that some knowledge of the reality of life in Christ may be discovered. One aspect of this discovery is almost surely a new awareness of the need for both corporate and individual discipline in obedience to Christ. Somewhere in the individualistic emphasis of contemporary Protestantism we have lost this awareness. Life in Christ demands that we submit our lives to the judgment and guidance of our fellow Christians through whom the Holy Spirit acts.

The staff of the Parish, made up of Christians who face common issues in their common calling, meets as a Group Ministry. This cannot take the place of our life in the con-

gregation, but it is the locus in which we have sought to
discover the direction for our work as ministers. In this
group we struggle together with the problems we each
face in the fulfillment of our ordination. We continue to be
amazed at the extent to which we continue to deceive
ourselves, and at the many subtle manifestations of our
own sinfulness. This fact itself has done much to convince
us that no Christian should dare to remain apart from the
criticism and discipline of his fellow Christians. In our
group, and not infrequently, the Holy Spirit does seem
to work to puncture our illusions and judge our achievements. Indeed, such groups as this, in which trust and
unity have been established, seem to provide a primary
context within which Christians may receive guidance and
direction from the Holy Spirit.

IV

There are many other issues which have come to the
surface over the past ten years. Some are settled; some are
unresolved and appear destined to remain that way for
some time at least. One persistent issue is the matter of
success and failure. What are the criteria by which the
ministry here is to be judged? We are frequently asked
what success we have been having and find ourselves at a
loss for a satisfactory answer. We are constantly referred
to in Protestant publications as one place where the
churches are meeting with power the challenge of the
inner city. On the other hand, we are faced with pointed
questions and criticism from many quarters, including the
seven supporting denominations, the seminary field work
students (no more critical group exists), and our wives.
Many crucial issues arise from the ambiguity of our situa-

tion. We are an experiment trying to become a church. We are an interdenominational mission project seeking to find our unity and yet remain faithful to our own denominational heritage. We are big and expensive and thus dependent upon generous mission giving. And above all we are committed to responsibility to the indigenous leadership of the Parish churches. All of those matters are, in their own way, important issues.

One sympathetic critic of the Parish is afraid that we have forged a theology of failure in the light of the results to date in the ministry of the Parish. Yet in the end we are led to affirm this: that God does not require of us success or failure, but asks only for our full obedience. But we are human and we do seek signs that our work is fruitful. Yet we know that we cannot depend for our strength and purpose upon our success in changing the world or overcoming evil or gaining new church members. Our only hope is to live in the world by God's grace, and thus to expose to the world the real meaning of evil. In the world of East Harlem we are witnessing to something that we know God has done. It is in the degree to which we reflect this, and not in the extent to which social improvements are made that we are faithful to our commission. When God gives us grace to labor with this perspective, to be faithful in the face of discouragement that is real and of defeat that hurts, then sometimes the world does respond. God gives signs, even as Jesus pointed out to the disciples of John when the sick were healed. But what signs do come serve not so much as proof of success as of doors of communication which have been opened.

A case in point is the narcotics program of the Parish. One of the ministers has given nearly full time for the last year and a half to work with young drug addicts. He has engaged in a many-sided approach to the whole issue of narcotics. But the heart of the program has centered in a community of laymen, some ex-addicts, some friends of addicts, and others, all of whom exercise a ministry within the household of faith. In the last year they have ministered to nearly five hundred addicts. Only a handful of these are now off drugs, and to date there have been no new church members. Yet here is a ministry to those in bondage that must be carried on. The success or failure of the narcotics program is absolutely in God's hands. (Over the door of the narcotics center is a simple sign on which a glass syringe is being smashed to pieces by a cross.) The witness of this ministry seems to some plain foolishness, but to others it may come as a witness to the foolishness of God which confounds the wisdom of this world.

The East Harlem Protestant Parish has been referred to as a dramatic, exciting, but sometimes off-beat experiment. Yet these emerging issues are the problems of the American churches, not just of this Parish. If the churches do not struggle with such issues, the gospel stands in danger not so much from the world as from the church itself.

CHAPTER V

URBAN SECT
AND CULT MOVEMENTS

INTRODUCTION

Nowhere is the proliferation of sectarian groups more highly visible than in metropolitan centers. These groups have been hailed as the "third great force of historic Christianity." Yet, for the most part, urban sects and cults receive far less serious attention from the established churches than their swelling numbers and vitality of fellowship would seem to warrant.

Many explanations have been advanced to account for the emergence of urban sects—their vitality, enthusiasm, and ability to exact a total commitment from their followers. One such theory is especially pertinent in the case of rural migrants to urban centers. It contends that sect membership often reflects a form of social reorganization in the face of a "culture shock" which the city dweller initially experiences. By turning to revivalistic sects and cults, the newcomer can recover a sense of security and find supportive group relationships in the new urban environment.

Other theories are explored in the selections of this chapter. These selections are written by individuals who have had first-hand contact with sectarian groups. They introduce the reader to the inner life, the social and spiritual dynamic, and the cultural sources, of urban sect and cult movements.

In "Store-Front Religion," G. Norman Eddy, Professor of Human Relations at Boston University, observes that store-front religious groups may be found in the transitional areas of nearly every large American city. The author identifies three basic types: transitory local groups, charismatic groups, and groups with a distinctive myth. These groups fill the emotional and spiritual void in the lives of many urbanites, who are not being reached by the more established, traditional churches.

"Sectarianism as a Response to Anomie" is written by Father Renato Poblete, S.J., of Santiago, Chile, and Thomas F. O'Dea, Professor of Sociology at the University of Utah. The authors suggest that sectarianism reflects a quest for community, a need to form communal, fellowship groups to offset the depersonalizing consequences of urban, technological society. Hence the formation of sects is a response to anomie, and sectarianism is a protest against the meaninglessness of life. This hypothesis is applied to analyze the Puerto Rican migrants to New York City. Membership in sectarian groups offers salvation from loneliness and isolation and provides meaningful social relationships and life orientation in the new urban setting.

"The Urbanization of a Holiness Body," by Val B. Clear, Professor of Sociology at Anderson College, is a striking case study of the dynamic transition which the Church of God, Anderson, Indiana, has undergone. Beginning as a rural holiness sect, this group has almost completely reversed its earlier patterns and is now predominantly an urban body. The author, himself a member of the Church of God, outlines the influence of urbanization upon the group's transformation. This article is a vivid reminder that sects are not inert and static. Rather, they are dynamic movements in interaction with urban culture.

Store-Front Religion

G. Norman Eddy

An ecclesiastical domain may be found in certain areas of almost every large urban community. The preachers—like their sermons and congregations—will vary somewhat, one from the other. But these groups all share one thing in common: their use of a store-front auditorium.

A more precise definition, however, would be of some value. More formally, I mean by this term "store-front religion" those groups found in the socially disorganized areas of large urban communities and generally housed in small secular buildings. These faiths are characterized by a more or less marked deviation from that of any established religious body. They differ in many ways from the denominations and ecclesia; specifically, in the relatively meager education of their clergy, in the lower economic stratification of their congregations, in the bizarre nature of their theology, and in their unpretentious store-front meeting places. Marked contrasts with the more traditional religious bodies are apparent both in their ritual and in their social and psychological objectives. Store-front religions range all the way from ephemeral groups to those which have a history of two or more generations. Some of these

Reprinted in abridged form from "Store-Front Religion," *Religion in Life*, 28 (Winter, 1958–1959), pp. 68–85. Copyright, 1958, by Abingdon Press. Used by permission of the author and the publisher.

groups are entirely independent, but a majority have at least a loose affiliation with other groups in an ecclesiastical organization. . . . All store-front groups, however, are characterized by the marginal, social, and economic status of their congregations.

Because of their variety, it is a formidable task to attempt any statistically accurate classification. However, I find three basic types. The first of these is the transitory local group. Usually, this group is emotional in character and does not have strong interchurch affiliations. The second type is "charismatic"; that is, it is the creation of a forceful leader who is able to sustain the loyalty of small bodies of people in several cities. And finally, there is a third type arising from a myth which unifies people socially by giving them a distinctive ritual and belief. While these divisions do not embrace all store-front groups and are not entirely self-exclusive, they do provide a workable framework for describing the essential characteristics of such bodies. The succeeding sections will describe three representative groups falling into these basic categories: (1) a primitive Pentecostal church; (2) *The House of Prayer;* and (3) *The Church of God and Saints of Christ* (also known as the Black Jews).

I. Transitory Local Groups

Careful observations over a period of years support the thesis that the number of store-front type buildings used for worship remains just about constant. Despite this, there is much evidence that the *churches* (i.e., the organized bodies of people themselves) constitute a very transitory phenomenon. They spring into being and dissolve again with a certain degree of regularity. Most of them are local in character since they are often the result of schismatic tension. Perhaps some church member has become offended by a particular doctrine being preached by his minister. Having the egotistic desire to preach, he may decide to organize a church of his own with those disgruntled members he is able to entice away from the original congregation. Since funds are usually very low, a store front provides a possible meeting place. After a longer or shorter period of vitality, the church frequently succumbs to economic or social pressures and another group takes its place.

The cyclical character of many store-front groups may be suggested by the following example. For several months I attended services in a rickety old building which displayed the sign "Pentecostal Church of Hope" crudely painted over the door. The minister, who referred to himself as Elder A., was converted three or four years earlier during the evangelistic services of a store-front group in another neighborhood. Elder A., an unskilled laborer, was about thirty-five years old, with a tall, thin, ascetic-looking frame. He had little formal education, and as he told me, had spent a wicked youth. He had drunk excessively, committed adultery, and brought disgrace upon both his family and himself. His conversion made for a radical change in his life. Not only was his entire outlook modified, but he sought for and received the "deeper blessing" of the Holy Spirit, i.e., he spoke in tongues and he danced in ecstasy before the Lord.

As a result, his passion for religious dedications knew no bounds. To remain a mere layman in another's church would not provide him with sufficient scope for his religious aspirations. He must preach. He felt himself called upon by the Lord, and preach he did. A sister's home where he was living provided the location for his first efforts, with members of her family and neighborhood friends making up the congregation. In this second-floor apartment opening off a dark hallway in an ancient tenement house, there was much shouting and praising of the Lord. Some received the gift of the Holy Spirit and testified in unknown tongues. But since not all the tenants in this dingy building were sympathetic to this type of religious worship, some became irate at the shaking of tambourines, the loud singing, and the jumping. There were services every night in the week, and sometimes these would continue until very late.

Eventually there was a complaint to the police, and as a result, they were ordered to desist. A store front seemed to be the only solution for their need of a new meeting place. Yet the congregation never exceeded more than thirty—and even this figure included some children. I got to know these people well enough to realize how difficult it was for them to raise the money for the piano, the folding chairs, and the monthly rent. I became inured to the pastor's impassioned pleas for even larger contributions. These were poor people and the outside pressure on them was strong. I returned one Sunday to find the church disbanded and a "For Rent" sign on the door. Altogether, the life span of this church had been something less than two years. Yet almost immediately after this group's failure, the building was occupied by another store-front group called "The Holiness Church of Christ."

Throughout the United States, there must be thousands of these little churches. What is their appeal? Why do these people worship in uncomfortable buildings when the denominational churches have more than enough room for them? Undoubtedly the answers to these questions are complex, yet three factors seem to be of particular importance—these groups provide: (1) a sense of status to the member, (2) assurance of spiritual healing, (3) opportunity for emotional expression.

The need for recognition is fundamental to most human motivation. It is only natural that persons of low economic status—who do not have the opportunity of participating in the expensive means of secular self-expression—should turn to the church to satisfy this need for recognition. Yet why is it that these people cannot gratify their wants in the larger churches? I asked two or three why they didn't attend an imposing church only a block from where they worshiped. One reply was, "Who would we be over there?" They gave other answers too—many of them theological; but I suspect that this was the real answer. Over at the other, larger church, they would have to compete with persons of considerably higher status—both economic and social. In the store front, they would be with their peers.

Yet equally significant to these people is the emotional release provided by their church. So important is this factor that church attendance occupies practically all of their free time. Emotionalism charges their testimony services and their singing as well as the sermons. In a typical store-front group, there are a few young people, but the majority are middle-aged or older. When they come in, many of them look haggard and beaten. Somebody—perhaps the deacon or the minister's wife—will begin a song. The drums, tambourines, piano, and the washboard (played with a claw hammer) take up a musical accompaniment. Everybody sings and claps hands to the rhythm. A few stamp their feet. Vibrations from the music

swell through the body. Their gospel songs are rollicking
jingles with endless stanzas.

> He'll never let you down
> He'll never let you down
> Though storms may come and
> Winds may blow
> He'll never let you down.

A jubilant atmosphere charged with deep feeling becomes inspired by the rhythm. This joyous feeling is
contagious.

I have asked some, "Have you had the gift of the Holy
Spirit?" Often enough, the answer has been, "No," although they hasten to add that they are looking forward
to it, or that they are trying to live so that the gift will be
vouchsafed to them. Whether or not they undergo this
experience, it is apparent that all have derived some ec-
static release from this kind of worship. In it they discover
an opportunity to lose their sense of frustration and failure
in the everyday world. And these people, with this fervid
cathartic experience, typify most transitory local groups.

II. The Charismatic Group

On the white-painted glass windows of a decrepit old
store front are lettered rather crudely the following words,
which I copied down exactly:

God has only one true house with one true name—the Bible
says even then will I bring to my holy mountain and make them
joyful in my House of Prayer. Is 56:7.

The church is not brick and wood, but people baptized with
the Holy Ghost and Fire who shout, speak with other tongues,
like the Bible says. We all must do this before we can be saved.

God's grace is a man. Titus 2:11. For the Grace of God bringeth salvation hath appeared to all men. Titus 2:12.

Although it may not be immediately apparent, these three sentences summarize the basis of the "charismatic" store-front religion: (1) a particular place of worship and (2) a particular type of worship and (3) a "divinely appointed" leader. The particular store-front meeting place from which the above quotations were obtained is especially conscious of this third factor, for it is the local branch of a national faith which is the creation of an extraordinary man who refers to himself as "Bishop C. M. Grace"—but who is known to his followers more affectionately as "Daddy" Grace. Because such groups as his publish little and make no serious effort to keep accurate statistics, it is almost impossible to say how many local *Houses of Prayer* (as his worship places are known) there are. It has been estimated that there are more than a hundred local groups which extend all the way from Massachusetts to Florida with over a half-million followers.

Bishop C. M. Grace is an example of what many sociologists would call a "charismatic" leader. Such a person is thought to have a divine gift for solving the most pressing problems and for working the most astounding miracles. His followers say, "We believe in the Father, in the Son, in the Holy Ghost, and in Bishop C. M. Grace"—but it seems to me that Daddy Grace is a more real deity to them than the Trinity. Indeed, one of his ardent followers told me that Jesus is gone now and it's easier to call on Daddy Grace. There are many reasons to believe that this comment is indicative of the divine status his followers believe Bishop Grace fills. On one occasion I listened to some of his group praying fervently for a friend who was ill—to

Daddy Grace. At the time, Daddy Grace was in another
city some distance away, and so I asked them, "Do you
really think that your prayers will be answered?" Almost
immediately they replied: "Certainly. Daddy always
knows when we pray to him. He knows everything we
need and he always helps us."

Once I asked him outright if he were God. In reply, he
said somewhat evasively, "Some people say that I am."
But whatever he may think about himself, his followers
give every evidence of their worshipful regard. In his
sanctuaries, he is pictured in the flowing robes associated
with Christ. Upon the bishop's breast is depicted a bleed-
ing sacred heart. At each meeting the people express their
thanks to "sweet Daddy Grace" over and over again. They
say: "Ain't he wonderful? Isn't he sweet?" To them, he
is their God.

The sanctuaries for the House of Prayer range all the
way from a large business-block establishment in Harlem
to the crudest, most dilapidated sort of store fronts in
some of the smaller Eastern-seaboard cities. Yet among all
those sanctuaries which I have visited, I have found the
following things in common: There is always a platform
supporting a large, comfortable-looking throne chair (surrounded by vases of artificial flowers) and a pulpit with
microphones—all for the exclusive use of the Bishop. No
one else ever stands on the platform. During Daddy
Grace's long absence from the local churches, protective
plastic covers are used to shield the objects on the platform. All around the walls on large placards are displayed
the Bishop's sayings intermixed with pictures of his homes
and other sanctuaries. In every meeting place there can
be seen a large photograph of El Dorado, which is reputed
to be the largest apartment house in the world and which

is said to be owned by Bishop Grace. On the platform itself, are large, life-sized cutouts of him. He is, without doubt, the author of their faith.

Of all the emotional groups I have known, this is the most extreme. The quite informal ritual consists of singing, testimony, marching, and compulsive dancing. There are services every night in the week, and from sunrise to midnight on Sundays. I was told that on Saturday night the faithful frequently become so much involved in worship that they continue through until one or two o'clock Sunday morning. Since little time is left to go home, the group just stays there to catch a few hours of sleep on the church benches. In this way they will be all ready for the sunrise services.

Perhaps the most distinctive thing about their services is the frenzied congregational participation. After a brief period of spontaneous singing, the young and old line up to take their turn at the microphone to offer testimony. It may be a long or short effort, but occasionally it becomes so emotional that a few lose control of themselves completely. Others start to clap their hands while the speaker moves around and around in ever-increasing tempo until eventually he jumps high off the floor. He throws back his head as if from a violent spasm. His actions are contagious and those waiting in line to offer their testimony begin to imitate him. If the Bishop is present at these occasions, he will simply sit there with an expression of benign indifference on his face. Sometimes, however, a member has to be restrained lest he injure himself. The emotional pitch of the audience must constantly reach toward greater and greater heights or else it will die away as quickly as it came into being. But after a period of relative calm, the audience may be aroused again by almost any portion of the ritual—a grand march, a chorus, or the remarks of the minister. For these people, direct emotional expression is the essence of religion. It is this expression which stirs them so that they feel they have been in touch with the Holy Spirit.

I have attended a considerable number of these services in various Houses of Prayer and have often speculated on the mechanisms essential to their appeal. It seems apparent that certain of the principles of dynamic psychology have a place in any explanation. These are poor people. In the face of an unappreciative and sometimes hostile social order, many such people unconsciously wish to regress. And it is clear that regression is an accepted form of behavior in the House of Prayer. Members may jump and shout and clap their hands together gleefully—like a child, without fear of censure. In the House of Prayer it is not always necessary to use the language of grownups—the speech of the hostile, unappreciative social order; rather, all are able to babble freely in nonsense syllables without arousing any adverse comment. Through regression, the faithful are able to leave the hostile world far behind.

Another psychological mechanism which also operates at the unconscious level is *identification*. The individual who worships Daddy Grace may live in a mean tenement in the worst slum, but "Daddy"—his friend and savior— owns the largest apartment house in the world. The individual may have nothing; perhaps he is pressed to pay his rent and to meet his grocery bill. Yet, through introjection, he becomes a part of Daddy Grace, so that now he, too, shares in a sense all that Daddy Grace owns. In other words, identification with Bishop Grace permits vicarious compensation for the ills and hardships of daily life. Moreover, by his acts of public worship in the House of Prayer, the humble individual has a further opportunity to compensate for the difficulties which life may have dealt him. Despite his lowly position in the external world, he can excel in the House of Prayer; he can testify and others will listen to him respectfully; he can wear the distinctive sash of high religious office; he can use the simple instruments of the orchestra without formal musical training.

Finally, the House of Prayer affords an opportunity for these people to vent their aggressive drives in a manner sanctioned by their friends and pastor. In every sanctuary there is a large illustrated placard bearing these words: "As the others go down, the House of Prayer goes up." Accompanying this message there is an idealized picture of the House of Prayer in a flamboyant architectural style comparable to a mighty Gothic cathedral. All about the building is a radiant halo of light. Beneath the cathedral is the rubble formed by the "churches of the world." Here is depicted the triumph of the true faith over the false. The members look up at this picture and all of their resentments can be channeled into approved feelings of hostility toward "other faiths." No doubt not all of these various factors motivate every individual, but perhaps they do suggest the satisfactions which the average member is able to find within the House of Prayer.

III. A GROUP WITH A MYTH—THE "BLACK JEWS"[1]

There is a third kind of store-front religion which is strongly oriented toward a sacred myth. This myth is the focal point for all the activity of the group. To these people this myth is not a fiction, but something in which they passionately believe—just like all those basic assumptions on which we ourselves act without giving them conscious thought. Perhaps this may be made clearer by defining the myth as an organized mental picture of the world. As such, it comprises those preconceived images in terms of which the world is perceived. The myth, therefore, gives both meaning and understanding to life. It provides an underlying stability and order to chaotic social phenomena by supplying a permanent frame of reference. For this reason, the myth makes for emotional solace in times of crisis. A myth may be either true or false in an absolute sense, but for our purposes it must be understood in terms of its function in the life of a people.

There is a Negro group which has a particularly dramatic myth—namely, black men are not Negroes. Rather, they are Jews! And on this belief, a whole way of life and a unified conception of the universe has been built. These people say that the so-called Negroes are, in reality, the descendants of the "lost" tribes of Israel. In the beginning, all the Jews were black-skinned, but as a result of interbreeding with Caucasians during the time of the Roman Empire, the Jews gradually began to lose the characteristic color of their skin. All this was revealed by a prophet, one William Crowdy, who had a call from God in the latter part of the nineteenth century to lead his people to the true religion. Today, those who hold his beliefs are not a large group. In two hundred or more churches scattered throughout the urban areas of the United States, there is a total membership of perhaps slightly over 35,000. Surely, this is one of the most distinctive and colorful of all storefront religions.

I became familiar with *The Church of God and Saints of Christ*, as it is called, several years ago when I attended one of their modest store-front sanctuaries. Later on, I became acquainted by visiting the headquarters in Belleville, Virginia. Since they think of themselves as Jews (although they believe that Jesus was the Messiah!), much of their theology and ritual has a Hebrew flavor. One of their leaders said to me, "As we come to understand our true heritage better, our practices become more and more Hebrew all the time." Therefore, it isn't surprising that the men wear *yarmelkes* (skull caps) on their heads. At the time of the important religious holidays, the presiding bishop will wear the costume of an Old Testament high priest. The Jewish calendar—with Hebrew names for the months—is used to determine the religious holidays. The Hebrew Sabbath is celebrated, beginning at sundown on Friday and terminating at sunset on Saturday. There is an annual observance of the Passover for a period of one week, which includes the slaying of the paschal lamb and the eating of unleavened bread with bitter herbs. This is a time of tremendous significance in the lives of these people —a period of great social as well as religious importance, when the membership comes to Belleville from far and near. Even the Hebrew custom of circumcision, which was not insisted upon originally, is now being performed increasingly on the younger males.

This faith presents a curious fusion of Old Testament Judaism and Christian theology; yet it goes beyond a mere blending of these culture complexes—for these "Black Jews" have created a faith and a liturgy all their own. This is evident from observing a tabernacle (as they call their place of worship), for both its ritual and its membership. Like the people who attend other store-front churches, these form a group from the lower economic strata, and their tabernacles reflect this poverty. Despite the lack of material pretension, the decoration of the church and the costumes of the congregation are really impressive. There

is the pulpit all covered with brown and blue silks, and
there is the great brass trumpet used to call the people to
worship. Seated on the platform are the officials of the
tabernacle, dressed in cutaway English walking-suits of
brown, with stiff, white shirt fronts and winged collars.

Many aspects of their ritual are striking. Perhaps the
most impressive of all is their music. No musical instrument
is ever used in the tabernacle. Stamping of the feet and
clapping of the hands provide an intricate rhythmic accompaniment to their elaborately developed melodies.
Frequently there is a gentle movement of their bodies to
the music, ". . . like wheat swaying in the wind to honor
the Creator . . . ," as they say. It seems pleasantly contagious. The little children in front and the older members
of the congregation who are not members of the choir also
sway with the singers. This is far from the violent, orgi-
astic, emotional demonstration found in most other store-
front groups. Rather, it is a happy and joyous display of
faith, somewhat sedate by comparison.

With these people, more than with any other group with
whom I am familiar, there is an elaborate ritual for giving.
At one point during the Sabbath, all other activities cease
and the men of the tabernacle bring portable tables into
the auditorium and set them up at predesignated spots.
When a signal is given from the platform, a number of the
women seat themselves at these tables and the financial
account books are placed before them. One of these
women is Secretary for Tithes, a second is Secretary for
Benevolences, and a third is Secretary for the Widows' and
Orphans' Home; there are, perhaps, ten others to take
care of the additional tabernacle demands. The rest of the
congregation arrange themselves in a single file and one
by one they pass before each of the tables, dividing their

offerings so that each secretary receives a portion. As a contribution is made, the name of the giver is read aloud. It is almost as if this ritual were designed to make the obligation of giving even more pleasant.

More than the transitory local groups or the charismatic people, the groups with a myth (as exemplified by the Black Jews) manifest a distinct way of life. It is their intimate and long association with one another—as well as their social idealism—which does so much to make them a cohesive unit. The institution of the Sabbath, for example, cannot help developing a social stability. Instead of attending services for an hour as do many churchgoers, these people are in continuous worship from sunrise to sunset. When exercises are not actually being held, as at lunch time, there is opportunity for friendly conversation which deepens the social bonds. In addition, the custom of going to Belleville for the celebration of the Passover leads to a greater feeling of unity with members from other tabernacles. Young people belonging to the church meet and many find marriage partners within the church. They do not find it difficult to carry out the injunction of the Bishop forbidding marriages with nonmembers. By so doing, each generation comes to think of The Church of God and Saints of Christ as *the* church and its ways as *the* way of all. It is for this reason that the Black Jews have been able to maintain a greater degree of stability than most store-front groups.

IV. CONCLUSIONS

In the process of making this impressionistic analysis, a number of conclusions about store-front religions emerged. These groups are characterized by a definite ecological distribution which seems to limit them, almost without exception, to transitional urban areas. Bishop Grace may have a fine home in the better residential section of the city, but the local House of Prayer is located in the slums. Although in some of the better districts of the community there are simple auditoriums with an electric sign reading "Jesus Saves," these churches belong, almost without exception, to the more organized peoples such as the Assemblies of God, which has reached denominational status in many parts of the country. As such, they are not true store-front groups. This ecological distribution may be related to the fact that store-front religions appeal to those classes and castes of our population which are socially and economically insecure. There is reason to believe that when a member achieves advancement in status he no longer requires the kinds of satisfaction offered by store-front groups. Because of these factors, a large proportion of the membership in such groups is Negro—although in each of the groups described above, there is a sprinkling of Caucasians.

With the exception of the Black Jews, most of these groups tend to be schismatic. For example, a small group broke away from the House of Prayer and took the name *House of Faith*. A similar body, also schismatic, is known as the *Latter House of the Lord for All People*. These schisms may be fostered by nebulous or even incoherent theologies. To attempt any systematic statement of their points of view is a task beset with many difficulties. Listening to sermons, talking with officials, and even reading the fragmentary materials which are very occasionally published by these groups disclose lack of coherence which is baffling to the serious inquirer. Even to say that they hold a position similar to Christian Fundamentalism would be far from easy to establish.

As these studies suggest, there is considerable variation in theological position among the groups. Moreover, they are not alike psychologically, socially, or even morally. They range from a psychopathic emotionalism (which seems to give the psychoneurotic and psychotic some place for haven) to groups such as the Black Jews, which emphasize wholesome personality development. There are some with a high ethical or moral purpose, such as one group which attempts to provide the children of the slums with a simple social program designed to keep them from the questionable society of the streets. On the other hand, my observations have led me to feel that there are some groups whose leaders and congregations subscribe to a questionable ethical code.

It seems reasonable to question the social values of the religion offered in many store-front groups. The extremes of behavior encountered in a number of such churches appear to be poor compensations for the difficulties the worshiper has found in life. At best, the broad answers to cosmic questions of destiny and mystery may be mere rationalizations to evade the stern realities of the social and economic world. To the degree that these religions are escapes from life rather than attempts to meet it realistically, they are not socially constructive. However, store-front churches exist, for better or for worse, largely because the great denominational bodies have failed to reach these people. If the large churches were satisfying them, they would feel it unnecessary to worship in such lowly places. It seems apparent, therefore, that such religious groups will continue until accepted religious or social institutions fill a void in the lives of the store-front people.

These religious groups are in general fragmentary and disorganized. To many observers it would appear doubtful that they are capable of making any lasting imprint on society either socially or theologically. However, before there is a categorical acceptance of this judgment it is well to recall that the social origins of the religious denominations and ecclesia of today were exceedingly humble. It seems likely that a contemporary might similarly have questioned their importance. Whatever position is assumed, it is evident that store-front religions must be further explored if we are to understand more fully their place in both the secular and the religious communities and their relationship to contemporary trends in American life.

Sectarianism
as a Response to Anomie

Renato Poblete, S. J., and Thomas F. O'Dea

The hypothesis to be explored in this paper may be
stated as follows. The development of sectarianism among
New York Puerto Ricans is a response to anomie. It is
furthermore a response that represents a positive quest
for community in the face of the loss of more traditional
social structures and the impersonalization of modern
American urban society.

The larger frame of reference in which this problem
must be considered is one that includes Western civilization as a whole. Modern man is haunted by the specter of
insecurity in consequence of the many reasons which we
have indicated above. "There is a decided weakening of
faith in the inherent stability of the individual and in psychological and moral neutrality; individualism has become
in recent decades a term to describe pathological conditions of society."[2] The release of the individual from the
traditional ties of class, religion, and kinship has made him
free, but on the testimony of innumerable works of our
age, this freedom is accompanied not by the sense of
creative release, but by the experience of disenchantment
and alienation. Erich Fromm has shown that it may be

Reprinted in abridged form from "Anomie and the Quest for
Community: The Formation of Sects Among Puerto Ricans of New
York," *American Catholic Sociological Review*, 21 (Spring, 1960),
pp. 18–36. Used by permission of the authors and the publisher.

accompanied by intense psychological anxiety.³ In fact the
theme of uprooted man seeking fellowship is as frequent
in our time as was the theme of the individual's emancipation from tribal or communal conformity in the past. Riesman speaks of a new need for "other directedness" among
Americans, and popular magazines exploit the theme of
"togetherness."⁴ The loss of what Durkheim called consensus is what Nisbet has called a loss of moral certitudes
and is followed by a sense of alienation from one's fellow
man.⁵ Industrial sociology has shown the importance of the
work community for the morale of the individual work-
man. Drucker has commented upon the "end of the economic man." Since the larger framework of human orientation includes what Paul Tillich has called "the ultimate,"
that such a loss of solidarity and consensus has religious
significance and that the response to it may take the form
of a religious quest is not difficult to see.

Today there is visible a reaction against the heritage of
the immediate past. Men seem to be seeking integration,
status, membership; there is a desire for recognition, for
the formation of small groups, for personal relationships.
This is a reaction against the impersonalization of a technological society characterized by urbanism. Toennies saw
the history of the West as the transformation of *Gemeinschaft* into *Gesellschaft*, what in Redfield's terms may be
called the transition from a folk to an urban society. Today,
American society seems to be reacting in an opposite direction. The much-heralded and quite ambiguous revival
of religion seems to be an associated phenomenon.⁶

If religion appears to offer a way out of this situation—
especially to a people whose cultural background is characterized by important religious elements—the reverse is also
true. Religious life requires the support and underpinning

of social solidarity. André Brien emphasizes the need of small communities in order that Catholic people may be able to live the faith.[7] He refers to the proliferation of sects in the popular milieu as a sign of the importance of the formation of small communities in the urban world of today. These groups, characterized by enthusiasm in the eighteenth-century meaning of that term, and sometimes to the point of fanaticism, are capable of evoking from the impersonalized man of our age a spirit of unity and sacrifice. The intense life of the group exalts the personality; the person caught up in the current of irresistible enthusiasm discovers in himself a force of life which previously had lain dormant. This gives the individual a feeling of participation and consequently of strength and worth.

THE QUEST FOR COMMUNITY

What we have reviewed so far would suggest that anomie is a fairly general problem in modern urban society and that reaction against it—attempts to escape it—are far from uncommon. We are suggesting that a similar condition is characteristic of the Puerto Rican migrants in response to the concrete conditions of their migration. At this point, in view of our general characterization of this phenomenon as a quest for community, it will be helpful to consider recent theoretical discussions of the meaning of that term among sociologists.

George A. Hillery, in his study of areas of agreement in the definitions of community used in sociological literature, states that "a majority of the definitions include as important elements . . . : an area, common ties, and social interaction."[8] For MacIver, a community is a social unity whose members recognize as common sufficient interest to permit the common activities and interactions of common life.[9] In his book *Society*, the same author states that we have community when the members live their lives wholly within the general group. He stresses community sentiment as the most important ingredient of community, since modern transport has made a territorial base relatively unimportant. For MacIver, this community sentiment has three elements: "we-feeling," that is, a sense of collective participation in an indivisible unity, a sense of belonging to the group which can use the term "we" with the same referent; role-feeling, a sense of status which consists in the fact that each person feels that he has a part to perform, a function to fulfill in the reciprocal exchange, involving a subordination of the individual to the whole; and dependency-feeling, closely associated with role-feeling, involving the individual's feeling of dependency upon the community as a necessary condition for his own life. It involves either physical or psychological dependency since the community is the greater home which sustains him. It is the refuge from solitude and the fears that accompany the individual isolation so characteristic of modern life.[10]

Toennies found the supreme form of community in what he called the "*Gemeinschaft* of mind" implying "co-operation and co-ordinated action for a common goal."[11] August B. Hollingshead concluded that the term "community" was defined in at least three different ways in current literature: (*a*) as a form of group solidarity, cohesion and action around common and diverse interests; (*b*) as a geographic area with spatial limits; or (*c*) as a sociogeographical structure which combines the first two definitions.[12]

The elements of these classical and contemporary definitions of most concern to us would appear to be those stressed in Toennies' *"Gemeinschaft* of mind" and Mac-Iver's community sentiment and represented in other terms in the other definitions.

A Test of the Anomie Hypothesis

Let us restate our hypothesis more fully at this point: The formation of sects is one of the known ways out of anomie, and the facts of Puerto Rican life in New York suggest the presence of such a condition among these new arrivals. The sect represents a search for a way out of that condition and is therefore an attempt to redevelop the community in the new urban situation.

In attempting to explore this hypothesis and to prepare for some kind of observational testing of it, a small area in the Southern Bronx was studied. This area coincides with St. Athanasius Roman Catholic Parish. In this area we were able to locate ten store-front churches and two larger churches of the same type, the Christian Church of Juan 3:16, at Westchester Avenue, and the Independent church, Iglesia del Señor, with characteristics quite like those of the Pentecostals.

These store-front churches did not have more than sixty members each. They have almost daily meetings with an attendance of half to two thirds of the membership present. It is quite difficult to get reliable figures on the exact membership since there are always some visitors at the services who either come from other store-front churches or who may be just curious outsiders. Each evening's services are organized by a different subgroup—the men's group, the women's group, or the youth group. The service begins around eight o'clock in the evening and lasts until

around ten. When a stranger attends he is greeted immediately, given a songbook, and offered a seat. The amount
of cordiality shown to the visitor is remarkable to the field
worker. The minister or some person from the congregation reads the Bible and explains what has been read. Accompanying the words of the speaker there gradually
develops a kind of spontaneous participation by the congregation. This takes the form of spontaneous ejaculations
such as "Amen, Alleluia, *Gloria a Dios, Gloria a Jesús, Dios
todopoderoso,* and *Alabado Dios.*" In this way the group
actively participates even in that part of the service in
which a leader has the structured ascendancy and initiative.

After the sermon, which is punctuated by such ex-
clamations from the congregation, the whole community
sings. Some of the melodies are old American folk songs
with special religious Spanish text or are translated Protestant hymns. Frequently somebody volunteers to sing a
solo or to play an instrument. The minister during this
period invites people to speak a few words or relate their
own religious experience or the history of their conversion.
Some members of the congregation express gratitude for
some favors received, or ask for prayers for some need.
This is followed by more singing.

The plans for evangelical work are proposed or reports
of current activities are heard. At the end everybody prays
in a loud voice and spontaneously. One can feel the enthusiasm and desire for the Spirit in the group. At times
an individual manifests the reception of the Holy Spirit
by "speaking with tongues." When that happens the members begin to shout incoherently or just to utter words.
The speech of the person who has the gift of tongues may
be "interpreted" by another member. Then the members

of the community thank God and pray that all may receive these gifts.

On Sunday, service lasts for two hours. Here the minister, either the regular minister or a guest, will have a more important role. He will give instruction to the people on the Bible or upon moral precepts.

In addition to using what sociologists call "participant observation" of these groups, ministers and members were interviewed. We were able to interview twenty-eight persons. The interviews were conducted in Spanish by the field worker, for whom Spanish is his native language. All but three of the twenty-eight were baptized Catholics. Yet these twenty-five did not have any real knowledge of the Catholic Church. There appeared to be no ground to assume that their conversion was in any intellectual sense a protest against the Catholic Church. The element of protest was not important in what they reported about themselves. Moreover, the interviews revealed that their knowledge of the ideology of the sect was rudimentary. The Bible is held to be the only norm of life, a point of view that involves a very fundamentalistic interpretation of the "Word." They all hold that we have been redeemed by Christ's death. They hold the importance of two baptisms, one of water and one of the Spirit. There is much emphasis upon a total way of life involving brotherly love and the rejection of sin. There is no systematic doctrinal body of beliefs.

The people interviewed talked very frankly about their conversion. They consider the frank revelation of the history of their conversion as a "testimony," bearing of witness to the Holy Spirit. The form of such testimonies shows that despite the spontaneity of communal religiosity there is a degree of stereotyping. It would appear that each convert has heard many testimonies and makes the attempt to interpret and fit in his own experience into a normatively desired pattern. They usually go in this way: "I used to drink . . . I was a drug addict . . . I used to run around with women . . . I was on the wrong path . . . but one day I received the Spirit, I got to know the 'Word.'" They always attribute a great sinfulness to their previous life. The form of the testimony emphasizes a great experience of sinfulness and the religious experience of being possessed by the Spirit. And the latter appears to give them a certitude of regeneration.

The formal "design" of the testimony reveals consciousness of sinfulness—conversion—regeneration. While this is not a spontaneous product of subjective personal disposition unaffected by social conformation to an expected pattern, there is reason to suspect that subjective experience lent itself readily to such conformation. That is to say, while these testimonies may be elicited in an interview situation without any direction suggested by the interviewer, the sectarian expectations do in fact act to standardize them. Yet they also seem to reflect something important of the experience of conversion which seems in itself (as well as in its retelling) to have been shaped for subjective awareness by the sectarian stereotype. Moreover, the original need dispositions of the subjects appear to have lent themselves to precisely this kind of standardization. Although it would be very difficult to separate the elements analytically and perhaps impossible to observe them empirically, there appears a measure of congruence between the "primitive" experience and the content of the sectarian stereotype. This bears obvious resemblance to the general sectarian conviction that Max Weber referred to in his treatment of "salvation religions." These people feel saved from something and incorporated into something new and clean and good.

Conversion—the classical phenomenon of religious psychology—is something that follows upon some months of attending services as spectators. When these interviewees were asked why they started coming to meetings, why they first became interested in the sect, their answers also revealed a degree of uniformity, and possibly one less affected by a cultural stereotype. "The first time I went there, I was impressed by the way everyone shook hands with me and the way everybody said 'hello' to me." "I was sick, they came to my home to say a prayer for me." "I used to go to the Catholic Church, there nobody knew me . . . now in my church they call me sister." A very typical answer was *"Me sentí como en mi casa"* (I felt at home). "I was lost here in New York, a friend invited me and I liked the way they sang and that we all could sing." "I like to read the Bible." "The first time I went, when the service was over, someone came to me and asked my name and invited me to come again." Participant observation at the meetings confirms the interpretation of warmth, welcome, and participation related by the converted.

The interviews strongly suggest that isolation is one of the things from which such people are saved by the salvation experience of conversion. Isolation appears to be associated with a loss of orientation in life. Thus the material offered by those interviewed would tend to support the contention that conversion offered a way out of anomie, both in terms of providing social relationships and giving meaningful orientations to the converted.

That the sect is a real community according to those elements stressed in the sociological literature is confirmed by both the content of the interviews and participant observation. For example the three elements of community sentiment stressed by MacIver are present to a high degree in the Pentecostal sect.

The presence of "we-feeling" is clearly evident in the way members talk about the sect. The church to which they belong is not something foreign or removed from them. The service is a common enterprise; the members support the group with great financial generosity; there is a real conviction of membership in a brotherhood. They all know each other by name: *hermano Juan, hermana María,* etc.

"Role-feeling" is also quite evident. Each member has a role in the community and so marked is such participation that one report concluded that "it is hard to know to what degree we can call these churches a lay association." The individual member has opportunities to direct the service, to tell his troubles, to recount his religious experiences, to ask for prayers and to give thanks for prayers said, or to ask for help. The members not only participate in religious services in this way but also take part in such work as visiting the sick. The minister of the East Harlem Protestant Parish, a parish divided into five small communities following the example of l'Abbé Michoneau in France, stated to us that the activity of the layman was in his opinion the clue to the success of these Protestant sects.

Moreover, MacIver's feeling of dependency is also present. Each person knows that he is a part of the group, that he needs the group in order to sustain his regeneration. He feels this dependency at the service when the minister asks the names of those who are sick, or the names of those whose birthdays fall in the coming week. If a person gives his name, the whole community prays for him.

It is important to note that the group solidarity appears to the converted not as a loss of individuality but rather as a chance to develop his own personality—to experience a worth-while fulfillment.

One indication of what has been said concerns the question of size. It would seem that such close in-group sentiment requires small groups and that a larger membership would inevitably introduce secondary relationships with concomitant impersonalization. In this respect it was interesting to find in the area of our study a large Pentecostal church with a membership of 800. This church had been founded in 1935 and began, as all such groups begin, as a small group with a small meeting place. By 1954, it had grown to 500 members and was able to purchase for $70,000 a reconditioned theater with a seating capacity of 1,800. Now two full-time ministers care for the community. At their weekly meetings they have between 200 and 300 persons. Though this figure in comparison with that of the total membership suggests a lower degree of participation, it is nevertheless remarkable to find there all the characteristics we found in the smaller bodies. H. Richard Niebuhr has developed the Troeltschian theory to show that sects in time also have to make some kind of compromise with the world in which they live and become routinized. Such a routinized sect he calls a denomination. This larger group in our area does not in the opinion of the observer show any impressive signs of such routinization, but our research has not proceeded far enough to answer the important questions in this respect.

While we do not consider our hypothesis unambiguously confirmed at this stage of the game, we do feel entirely justified in stating that a hypothesis based upon such a firm body of sociological theory as this one is provides a very helpful device for understanding the phenomenon with which we are dealing. Moreover, the evidence to date does bear a striking congruence with the hypothesis itself. Since the hypothesis is based upon a body of theory that has considerable congruence with religious life as it has been studied in a multitude of different concrete settings, the congruity of our preliminary material with it gives us greater confidence than would be the case were our hypothesis merely an *ad hoc* construction unrelated to a larger body of theory and empirical generalization.

The Urbanization
of a Holiness Body

Val B. Clear

In the period immediately following the Civil War a rash of spontaneous revivalistic movements arose. Some flourished and eventuated in permanent religious associations while others faded and died. Those that persisted were for the most part the bodies we know today as the "Holiness Churches."

The holiness people of this period were predominantly rural people. They tended to be the more devout persons in the rural churches, for the holiness movement was aimed at proselyting rather than at winning sinners to righteousness. Its main appeal was to the main supporters of local churches and it exploited fully the unsatisfied hunger found in the hearts of devoted persons of all ages.

But rural America moved to the city and with it moved many holiness people.

THE OLD PATTERN

The effect of this environmental change can be illustrated by a close look at the changes occurring in one religious group emerging out of the National Holiness Movement: the Church of God (Anderson, Indiana).

Reprinted in abridged form from *The City Church* (July-August, 1958), 2–3, 7–11. Used by permission of the author and the publisher.

The traditional position of this group denies itself denominational status. It refers to itself as a movement and conceives its function to be a testimony to the true nature of the church that Jesus founded—undivided brotherhood of all the redeemed. It maintains no membership rolls (except where state law requires it) and studiously avoids the use of terms like "denomination" or "sect" in self-reference. The avoidance of these terms is so unanimous as to amount to a shibboleth in identifying strangers and friends, even yet.

The urbanization of the body brought extensive changes at many points and complete reversal of position at some points.

The effects of urbanization have not appeared without resistance. Change rarely does. And where the values of the past have a religious character normal resistance is strengthened further by deep emotional attachments to the faith and patterns of the past.

One of the earliest portents of future stress over urbanization's influence came at the national camp meeting of the Church of God in 1910. In a forceful editorial the official weekly, the *Gospel Trumpet,* described what happened when the generally accepted standards were relaxed. The point at issue was the wearing of neckties.

In a rural environment it was not very difficult to preach against the wearing of neckties, termed "superfluities of naughtiness" from James 1:21. Neckties were symbols of the sophistication of the city, which is always resented in rural society; and holiness people in rural areas were generally opposed to them as evidence of ungodly pride.

Church of God people had opposed ties from the beginning of the movement in 1878, but by 1910 there were a few brave souls who dared to challenge the pattern. One of these was a Pittsburgh banker who was also a lay preacher. Later he became a full-time minister and retired a few years ago as general manager of the publishing house of the Church of God.

Because of his employment in the banking business, in which he dealt constantly with highly sophisticated people, A. T. Rowe had to wear a tie. He did so, but whenever he went to a religious function he removed it. The inconsistency of this behavior was not lost to him, and finally he argued that if he could be a Christian businessman during the week while wearing a tie, he could be a Christian minister over the weekend while similarly adorned. In 1910 he and a few other ministers appeared at the annual national camp meeting with neckties on.

The editor of the *Gospel Trumpet* joined battle. He wrote scathingly that

It is a matter much to be regretted that two or three ministers in this reformation have been so blinded by such a spirit of compromise as to don their superfluous paraphernalia and take the pulpit even at a camp meeting and upbraid as fanatical the saints who would not fall in line with the same. There may be circumstances where such an article of dress would not be objectionable when required in holding a business position, but it is a superfluity in assemblies of the saints.

A key to succeeding changes is to be found in the last sentence above: "There may be circumstances where such an article of dress would not be objectionable when required in holding a business position. . . ." When compromises are justified on the basis that the business world requires them, the day of the bourgeois church has dawned.

Other changes followed. Increasingly, the growth of

adherents occurred in urban centers. A device intended to meet the challenge of the cities was developed, called the Missionary Home. Before 1900 one was established in Chicago in Plymouth Court, across the street from what is now the Board of Trade Building. One of the annoying aspects of the location was the presence in the same building of a house of prostitution. Workers in the Home, virtually all of whom were recently from the country, came face to face with urban patterns at their worst.

By 1910 there were Missionary Homes in at least nineteen cities from New York to California. These were permanent establishments with a permanent core of mature leaders who devoted themselves to training young workers and to doing evangelistic work on their own. Eventually most of these Homes became congregations. The one in Chicago, mentioned above, has moved by several stages from the Loop south to 81st Street, where a few years ago it erected an impressive Bedford stone church of traditional design. The congregation has now lost all semblance of its original pattern and operates a family-centered program similar to that of its neighboring Protestant churches.

The Missionary Homes were staffed by persons with rural background, and they were most successful with persons of rural background; but any group which rubs shoulders with urbanism for several years necessarily finds that some of it rubs off, and in the case of the Missionary Homes this unmistakably was the outcome.

Another area in which the move to the city affected the Church of God was its pattern of behavior before an audience. The degree of cause-effect relationship here is difficult to assess. I am persuaded of the validity of Richard Niebuhr's thesis that sects tend to change because of a strong impulse toward respectability, and evidence is unmistakably clear in the history of the Church of God. Before moving to the city it was customary for brethren to greet each other with the "holy kiss" (man-man and woman-woman, but never man-woman), and the raising of "holy hands" was almost given the status of an ordinance.

Dietary considerations also were to feel the effect of the cityward migration. The common formula was to deny in the same breath the use of narcotics, coffee, tea, and alcohol. All were taboo. And, one might point out, not readily available in an area of self-sufficient farming.

The pattern of public worship was another facet to feel the effect of urbanization. Simplicity was the keynote before the move to the city. Previous to 1890 settled pastors were almost unknown. All ministers conceived of their function to be "guerilla evangelism" (their term), by which they meant swooping down on a community without advance notice, holding a series of meetings (in the schoolhouse if possible; if not, in a nearby grove), blasting the devout loose from their churches, then moving on. The converts were left in an ecclesiastical vacuum. They had withdrawn from their churches, but no attempt was made to establish a local fellowship to which they could resort. In many places they did come together regularly and form an unstructured association, but without a pastor.

The New Pattern

Contemporary Church of God behavior cannot be understood adequately without realizing the background

presented above in abbreviated form. The changes have
been broad and profound.

Perhaps the point of maximum accommodation has
been in the area of interdenominational co-operation.
Early leaders of the Church of God refused to extend the
hand of fellowship to, or to co-operate on any level with,
ministers of other religious bodies. All religious organizations, they said, were conceived by Satan and no true
Christian could have anything to do with them once he
recognized them for what they were.

Urbanization brought an opportunity to observe the
genuineness of persons in other religious groups. Honest
appraisal of the vitality of the faith and the validity of
the works of their neighbors led ministers and laymen
alike to revise their attitude toward those of the outgroup.
Perhaps the painful presence of intragroup tensions, with
resultant schisms in numerous Church of God congregations, made them self-conscious about claiming purity.

At any rate, the voice of protest was muted. The program of the local church became more and more an evangelistic outreach toward the unredeemed and less and
less an appeal to the already churched populace.

Co-operation replaced combat. Pastors engaged in interdenominational programs of various kinds, congregations became members of councils of churches, and
ministers joined ministerial associations. In the majority
of cases, urban Churches of God are now well integrated
in local interdenominational programs, with many ministers carrying major responsibilities.

Co-operation on the interdenominational level is reflected by the presence at Evanston and Oberlin of ac-
credited observers. Each of the general agencies of the
Church of God is integrated into the appropriate division

of the National Council of Churches of Christ. The body is not a member of the National Council, largely because there is no national organization that feels it is legally authorized to take the step. But on every level the Church of God is a part of the organization of the National Council. Executives of the general agencies of the Church of God hold several responsible positions in the divisions of the Council.

So the cycle is completed. In a rural society the message preached rejection of all ecclesiastical organization because such human machinery was a cancer in the body of Christ. With urbanization came socialization and assimilation until today some of the hands that push the buttons of that machinery are those of Church of God executives.

Perhaps less crucial, but quite symptomatic, has been the change in group customs regarding dress and diet.

It was a simple matter in rural America to condemn the wearing of decorative attire: lace, bright collar buttons, jewelry. But when the people moved to the city they found neckties essential to certain occupations. Some perceptive souls pointed out that *not* wearing a necktie might also be an act of pride, and that one dressed too severely might well be guilty of the pride of self-righteousness and therefore be as bad off as the vain one who decorated his person. This created a quandary which was gradually solved by rationalizing acceptance of the majority group patterns. As late as 1930 some question was raised as to the propriety of wearing gold frames for eyeglasses, but when the memorial church in Washington, D.C., was dedicated a decade later a gold cross was placed on the altar. The change was further demonstrated by the gift which a leading minister gave his wife on their twenty-fifth anniversary. He gave her a gold wedding band, the first wedding ring she had ever had. Gold was no longer a carnal metal. Today most urban congregations are quite receptive to diamond engagement rings and wedding bands, and in many urban congregations Sunday morning finds a number of worshipers wearing earrings, scatter pins, and similar jewelry.

The change is less evident in the rural church, although there has been some change there also. In general, rural Churches of God tend to follow the pattern of the neighborhood in which they are located. Kansas congregations, for example, may frown on mixed swimming of both sexes, but in California young people's societies may have their meetings on the beach with swimming a part of the program.

The intensive evangelistic drive of the people newly moved to the city has changed from the aggressive door-to-door and street-meeting approach of the Missionary Homes to a much more sophisticated pattern. To be sure, there is still an interest in evangelism and most congregations have a "revival meeting" semiannually, which is aimed ostensibly at reaching the unredeemed.

Increasingly, however, emphasis is placed on Christian education in the program of the local church. Christian Family Week, Youth Week, World Communion Sunday, The World Day of Prayer, Holy Week—these are now the focal points of the church calendar, whereas previously congregational life revolved around the revivals that performed ritual and festive functions in the group.

Sophistication has become a necessary part of accommodation to city life. One of the forces bringing this about—and the major force, probably—has been the problem of conserving the next generation.

For city people who had been reared in the country a church program did not have to differ greatly from what they had known. It is a truism, despite the humor, that you can take the hick out of the country but you cannot take the country out of the hick. Some modification is needed in a city church serving rurally oriented people, but nothing drastic. Its function is to bridge the gap, to facilitate transition.

But the children of the migrant are another matter. They have been reared in the city. They do not have a reservoir of rural ideas and thought patterns. They constitute a totally different set of problems for the church, and one of them is prestige. To hold the next generation the church of the migrants must become eminently "respectable," otherwise the young people will go either to another church or to none at all.

So the church relaxes its program of grab-him-by-the-lapel evangelism, puts robes on the choir and candles on the altar, divides the chancel, replaces folding chairs with oaken pews, and calls a college-trained minister. The most dramatic step comes when it moves out of its plain, rectangular white frame building into a stone Gothic or redwood contemporary structure. It is now respectable.

Urban pastors with considerable prestige tend to place great emphasis on either preaching or counseling. From the 1890's, when a sermon dared not be prepared in advance in order to avoid harnessing the Spirit, to today's plan of sermons projected sometimes months in advance, is a long way. But the city congregations have desired trained ministers, and in their training the young men have learned professional standards. Sermons are prepared with care and diligence. Many write out the messages almost verbatim, but no one actually reads the manuscript. One pastor, a man who has done all his residence work toward a doctorate at Union Theological Seminary in New York City, charges professional rates for personal counseling and has a thriving clientele.

Salary-wise, the ministry of the Church of God reflects professionalization, as well. No figures are available for publication, but an enlightened guess is that the average salary of pastors of thriving urban churches would be in the neighborhood of $7,000. A number receive a pastoral salary of over $10,000, in addition to income from other sources.

One of the reasons for this salary scale has been the short supply of trained ministers capable of successful city service. And with the growing number of managerial, business, and professional men on the boards of trustees, competitive salaries have mounted. Urbanization has produced a cyclical effect: winning urbanized laymen to the church has produced a desire for a more sophisticated minister. The more sophisticated minister has been better able to win professional, managerial, and business men. In turn, they have sought professionally trained clergymen. And so ad infinitum. In seventy years the Church of God has come from the pattern of no pastor for any church to the point where one congregation has four and a half ministers.

IMPLICATIONS

A year ago 26 per cent of the constituents of the Church of God were in rural churches. Urban centers of under 10,000 had 17 per cent. The cities of 10,000 and over held 57 per cent of the constituents of the body. In congregations, the rural churches were exactly offset by those in cities of 10,000 population and over: 40.5 per cent for each. An additional 19 per cent of the congregations were located in smaller cities (2,500–10,000 population). Starting as a rural, amorphous movement, the group in its eighty years of development is now decidedly an urban body.

With the urbanization of location has come an urbanization of behavior patterns. Taboos reflecting a rural environment of the 1880's have become obsolete in an urban environment of the 1950's. Prohibitions have been dropped and a new dynamic for prestige has developed.

But what now happens to rural in-migrants to the city? Radio, television, centralized schools, magazines, and other factors have reduced the differential gap between rural and urban cultures, perhaps, but the basic problem of acculturation is still an important one. As churches in the city's port of entry make continuous adaption to urban ways, their effectiveness in serving the needs of the rural in-migrants diminishes. In many cases the churches themselves join the exodus to the suburbs. We must find some way to meet on his own level the rural person whose roots have been torn up in his move to the city. An effective church program will aid his adjustment to city life, but in doing so the church itself will be changed. Some provision should be made to replace it with another institution that can speak meaningfully to the condition of his successors in the cityward movement of population.

CHAPTER VI

DILEMMAS OF URBAN CHURCH ORGANIZATION

INTRODUCTION

Urbanization is surely one of the contributing factors to the proliferation of organizations and the need for co-ordination among large collectivities. In a sense organizational life constitutes a powerful antidote to the dehumanizing effects of urban society. As an acute observer noted: "What a man belongs to constitutes most of his life career and all of his obituary." Moreover, without organizational affiliation a person is isolated and impotent; likewise, a community without organizations is paralyzed.

From a negative standpoint, however, organizations tend to breed overconformity to established procedures. They run the risk of inflexibility and of separating laymen from the centers of institutional power. If organizational life maximizes personal achievement, it can also devaluate the sense of personal worth.

The dilemmas of organizational life are posed no less for the church and the ministry. Indeed, at a time of rapid church expansion and institutional vitality, the organization of the church is looming as one of the most critical problems confronting American Protestantism. Just as the church must clarify its purpose and task, so too the minister must search for self-understanding of who he is and what he is doing. He must work out a doctrine of the church and the ministry which is integrated with a sociological definition of his role. The selections in this chapter should stimulate discussion of these themes.

219

"The Organizational Dilemma in American Protestant-ism" is written by the editor. *The dilemma facing religious organizations is that the very organization necessary to fulfill the purposes of the church may at the same time detract from the purpose it is intended to serve. Despite efforts to escape from this dilemma by defining the church so as to avoid the conflict, the problem remains and is increasingly serious because ecclesiastical organizations have expanded in scope and size. Nowhere is this dilemma more evident than in the large urban parish, where koinonia is virtually lost sight of in concept and in practice.*

Samuel W. Blizzard's article "Role Conflicts of the Urban Minister" has stimulated spirited discussion on the minister's role ambiguity. *The author, Professor of Christianity and Society at Princeton Theological Seminary, explores the conflicting role expectations in the life of the urban pastor. These recurring dilemmas include: the saintly versus the prophetic role, man of action or scholar, counseling skills at odds with preaching role, local parish orientation set against denominational orientation, family loyalties as opposed to job demands. These tensions in the minister's self-image of his role are potentially dangerous for the mental health of the clergy.*

The social structure of an urban congregation is as variable and complex as the proverbial fable about the seven blind men, each of whom took hold of one part of the elephant and concluded that his partial description defined the whole. In "Conceptualizations of the Urban Parish," Joseph H. Fichter, S.J., Professor of Sociology at Loyola University of the South, suggests seven frames of references for viewing the Roman Catholic urban parish structure: a legal corporation, a superimposed association, an institutionalized association, a communal group, a cluster of subgroupings, a series of statistical categories, and a system of kinship groupings. The article is also suggestive for analysis of urban Protestant churches.

The Organizational Dilemma in American Protestantism

Robert Lee

I

Like other social institutions on the contemporary American scene, Protestantism is deeply implicated in what Kenneth Boulding calls "the organizational revolution." In an age of large-scale organizations and centralized agencies in various spheres of life, churches too are organized on a similar basis if they seek to be relevant to the new *Zeitgeist*—not to mention the strain toward survival endemic to the career of most organizations.

The elaboration of organizational apparatus in American Protestantism brings in its wake many pressing issues; for it seems a truism that the virtues of religion can seldom be as well organized as its vices. One of these key issues, which I shall call the "organizational dilemma," goes to the very core of the faith and challenges its integrity. Unlike the rather commonplace dilemma of the gap between an individual's profession and his practice (which is less an intrinsic dilemma than a commentary on the givenness of the human situation of finite man), this dilemma, of which we speak, is structural; it is part of the

Reprinted from *Challenges to Traditional Ethics*, edited by Harold D. Lasswell and Harlan Cleveland (Conference on Science, Philosophy, and Religion, New York, 1961). Used by permission of the Conference on Science, Philosophy, and Religion of The Jewish Theological Seminary of America.

very make-up of the church which exists in a particular social context and interacts with its surrounding culture.

The dilemma is simply this: on the one hand, if the church is to take seriously its obligation as a missionary and witnessing movement, it must maintain some semblance of continuity, stability, and persistence; it must develop appropriate organizational and institutional forms. Yet, on the other hand, the very institutional embodiments necessary for the survival of the church may threaten, obscure, distort, or deflect from the purposes for which the institution was originally founded. Thus it is hardly sufficient to say that the task of the church is to be obedient or to be faithful if obedience and faithfulness are detached from the question of institutional self-maintenance.

In a very fundamental sense, the critical problem of the church is the problem of community. And community always involves the rational organization of human resources and more-or-less defined patterns of group interaction governing the life of its members. We may speak heuristically (not literally) of the church and community problem by reference to this familiar aphorism: "After the doxology, comes the theology, then the sociology." After the initial religious experience or the original creative impulse (doxology), soon there sets in the need to define and formulate a systematic body of teachings, a codified and articulated set of doctrines (theology); then follows the necessity of preserving and perpetuating the original experience through the organization of a community (sociology).

After the Spirit-ruled (charismatic) church of Pentecost, there soon develops the institutionalized church of early Catholicism. After the prophets come the priests.

Or, in the much-quoted words of Max Weber, with the passage of the charismatic leader, attempts are made to preserve the benefits of charisma, resulting in a "routinization of charisma." The holy must necessarily be related to the profane. Indeed, "we have this treasure in earthen vessels." There must necessarily be a *manifestation* of the *essence* of the church. And, in the very process, the instrumental purposes of organizations become exalted as ends. Paul Harrison states this dilemma cogently when he points out, "The results are paradoxical, since the goals which the organization was created to achieve tend to be displaced by the goal of organizational self-perpetuation."[1] And Philip Selznick pinpoints the dilemma by the term "organizational imperatives." The organization must satisfy its own self-generated needs before the group can attend to the goals for which it was established:

We can say that once having taken the organization road we are committed to action which will fulfill the requirements of order, discipline, unity, defense, and consent. These imperatives may demand measures of adaptation unforeseen by the initiators of the action, and may, indeed, result in a deflection of their original goals.[2]

In other words:

Running an organization, as a specialized and essential activity, generates problems which have no necessary (and often an opposed) relationship to the professed or "original" goals of the organization. The day-to-day behavior of the group becomes centered around specific problems and proximate goals which have primarily an internal relevance. Then, since these activities come to consume an increasing proportion of the time and thought of the participants, they are—from the point of view of actual behavior—substituted for the professed goals.[3]

At present there are several prominent efforts to avoid
or escape from the organizational dilemma confronting
churches. One such approach would define the church
solely in terms of its essence, in terms which focus on the
"invisible church," or on the "bride of Christ." (As D.T.
Niles quips, "Who wants to marry an invisible bride?")
Hence the church is defined in terms of its being and not
in its organization and action, as if God were involved in
the former but not the latter. Such a view is essentially
maintained by Emil Brunner in his *Misunderstanding of
the Church*, which, indeed, has misunderstood the church.
For it makes of the church something of a disembodied
spirit floating about, perhaps in outer space. According
to Brunner, "The New Testament *Ecclesia*, the fellowship
of Jesus Christ, is a pure communion of persons and has
nothing of the character of an institution about it."[4] We
would do well to remember, as Jacob Taubes reminds us,
that "man is not content to let the heavenly city remain
an abode in the clouds, but longs for an earthly setting."[5]

The other alternative, which does equal violation to
the "reality of the church," is to focus exclusively on the
institutional and organizational aspects of the church.
For ecclesiastical structures, in Protestant thought, do
not exhaust the Protestant conception of faith. Indeed, as
H. Richard Niebuhr observes, "Protestant religion centers
less in the ecclesiastical establishment than in the Bible
and the proclamation of its message, and in the personal
religious experiences and attitudes of its adherents."[6] To
view the church simply as a social organization is already
to judge it by a set of assumptions which may be covert
or explicit. Thus the American Institute of Management's
1955 study of the American Baptist Convention concludes
with this professional appraisal: "Viewed against the

background of the modern business corporation, the management practices of religious organizations are appallingly archaic."[7] Again the report states, ". . . Religious organizations may be compared to corporations which concentrate on product development to the virtual exclusion of executive development."[8]

Note that the Institute's first generalization is made after a study of a single Protestant group. But even if such a judgment were accepted at face value, there remains the problem of whether a religious organization can legitimately be evaluated solely "against the background of modern business corporations." Religion cannot be treated as a "product," a commodity to be developed, processed, packaged, shipped out, and sold by a band of supersalesmen-evangelists. To be sure, there is no excuse for wastefulness, slovenly work habits, and the like. But that a business should be the model for a church to conform to is to forget the purpose of the church; it would be similar to the hazards involved if higher education were evaluated solely in terms of business standards without regard for educational goals and traditions.

In point of fact, the real danger of large organizational development in the churches does not inhere in the organizational structure per se, but rather in the ethos that often accompanies mass organizations. Religious groups not merely conform, but sometimes overconform, to the worst features of a business ethos. For example, one Protestant agency has adopted the symbols of status of a corporation hierarchy to the extent that there are four different shapes and sizes of desks, each of which is assigned to denote a particular status in the hierarchy of the organization. In another agency there is an unusually great social distance between those on the executive and those on the secretarial staff, so that it would be unthinkable for executives who bring their lunch to eat in the same room with the secretaries who bring theirs. It is interesting to note that the terms used to designate leaders of most ecclesiastical structures are adopted from the business world: executive secretary, executive vice-president, treasurer, board of directors, board of managers, etc.

The seeds of the organizational dilemma are contained in the very institutional structure of the church as it interacts with the culture. This inescapable problem is not derived from the fact that churches attract to their ranks persons of prestige and power. Such a notion, advanced by Elizabeth Nottingham in her book, *Religion and Society*,[9] neither does justice to the complexity of the dilemma nor to persons of prestige and power. Even if church membership consisted of those of lowly estate, the organizational dilemma, as we have portrayed it, would still persist. Indeed, in some sect groups and lower-class denominations and conventions, the dilemma is particularly acute.

Let it be clear that our remarks should not be construed to mean that organizational structures are evil in themselves. To hold that organizations and human institutions are inherently corrupt would be untenable from the standpoint of both theology and sociology. For rational forms of procedure may, indeed, enhance and facilitate the better performance of purpose and functions; this is certainly their intention. And to focus exclusively on the dysfunctions of large-scale organizations surely neglects the ways in which such organizations are conducive to the realization of purposes in the modern world. Large-scale organizations usher in new possibilities for creativity, and at the same time new institutional vulnerabilities and hazards.

It would be a mistake to assume that the organizational dilemma is a new phenomenon. It is at least as old as the church itself. Indeed, the apostle Paul may be considered a remarkable church organizer and administrator, whose visits and letters constantly reminded Christian communities, particularly at Corinth, of the tension between the kerygma and communal response. Although essentially a perennial problem, the organizational dilemma today clamors for urgent attention because church organizations have expanded immensely in scope and size. For our day, the search for that theoretical point which will allow the church to remain true to its purposes and yet operate through viable institutional forms that will preserve its gains and extend its influence must be an ongoing, never-ending quest. While there can be no simple resolution of the dilemma, it may become easily obscured, or perhaps, misunderstood, so that equally truncated views are adopted—views which interpret the church only as an organization or as a spiritual entity devoid of organization.

II

By no means is the organizational dilemma confined to the interdenominational administrator or the denominational board secretary in some big city headquarters. It is very tempting for many local pastors to sneer at the "bureaucracy" in their denominational agencies or in the National Council and yet fail to recognize its existence in their own local situation. We have only to remind ourselves of the widespread discussion of the multiple roles of the modern minister and the drift toward assuming administrative and organizational functions even in small parishes—what Charles Page calls a "one-man bureaucracy." With the increasing specialization and segmentation of the local clergyman's role, there develops a gap between the man in the pulpit and the man in the pew, between leaders and rank-and-file members. Social distance may exist between pastor and parishioner as administration supersedes ministration. In short, there is no escape from the organizational dilemma.

Perhaps nowhere is this dilemma more evident than in the large urban or metropolitan church. In terms of goal displacement, one is tempted to argue that these large congregations tend to make conventional Christians of their members, who increasingly become spectator-worshipers.

The large urban church is symptomatic of the shift in our society from a communal to an associational pattern. That is, segmental participation or partial involvement in many special interest associations takes the place of a community-centered focus. "This means," in the words of Robert T. Handy, "the church tends to get reduced merely to one of the many groups in which persons, detached from locality, associate together with segments of their personality. In this segmentation of culture, we find . . . the substitution of multiple moral standards for a single communal standard."[10] With increased specialization of roles and multiple-ministerial staffs in our large urban churches, face-to-face primary group relationships are weakened and replaced by associational relationships.

Martin Luther once defined the church as a sustaining fellowship of "mutual conversation and consolation" in which the members love one another and share one another's fortunes and burdens. Yet this is hardly possible in the modern situation in which the church is a part of mass culture. Like its urban ethos, impersonality, anonymity, and mass participation are prevalent in the large urban church. In tune with the rapid pace of urban culture, church members rush to church for a brief hour a week and then are just as quick in leaving its doors. The congregation on a Sunday morning is a sea of more or less impassive faces. Everyone is alone in the crowd, be it subway or sanctuary. Strangers they come and strangers they go.

For the most part, there are few available opportunities for "mutual conversation," except among the inner circle of members. Greetings and comments which do get exchanged are usually "fatuous sayings" employed in order to fend off any deeper involvement. Contacts are fleeting and superficial. As a rule, the larger the size of the congregation, the fewer the opportunities for interaction on a meaningful level. The church as *koinōnia* (community) is virtually lost sight of in concept and in practice.

In place of koinonia, we have an association of dues-paying members, the majority of whom are on the fringes of church life. These, then, are apt to be conventional Christians who may come and go, but whose Christian fellowship in any corporate sense is devoid of vitality. I suspect their numbers are legion. It may well be that the sheer size of many large urban congregations makes them "unassimilable."

With growth in size of membership, it is quite possible that churches reach an ecclesiastical "point of diminishing returns." Adopting an analogy from the growth of biological organisms, Kenneth Boulding suggests that "as an organism grows it absorbs more and more of its environment, and eventually it uses up the more favorable parts of its environment, and the environment turns increasingly less favorable."[11] What Boulding calls the "principle of increasingly unfavorable environment" may well apply to human organizations. For as a church increases its size beyond a certain point, it becomes exceedingly difficult to maintain adequate communications between leaders and members and an adequate sense of community among the members. Since the membership size is a symbol of "success" in our culture, it would appear that the large urban church is a victim of its own success. Thus the consequences of the organizational revolution for the large urban church call into question the very meaning of church membership.

III

Another aspect of the organizational revolution is its impact on charismatic leadership. Charisma, as originally defined by Max Weber, is an "extraordinary quality possessed by persons (or objects) which gives these persons a unique, magical power."[12] In recent sociological usage the term refers more broadly to a gifted leader with a dynamic personality, capable of commanding a following and usually exercising prophetic leadership.

A full exploration of the consequences of large-scale church organizations on the charismatic-prophetic *person* would be highly desirable, since this is an area of limited knowledge based on research. In addition, there is the problem of "institutional charisma." For Weber did not confine the concept of charisma to a single personality, but also spoke of the "depersonalization of charisma"— that is, the shift from a sense of an extraordinary personal gift to an impersonal capacity that in principle can be taught and learned.[13] Such an exploration might examine Weber's contention that "in institutional charisma the typical problem of deterioration is the drift of functionaries and their education toward specialized performance at the expense of personal inspiration or substantive rationality."[14]

More evidence is certainly needed before we can state categorically with Robert Michels that "bureaucracy is the sworn enemy of individual liberty, and of all bold initiative in matters of internal policy."[15] Michels' statement runs the risk of being a kind of slogan in which one can easily single out a highly visible target for attack. Yet when one views some of the top administrative posts in Protestant bureaucracies, one cannot help being impressed by the truly charismatic qualities of the persons who hold these offices. Think of men like the late John R. Mott and William Temple; James Pike, Lesslie Newbigin, W. A. Visser 't Hooft, Truman Douglass, G. Bromley Oxnam, Hermann Morse, David W. Barry, Roswell Barnes, and others. Of course, it may be argued that these are the exceptional individuals and that scores of other top leaders and those in the "lower-upper" echelons of ecclesiastical leadership leave something to be desired in the way of prophetic and imaginative leadership.

In order to identify this problem more clearly, let me cite three examples of the failure of personal charisma and of institutional charisma. These examples should not be taken as conclusive evidence of the decline of charisma, but merely indicative of the possible consequences stemming from organizational preservation and elaboration.[16]

1. In their study of the clergymen's role during the

Little Rock school crisis, Ernest Q. Campbell and Thomas
F. Pettigrew show that when ministers are faced with an
"idealistic" as contrasted to an "organizational" alternative, they will choose the latter to a degree that impairs
a prophetic ministry.[17] Ministers tend to "ease out of this
conflict" by appealing to various "reference systems."
One of the chief forms of appeal is the "organizational
reference system" in which a prophetic role is eschewed
for the sake of maintaining organizational equilibrium or
survival. Taking a leadership role may "rock the boat,"
alienate powerful contributors, or interfere with a building fund campaign, etc. For the sake of maintaining institutional stability, the clergy, by and large, played a passive role. The goal of prophetic leadership was clearly
incompatible with the desire to maintain organizational
growth and stability.

2. Individual action is increasingly geared to conform
to expectations of denominational leaders, who gain personal power either by ascription or by appropriation.
Thus many local ministers become more interested in
making a good statistical showing in reports to their denominational headquarters than in the nurture of souls
or in a prophetic ministry. Conformity to denominational
expectations may operate in very subtle ways. Consider
the case of the local minister who is asked by his denominational executive to assume a particular responsibility
(e.g., chaplain for a family summer camp) which happens to conflict with a prior commitment he has scheduled
for his church. If he should have several such conflicts,
it is likely that he will gain the reputation of being a
"non-co-operative" person in the eyes of the denominational official. Thus local men often feel compelled to
"play ball" with denominational officers, who either have

a power of appointment, should another position be available, or who can put in a negative word that has the power of blocking advancement to another post. In a sense, the local pastor is part of the "captive constituency" of the denominational administrators.

3. An example of the problem of institutional charisma is contained in the statement of a church building and extension secretary of a leading denomination. He stated very bluntly that in looking for men to staff the new so-called "high potential" suburban churches, his committee was "considering only the 'good organization men'—middle-aged men who have a large barrel of sermons to draw from and who won't have to spend too much time in their studies, men who can build up a church so that it will be on a self-supporting basis before long, men who can begin from scratch and have at least two hundred members within the first two years." The search for such men is certainly along the lines of Weber's concern that there is a drift in leadership "toward specialized performance at the expense of personal inspiration or substantive rationality." Theology is expendable and spiritual vitality becomes secondary, as long as the marks of institutional success are visible.

IV

The organizational dilemma in American Protestantism cannot be simply resolved. Obligations stemming from organizational needs cannot in all cases be perfectly compatible with the obligations of religious vocation and commitment. What we can hope for is that the tension, which is implicit in the organizational dilemma, be kept alive.

To obscure this tension is to court institutional inertia and ossification. It is to take over without criticism whatever organizational forms and devices happen to prevail in the culture. This does not mean that the church is to develop a strategy in its organizational patterns which is always "against the stream." Such action may prove fruitless and irrelevant when the tide is flowing the other way. But it does mean a frank and conscious recognition of the dilemma, an appraisal of the opportunities and hazards of organizational life, and a periodic re-examination of ecclesiastical structure which will allow for flexibility, experimentation, and new patterns to emerge.

One of the great needs of large-scale ecclesiastical structures is a built-in self-evaluation process, which encourages critical reappraisal of organizational means in the light of purposes and goals. This process should enhance institutional self-understanding and enable a degree of self-transcendence, which may save ecclesiastical structures from becoming ends in themselves, and, if necessary, transform them better to carry out the purposes of the church in the modern world.

I take it that this, too, is involved in Philip Selznick's thesis that preoccupation with questions of administrative *efficiency* does not lead to the knottiest and most significant problems of leadership in large organizations.[18] Instead of efficiency, the focus ought to be on leadership. Large-scale organizations are desperately in need of statesmen, of leaders who lead. The "absence of spirituality among spiritual leaders" does not enhance the quality of the institutional life of ecclesiastical structures.

We cannot escape or withdraw from the organizational dilemma in American Protestantism. The benefits derived from large-scale ecclesiastical structures cannot be minimized. Nor can the ever-present hazard of enslavement to the organizational imperatives be denied. To be sure, we may eliminate some of the unnecessary dysfunctions and mitigate some of the abuses of organizational life. Responsible as we must be for living within this dilemma, its final resolution is not of our own contrivance, but surely within the province of our hope.

Role Conflicts
of the Urban Minister

Samuel W. Blizzard

I

Role conflicts are a basic, root problem of the ministerial profession. This is one conclusion suggested by research now under way among a national sample of Protestant clergymen. Parish ministers who desire to be effective in these times are aware that there is much ambivalence about the many roles they are expected to perform.
Clergymen are also aware that ambiguity characterizes
their personal, family, and community lives as well as
those duties that are professional.

The understandings about the role conflicts of the Protestant minister that are presented in this article have
been secured with the co-operation of 345 urban parish
clergy. The Department of the Urban Church, National
Council of Churches, and denominational urban church
executives have sponsored this phase of the research by
selecting the parish clergymen who have co-operated in
the project. Each minister furnished information for the
research by granting a mail interview. They are one group
of clergymen who are participating in a comprehensive
study of the functions of the Protestant parish minister

Reprinted from *The City Church* (September-October, 1956),
pp. 13–15. Used by permission of the author and the Department of
the Urban Church, National Council of Churches.

in the United States. This research is being conducted under the joint auspices of Union Theological Seminary, New York, and the Russell Sage Foundation.

II

A thumbnail sketch of the co-operating urban ministers shows that their average age is 46.8 years. Ninety-seven per cent are married and there are on the average 2.4 children in the family. The typical year of their ordination was 1935. They have been in their present parish an average of 7.9 years and 97 per cent have the status of minister in charge of the parish rather than that of associate or assistant minister.

All of these ministers serve urban churches. However, four out of five of the churches are located in metropolitan areas, rather than in the nonmetropolitan areas. They are located in all the regions of the United States. Twenty-one Protestant denominations are represented among the ministers in the panel. The average church staff in man years is 4.73 persons. The average number of ministers in each parish is 1.47. Nearly one half of the churches (47 per cent) have a part-time lay professional worker (religious educator, choir director, church visitor), who receives remuneration. Four fifths have some secretarial help, and 18 per cent have no paid janitor. The average church served by one of the informants has 960 members and 465 in the church school. The average local budget is $37,646, and the average benevolence budget is $12,820.

III

The roles of the urban minister are characterized by diffuseness rather than specificity. Role ambiguity, therefore, is inherent in the profession. In the context of conflicting role expectations the urban clergyman faces the problem of emotional maturity and the desire for self-understanding. He is expected to be a man of belief, a saint, but his right to completely express ethical judgments based on his personal understanding of and commitment to the Christian faith are often challenged and jeopardized. He is expected to be a man of action, a practitioner, but he is also expected to be a scholar of religion, a contemplative role. The practitioner roles are both privately and publicly focused (pastor role vs. preacher role). They are oriented to a message or ideology as well as to helping people (teacher vs. organizer). He is expected to perform in his profession as a general practitioner, but the success image emphasizes specialization in one role. The definition of an effective urban parish minister is often in conflict with the image of success in the denomination. Contrasting and sometimes contradictory goals are urged on him. A clergyman is expected to be a professional man, but his family life may be crowded because his job demands long hours of duty. His professional responsibilities are primarily to one institution in the community (the church), but many extraprofessional demands are made on him as a community organizer and a leader. It is the purpose of this article to explore some thematic expressions of role conflicts in the professional life of the urban Protestant parish clergyman.

Urban clergymen are seeking self-understanding. This theme occurs in response to several questions in the survey as ministers examine their present parish situation or recall previous parishes and nonclergy occupational experiences. More than one fourth of the ministers mentioned that their experiences in nonclergy occupations had influenced their way of being a minister by giving them a greater understanding of people and human nature. One fifth found that this occupational experience had also given them a greater understanding of self. Almost as many considered personal emotional inadequacies as a problem in parishes previous to their present assignment. One minister expressed it: "Myself is the greatest problem." The same proportion gained personal emotional growth as they functioned in ministerial roles in previous parishes. More than one fourth were able to gain a better understanding of interpersonal relations and to learn to identify themselves with people in parishes prior to their present location. But in their present parish nearly a third of the ministers considered a sense of self-inadequacy as a problem in their professional life. They spoke of "insecurity," "always being honest with myself," "overcoming self," and "feeling rejected." More than one fifth are critical of other ministers because of their emotional immaturity.

The role conflicts of urban Protestant parish ministers are reflected in several themes. The first role conflict is that of the believer or the saint vs. the prophet. The minister feels that he is expected to be a man of belief, but that ethical judgments that he derives from his understanding of the Christian faith are at times challenged. The saint cannot always play the role of the social prophet. More than one third feel that time for self-maintenance of the spiritual life is a problem in their professional life. Ministers in the urban panel devote one hour and eleven minutes a day to spiritual growth (meditation, prayer, Bible-reading). One in twenty recalled that this was a problem in previous parishes. Twelve per cent are

critical of other ministers because they feel that their
spiritual life as a believer is inadequate. In the pastor
and counselor role the minister-believer becomes aware
of social questions and ethical issues. More than one fourth
of these questions deal with ethical issues involving individual parishioners. Fewer issues involved the local
church. Seventeen per cent reported counseling situations
involving the application of Christian beliefs to community problems. In the matter of taking a stand on
controversial issues, only 1 per cent felt free to speak on
local church issues and 28 per cent on community issues.
However, 78 per cent felt free to speak on general controversial issues. Some suggested that they "preach the
Bible and do not engage in issues." There is a general
feeling among the informants that the minister is expected to be a model to other believers but that he is not
expected to take stands on specific issues involving religious ethical judgments. The saint and the prophet roles
are in conflict.

A second theme in the conflicting role images of the
Protestant urban minister is that of the practitioner and
the scholar. The urban parish ministers in this panel work
an average of 10 hours and 32 minutes each day performing the practitioner roles (administrator, organizer, pastor, preacher, priest, and teacher). They devote 27 minutes a day to general intellectual activity. An additional
38 minutes each day is spent in sermon preparation. Time
for self-maintenance is seen as a major professional problem by these ministers. When they were asked to name
any persons whom they admire or who have greatly influenced the way they think and act as a minister, one
half mentioned seminary professors and a somewhat
greater proportion mentioned well-known religious authors. They have the scholar image of their mentors. How-

ever, they spent the major portion of their time as practitioners, men of action, rather than as scholars of religion, a contemplative role.

The practitioner roles performed by parish ministers have built-in expectancies which foster role discrepancies and conflict. In the pastor-counselor role, the minister is expected to respect confidences. The relationship with the counselor is a private affair, but nearly one fifth of the informants were critical of the way in which ministerial colleagues practice in this role. In the counseling situations the minister is expected to have a permissive attitude toward the parishioner. The preacher role requires the clergyman to perform in an altogether different mode. Preaching is a public role. It is easy for parishioners to pick up a reference to a counseling relationship if it is alluded to in the sermon. The preacher role tends to call for an authoritarian approach. It is directive rather than nondirective. Hence the foci of these two practitioner roles basically conflict. Furthermore, three of the practitioner roles place the minister in the position of an actor before an audience. This is the case in preaching, teaching, and liturgical duties as commonly performed by the clergy. The administrator, organizer, and pastor roles involve the minister in interpersonal relations and intra- and inter-group relations. This calls for a different orientation on the part of the minister. It may also be noted that the same grouping of practitioner roles may be viewed as being ideological or message oriented as contrasted to ministering to the needs of people. Hence, as the minister shifts from role to role he must reorient himself to avoid conflicting role expectancies.

The typical urban parish minister is a general practitioner rather than a specialist. Very few (6 per cent) urban churches are served by three or more ministers.

Hence, as the principal professional leader in the parish the minister must be prepared to perform the whole gamut of practitioner roles. The image that he has of success in his denomination places a high value on having a special proficiency in one of the roles. This is cited by more informants in their image of success than any other factor (43 per cent). They feel that they may be a success in their denomination if they are a "good preacher," or a "good pastor," or a "good administrator." The single role approach of the specialist is a part of their success image, rather than the multiple role approach of the general practitioner.

The image of an effective minister is oriented to the parish. The image of the successful minister is oriented to the denomination. These images are in some respects in conflict. Character or integrity, an outgoing personality, spiritual maturity, and abilities in the practitioner roles are characteristics of both the effective and the success image. The ranking these characteristics receive differs sharply. Character is rated first for effectiveness, but it is fifth in the success pictures. Ability in performing ministerial roles is first for success, but these roles are last in the effectiveness scale. Spiritual maturity is third in the effectiveness image, but it is last in the success ratings. Self-understanding is reported to be important by informants in their effectiveness image, but co-operation in denominational programs is given a higher rating in the success picture. The dilemma that this conflict in role expectancies creates for the minister is often a choice between doing a job in the local parish and doing those things that will result in his professional advancement in the denomination.

The urban parish minister plays a role as a member of a family. In a waking day of 16 hours and 17 minutes he spends 1 hour and 46 minutes in family activities. This includes spiritual life (5 minutes), family fellowship and recreation (59 minutes), family care (24 minutes), and maintenance (18 minutes). Urban panel informants spend 33 minutes a day less with their family than do rural ministers. These facts focus on the conflict the minister faces between his professional roles and his role as a family man.

A final theme that reflects the role conflicts of the urban Protestant parish minister focuses on his professional and extraprofessional roles. As a professional leader in the community, the minister's primary responsibility is to the church as an institution. Certain services are expected of the urban minister that may be a part of his technical training and experience but are not strictly a part of his professional duties. Urban ministers devote an average of 29 minutes each day to community organizations. It is expected that he will devote time to educational groups, health and welfare agencies, and youth and character organizations. He is expected to be a "chaplain" in many of these organizations. For others he will function as a member of the board of directors, and for other groups he will sanction fund-raising campaigns. Ministers feel pressures are placed on them in the community to perform these and other extraprofessional roles. A few resent the time that this requires, and others ask themselves questions about how these roles further their basic religious functions in the community.

IV

The ministry is a free profession with diffuse role definitions in a voluntary institution. Diversity of role performance and lack of clarity in role expectancies is to be expected. In the case of the urban minister the situation is magnified by the number of people each minister serves and the long hours he works. It is also exaggerated by the heterogeneous features of urban life and the mobility of the population. Hence urban ministers must minister to people on the basis of relatively short acquaintances and secondary groups, rather than face-to-face relations. The resulting wear and tear on the professional leader is apparent. This seems to indicate a need for a more probing understanding of the stresses, tensions, and conflicts in the ministry than clergy and laymen in the church have yet displayed. The future of the church may stand or fall on the mental health of the clergy.

Conceptualizations
of the Urban Parish

Joseph H. Fichter, S.J.

The social structure of an urban Catholic parish is highly complex. At first glance this would not seem to be true because the casual observer probably sees nothing but a large number of people who satisfy their religious needs at a particular parish church. On closer analysis, however, it will be noted that any social unit of a few thousand persons logically structures its social relations according to multiple patterns. It seems true also that the researcher not only can but must conceptualize the parish in multiple ways in order to achieve meaningful analysis.

The normal large urban Catholic parish may be studied under the following aspects, even though each varies in importance as a conceptual frame of reference for research. The parish may be called (*a*) a legal corporation, (*b*) a superimposed association, (*c*) an institutionalized association, (*d*) a communal group, (*e*) a cluster of subgroupings. It is also helpful for some purposes to conceive the parish as (*f*) a series of statistical categories and (*g*) a system of kinship groupings.

Reprinted from *Social Forces*, 31 (October, 1952), pp. 43–46. Used by permission of the author and the publisher, The Williams & Wilkins Company. (An extended version of this article appears in the author's book, *Social Relations in the Urban Parish*. University of Chicago Press, 1954, pp. 181–194.)

(*a*) As a *legal corporation* formed under the laws of the state, the urban Catholic parish has as its purposes and objectives: "The holding and administering of property, real, personal, and mixed, so that the same may be devoted to religious services, charitable, educational, and literary purposes, for the benefit of those who attend the Roman Catholic Church belonging to this corporation."

The members of this ecclesiastical corporation also constitute the Board of five Directors who manage, administer, and control it. These are the legal officers of the parish. The Bishop is ex-officio President, the Vicar-General of the diocese is the Vice-President; the Pastor holds the combined office of Secretary and Treasurer. The two remaining members of the Board are lay parishioners, sometimes called "trustees," who are appointed by the Bishop, usually for a term of two years. They are almost always successful professional or business men.

In practice, all legal and fiscal business of the parish is conducted by the Secretary-Treasurer, the Pastor. The corporation charter forbids him to contract any debt over two hundred dollars and stipulates that "no real estate belonging to the corporation shall be sold, mortgaged, or disposed of in any way, without the vote and consent of all the five Directors."

The obvious intent of this parochial charter is that the effective legal and financial control of the parish be in the hands of the clergy. The history of lay trusteeship in the United States has demonstrated the wisdom and practicality of this arrangement. The Pastor, who is himself subject to higher authority in the administration of the parish, usually recognizes that the practical advice of the lay trustees can be very valuable. At the same time he usually makes it clear that their function is consultative and not directive. The Pastor is obliged to meet with the trustees only on important financial decisions.

It is evident that the lay people in the Catholic parish are not stockholders, or members in any way, of this corporation. They contribute the money and the properties which the corporation administers. They may be termed "beneficiaries" of the religious services, and of the charitable, educational, and literary purposes for which the corporation was constituted. The two lay members of the Board are not their elected representatives. Viewed in this legal light, the American urban parish is neither a spontaneously organized social structure nor a mass-controlled organization. The lay people have no formal authority, direct or indirect, over the parochial corporation, but the corporation is an instrument of service to them.

(b) The urban Catholic parish may be called a *superimposed association* in the sense that the conditions for its existence are fixed by Rome through the local Bishop. Canon Law 216 points out that every diocese must be subdivided into definite territorial areas, each with its own permanent pastor, people, and church.[19] Thus, the religious association of lay Catholics in any given parish is not a matter of choice by the people themselves as long as they reside within the designated boundaries. In practice, of course, some of the lay persons in any parish attend neighboring Catholic churches for religious services, and some participate in other parochial activities there, but a formally imposed and morally obligatory relationship still remains between them and the Pastor of their own parish.

Of more importance than the territorial assignment of people to a definite parish is the fact that the general framework of their religious functions and objectives is also prescribed by church authorities outside the parish. This means that whenever the parishioners assemble for religious activities they follow a pattern of worship and devotion which is *essentially* the same throughout the whole Catholic Church. The liturgical rituals of the church, in so far as they are designed for public and corporate worship, can be termed ideal patterns of social relations. The moral and social behavior of parishioners, normatively posited in commandments, precepts, and rules of the church are also superimposed.

(c) The Catholic parish may also be conceptualized as an *institutionalized association*.[20] This is the fact which makes the parish a unique social phenomenon, different from every other parish. In other words, the patterned relationships in the urban parish have become institutionalized *locally,* by and for these particular people over a period of several generations in this designated territory of so many city blocks.

As Joachim Wach remarks, "The sociologist of religion, interested in the study of the cultic group, cannot be satisfied with reviewing its theology as the foundation of the theory and practice of fellowship among its members."[21] Even the most sympathetic observer will note that the facts of social life in the urban parish frequently fail to conform to the expectations of social thought and behavior implied in the moral and dogmatic teachings of the Catholic Church.

This is simply another way of saying that while there are many similarities among Catholic parishes all over the world there are also distinctive features in each. The associative processes and patterns are formed, maintained, and transmitted by these particular parishioners. They are affected by the age and sex, and by occupational, marital, economic, and class status of the parishioners, as well as by the manner in which the parishioners perform the roles consonant with these statuses. They are affected by the various personalities which individuate each human interaction, by the goals toward which the roles *actually* function, and by the strong secular values of the American urban and industrial milieu.

(*d*) The fourth way in which the Catholic parish may be conceptualized is that of a *communal group*, that is, of a number of people who are held together primarily by their high religious values. Everett Clinchy, who is a close observer of religious behavior, says that "the central element in the structure of a group's existence is religion. . . . The heart and will of every culture lie in the beliefs of the group: that is, its religion. Without convictions about what is good, and without specific beliefs about its goals and the means to attain them, the group's *esprit* will decline, and the group will perish."[22]

This concept of the parish as a communal group rests upon the negative notion that the group will perish unless it holds values of a high order. This is one of Sorokin's most emphasized sociological principles: that people are truly integrated by their "systems of meanings and values."[23] Znaniecki also uses this principle when he calls a parish "a kind of great family whose members are united by a community of moral interests."[24] Finally, Donovan remarks that "the members of the parish, both clerical and lay, share in a unity which stems from their common religious beliefs and which finds expression in their joint participation in group functions."[25]

These observations constitute the hypothesis that the *sharing of common values* is the essential sociological and psychological factor of the Catholic parish as a group. Our empirical research indicates, however, that the *sharing of functions* is a much more practical factor of unity. In simple terms, this means that when people do things together which they think are worth doing they tend to be drawn together. The interacting influence of co-operative functions seems to increase the group appreciation of values, and this again leads to progressive interaction.

It is quite possible that smaller village parishes tend toward the ideal of the communal group. In the large urban parish, however, the great majority of lay persons use the local church as a kind of "service station" for their religious needs: a place to go to Mass and confession, to get married and have their children baptized, and to have their old folks buried. Their communal "social" bond with the priests and other parishioners is analogous to that which an automobile owner has with the gas station manager and with the latter's other customers. It is somewhat like the professional relationship between dentist and patients.[26]

While the concept of a genuinely integrated communal group does not apply to the whole urban parish as a social aggregate, this does not mean that there is no nuclear group which cannot be so conceived. As a matter of fact, there is at the heart of every urban parish a group of parishioners who are united primarily through their high religious values. It appears that only these can fulfill Znaniecki's definition of the parish as a "great family."

(*e*) The fact that various functions are performed and various objectives attained in an organized way leads to the fifth concept of the urban parish as a cluster of *subgroupings*. Each of these has its own objectives, activities, and membership. The Pastor is theoretically and ex officio the highest authority in all of them. Their ultimate objective must in some way conform to that of the parish as a whole: the sanctification and salvation of souls. But their immediate objectives help to specify the various groups.

It has been noted that the total parochial association is superimposed and maintained according to universal standards of the Catholic Church. Much more latitude is allowed in the origin and maintenance of the parochial subgroupings. The original impetus for the formation of a group comes sometimes from the people, and sometimes from the pastor. Occasionally its formation may be requested by the Bishop.

These "parish societies" may be classified in many ways, according to age and sex composition, marital status, and religious conditions of membership, although these norms are not in every instance defined. They may be placed on a continuum indicating the degree of success or failure they experienced in striving for their objectives. They may be divided as formally imposed or locally initiated, who originated them and where.

Probably the most useful sociological approach is that which considers the main functions and goals of the parish organizations. (1) the *liturgical* groups are those which assist at the religious services performed in the church itself. The Acolyte Society, the Choir, and the Ushers, take a more or less direct part in the services; the Ladies' Altar Society provides the appurtenances of the sanctuary. (2) The *sociospiritual* groups are sufficiently distinctive in their functions and objectives that they may be considered separate from those in the above category. They are organized into social groups for the primary objective of sanctification. They are Children of Mary, Sodalities, Junior and Senior Holy Name Societies, Nocturnal Adoration Societies. (3) In the category of *educational* groupings are included the Parents' Club, the Confraternity of Christian Doctrine, and study clubs of various kinds. (4) The *ameliorative* groups do the corporal works of mercy, St. Vincent de Paul for men and the Daughters of Mercy for women. In a sense they act as the "relief agencies" of the parish for the needy families and individuals of the parish. (5) Finally, the primarily *recreational* objectives are pursued in the Boy and Girl Scouts, Brownies and Cubs, Boys' and Girls' sport teams, and in the adult committees which promote these groupings.

Besides the five general conceptualizations described so far it seems useful to think of the urban parish (*f*) according to the statistical categories into which the membership falls and (*g*) as a network of kinship and family relationships.

The purpose of the classification of parishioners is the comparison of one category to another and of each to the religious ideals and practices which the parish is promoting. In the first volume of the *Southern Parish* series these categories were employed in many ways according to age, sex, marital status, socioeconomic status, length of residence, amount of schooling, nationality background, and so forth.

The concept of the parish as a network of family relations is more subtle and more difficult to actualize. While it is probably false to assert as a generalization that "religion runs in families" we have found that participation in the parochial programs is frequently a "family affair." We noted this particularly in the parish organizations; the youths tend to be active in their groups when the parents are active in adult societies.

In the abstract analysis of an urban parish according to these various seven conceptual frameworks there is danger that the social roles of the persons-in-action may be neglected. For example, there can be no question that the key persons in the operation of any Catholic parish are the priests. This is true not only of the direct "care of souls" but also of the whole problem of maintaining the social structure as a going concern. Thus the pastoral roles may be separately analyzed.

At the same time, a parish is nothing without its lay membership. According to the theory of "organized Catholic Action" the lay people participate with the priests in the work of the hierarchy. The democratic ideology of the urban American culture is a social fact which cannot be neglected. In other words, the urban parish in America seems to steer a psychologically difficult course between the "congregational approach" wherein the lay people run the church, and the "authoritarian approach" wherein the lay people are passive subjects of church administration.

CHAPTER VII

URBAN CHURCH
AND COMMUNITY CONFLICT

INTRODUCTION

Conflict is one of the facts of life in urban society. The only community where conflict is absent is likely to be a dead one. Moreover, community tensions need not necessarily be destructive but can be creative and salutary.

At least controversy reflects personal interest and involvement in public issues. This reveals the inadequacy of the popular image of the urban scene as one of mass apathy and unconcern. At best, conflict is the matrix wherein policy decisions that lead to social change and progress are forged. Surely the cutting edges of a democratic society are at the points of conflict and tension rather than in those areas where the issues have been solved and settled.

The urban church that evades conflict in its own household or in the community will be unable to see it as the potential birth pangs of new life in cities and churches. Such a church will likely be socially irrelevant. Fear of conflict or avoidance of stressful situations often prevents churches from understanding the nature of community conflict and from exercising a creative role in them.

This chapter seeks to lay bare the nature of the problem of community conflict facing the urban church. Its selections bring insight into how conflict is faced and into how urban churches must bring honest reconciliation to heal the hatreds of community conflict. The selections are limited to three major areas: racial, class, and religious tensions.

During the Little Rock, Arkansas, school controversy,

two sociologists, Ernest Q. Campbell and Thomas F. Pettigrew, now professors at the University of North Carolina and Harvard respectively, conducted a case study of how ministers respond in a community crisis. "Community Action and Inaction: Ministers in Racial Crisis" presents a series of vivid composite vignettes which depict the various roles assumed by clergymen during this crisis. The article strips bare the real motivations of many American ministers, not simply those in Little Rock. Indeed, it is a paradigm of ministerial behavior in instances of community conflict.

In "The Fellowship of Class," David W. Barry suggests that the church is captive to prevailing forms of human association in the city. Nationality and ethnic ties have been transplanted to urban areas and find expression in a divided Protestantism. With the ascendancy of the third generation, older ethnic loyalties have largely eroded. But another form of divisiveness has emerged: class status. This orientation to social class shapes the values, curriculum materials, and practices of urban church life. The fellowship of class is an alien intrusion, a millstone around the minister's neck.

Will Herberg, Professor of Judaic Studies and Social Philosophy at Drew University, discusses "Protestant-Catholic Tensions in Pluralistic America." The author argues that religious tensions are the most pervasive kind of conflict in America. He sets these tensions within a historical-sociological context. Contemporary attitudes are largely conditioned by these background factors. The author then examines some of the typical stereotypes about Roman Catholicism and subjects them to critical scrutiny.

Community Action and Inaction: Ministers in Racial Crisis

Ernest Q. Campbell and Thomas F. Pettigrew

These vignettes, most of which are composites, were written in the conviction that the greatest potential influence for peaceful and constructive change in the South rests with the Protestant ministry. The relative prestige of the minister is higher in this region than in others, and in all regions the minister is uniquely qualified to tap the domain of guilt. The national stands of the major denominations regarding the Supreme Court decisions on desegregation have been unequivocal and forceful, and many Southern ministers fully accept the position of their governing bodies. It is therefore constructive and important to determine through empirical study the nature of ministerial action and response at the community level during periods of racial crisis. This is the purpose of our Little Rock study.

I. Study in Consensus

The Rev. Hard Core Resistance was about to address his Dissident Baptist congregation from the pulpit of his simple cinder-block church. His listeners were sincere people of modest means. Many of them had migrated to

Reprinted in abridged form from "Vignettes from Little Rock," *Christianity and Crisis* (September 29, 1958), pp. 128–136. Used by permission of the authors and of *Christianity and Crisis*.

Little Rock from rural Arkansas in recent years, bringing their fundamentalist faith with them. Virtually none had attended college. They worked at semiskilled and skilled blue-collar or minor white-collar posts—clerks, mail carriers, carpenters, electricians, railroad men, service station operators.

Resistance himself had gone directly from a rural high school to the local Dissident Baptist seminary (not recognized by the Southern Baptist Convention). Granted a Doctor of Biblical Literature degree from this unaccredited school, he now instructs in homiletics at the seminary in addition to his pastoral duties.

It was the fateful fall of 1957. And he gave his congregation the same interpretation of the city's crisis that he had given the press and the local Citizens' Council at other times:

"My friends, right now I could go back to my home county in southern Arkansas and the nigras there would greet me as a friend. I am their friend; I have no animosity toward them and I have their best interests at heart. Anyone who says I hate them is a liar.

"The nigras know I have their best interests at heart. They don't want this integration any more than I do. This fellow who preaches over here at the nigra Baptist church —I give him Bible lessons—he told me he bet you couldn't find a handful of nigras that want to go where they aren't wanted. It's just a few of them that belong to this National Association for the Agitation of Colored People that's causing all the trouble.

"There are a lot of preachers in these uptown churches, my friends, who've been telling us that God is an integrationist. The trouble with those fellows is that they just aren't good Bible students. Matter of fact, I've never known an integrationist who was a good, sound student of the Bible. All they learn is a watered-down modernistic version of the Bible. Even so, I notice not a single one of them has any nigras coming to his church. It does look to me like they ought to integrate their churches if they want to go around telling us to put the nigras in our schools.

"Then, too, those uptown preachers get their money from the swanky people up on the Heights, and those folks up there are lukewarm about integration at best. 'Course they got no cause to worry. They've got their brand-new high school, just opened up last fall, Hall High School it is, and not a nigra in sight 'cept for sweeping the floors. It's us common people who're told to send our kids to school with colored kids at Central High. Those swanky folks on the Heights are the most prejudiced of all, because they're prejudiced against white folks like us as well as against the colored folks.

"Now, in closing, I want to give you some advice. People who walk down the streets in Little Rock, or stop to look in a store window, are liable to be called a mob these days and arrested. So be careful. There are FBI agents all over the city, and Army helicopters swoop down on innocent bystanders. I'm against violence as much as the next man. No matter how provoked you are, don't retaliate; turn the other cheek. Right will win; the South will not stand for integration. The white man is the best friend the nigra ever had; we are all creatures of the Lord. Why, here in Little Rock the nigras have a fine new high school, the finest money can buy, and who gave it to them? The conclusion, my friends, is that the Lord smiles on segregation."

Resistance's congregation felt reassured, convinced, secure. Many stopped to thank him for making things so clear to them. Their enthusiastic response, high morale, and generous contributions indicated their support for his position on race. His congregation was with him; his ministerial associates were with him; his conscience was with him. God, he was convinced, saw things his way. He had a sense of mission. He had no worries.

II. A STUDY IN CONFLICT

The services at Centenary Protestant Church began routinely enough on that September Sunday morning. Attendance was off a little, and in the small congregation this was a noticeable matter. The opening hymn had been sung when an usher came down the aisle and, in obvious agitation, called the minister aside. For the moment, worshipers did not know what had happened.

Outside, in the vestibule, a well-dressed Negro couple stood, expecting to participate in the church service as invited guests. The usher had detained them while he conferred with the minister. While this conference took place, the leading layman of the church went into the vestibule and exchanged pleasantries with them.

The harried usher reported to the minister that the Negroes were in the vestibule and that they expected to join the congregation in the morning worship. But Negroes had never before attended services here. And furthermore, the Negroes claimed to have been invited. The pastor's wife, they said—at least a woman who *said* she was his wife—had called their minister the previous afternoon to ask him to send representatives of his church "as a gesture in racial good will." Centenary members would return the visit on a later Sunday, the caller had explained. What, pleaded the usher, was he to do with the visitors?

Mr. Troubled, the minister, advised his usher to tell them that there must be some mistake, that no authorized person had made such a phone call, and that no plan for an exchange of visits had even been discussed by the

members of his church. He further advised him to tell the
Negro that his church had taken no official stand on integration and that until such time as it did, perhaps it
would be better if they went somewhere else to worship.
This message was relayed to the visitors. The lay leader
accompanied them to their car. As they prepared to leave,
a car drove up containing several other Negroes who also
were responding to the "invitation." These Negroes de-
parted without getting out of their car.

The usher later reported to the congregation that the
visitors were extremely polite and very understanding.
They realized, he said, that a trick had been played.

Thus it came to pass that one of the fifteen Little Rock
ministers to issue a proclamation condemning the governor of Arkansas for turning away Negro students from
Little Rock's Central High School himself turned away,
less than three weeks later, five Negro adults who came
to worship in his church. And this minister has in his desk
a small clipping from an out-of-state newspaper that upsets
and confuses him. The dispatch concludes a description of
the incident with these words: "Perhaps these Negroes
mistook this church for the House of God."

The people who perpetrated this hoax had chosen their
target well. The church to which they "invited" these
Negroes is surrounded by small churches representing a
variety of fundamentalist sects, with which it is in active
competition for member loyalties. Of all the churches
whose ministers publicly protested Governor Faubus' in-
terference with educational integration, this one is the
smallest and the least affluent. It is, in other words, the
most vulnerable. Members already were making known
their distrust of the minister's racial postures, and attendance was off. The hoaxers knew what they were up to.

The incident placed the minister in serious conflict. After

turning the Negroes away, he explained extemporaneously to his congregation that there was really no reason why they should come unless to cause embarrassment or as the result of a trick. Yet, he told his church, we must remember that we are *all* children of God and because we are children of God we are *all* brothers. He concluded his remarks with the exhortation: "We'd better be mighty careful how we push God's children around."

Later in the fall, Troubled attended a national conference of his church as an official representative from his area. He talked, dined, and worshiped with Negroes at the conference. Everyone there, it appeared to him, was in favor of integration of the churches and vocally critical of segregation. What these people think, representing his church as they do, is important to him.

He is a Southerner as well as a minister—a product of the Southern culture, and of its rural areas at that. He has an emotional commitment to segregation—"To tell the honest truth, I'd rather things stay the way they are. I'd rather have segregation"—that he cannot intellectually justify. As a minister he believes, as he told his congregation, that God is no segregationist, and that you have to twist the Bible to find anything in it that supports segregation. He is caught in the middle between pressure from his local congregation and the important relation he has to his national church body. Actions that are prompted by his identification with his church at the national level alienate him from his local congregation, thus reducing his influence and interfering with his pastoral work. Yet this identification is strong enough that silence and inaction frustrate him.

"My spirit is not satisfied," Troubled admits sadly. "I just know that Jesus never would have turned anybody away if he had been in my pulpit."

III. A STUDY IN COMPROMISE

Mr. Power is a cordial and impressive man in his fifties, born and educated in Arkansas. His able leadership of the large and affluent First Metropolis Protestant Church for over a decade makes him one of the most influential ministers in Little Rock. In addition to his persuasive sermons, Power administers a major enterprise with considerable skill. Indeed, there is the atmosphere of the major executive about his handsomely appointed offices. The flurry of secretarial activity in the church office, the countless meetings day and night of committees and organizations in various parts of the plant, even the Chamber of Commerce plaque above his desk—these suggest the operation of a vast business firm.

Sincere, direct, and candid, he knew the visitor would be primarily interested in the racial crisis and he came right to the point. Yes, he believes the nine Negro children had every right to attend Central High School, and he wanted to see them kept there. No, he would not go so far as to call himself an integrationist.

"Gradualism describes my position best, sir. All of the truly responsible leaders in Little Rock, both Negro and white, are gradualists too. But one of the horrors of this terrible situation, I tell you, is that the good terms 'moderate' and 'gradualist' have become despised epithets hurled at you by segregation extremists as if you were some sort of Communist traitor.

"I see you smiling, sir, and I know what you are thinking. You are wondering what Christian leadership has been offered in all of this mess. In my opinion, most of Little Rock's ministers have been most courageous, everything considered. Most of us had given sermons before the trouble. I gave a pretty direct talk once or twice myself, but I'm not sure they had much of an effect. Raised a few segregation backs in the congregation at least. And now I'm widely known as opposing segregation in principle.

"I'm proud of the people in my congregation too. Not a member of my church was in that awful mob at Central High School. They wouldn't think of doing a thing like that. They believe in law and in orderly processes for settling differences.

"Well, sir, when all this trouble started this fall, you just can't imagine how explosive the whole thing became. I signed that ministerial protest against Faubus calling out the Guard, but I can't see that our announcement did any good at all. It looks like people have got into the habit of respecting religion but not listening to it. After that, it seemed obvious to me, sir, that this wasn't going to do anything to help the situation. I did say something on a radio program about these addlebrained segregationists outfits we've got around here, and it started an awful ruckus around here in my church.

"I can't impress on you enough how strongly some of my people believe in segregation. They have Christian love in their hearts for the Negro, but they have a lot of irrational fears about desegregation. Like I said, I got into a little trouble myself—all passed over now, I saw to that— but I've heard that some of the most outspoken ministers are in terrible difficulty. It takes a lot of plain old-fashioned fortitude to do what they've done, but they've paid a stiff price. Membership off, pledges off, attendance off; driving people away is no way to build a church.

"So I haven't talked about race directly since all the fuss began. Debate just wasn't going to help. Good Christians can believe in either segregation or integration. Obviously, the first step, sir, was to get all the Christians in the community to return to God. And this is what we tried to do

with our city-wide prayers for peace. Reconciliation—
that's what we needed. The theme we needed is right here:
St. Paul's Second Epistle to the Corinthians, fifth chapter,
eighteenth and nineteenth verses. 'And all things are of
God, who hath reconciled us to himself by Jesus Christ, and
hath given to us the ministry of reconciliation; To wit, that
God was in Christ, reconciling the world unto himself, not
imputing their trespasses unto them; and hath committed
unto us the word of reconciliation.' That's it, reconciliation.
A powerful Christian term it is too. The newspapermen
misunderstood it, I'm afraid. Because we didn't have the
prayers support either side, or condemn anybody, the press
thought reconciliation meant neutral and compromising.
They simply missed the point.

"I think those prayers were the best thing we could have
done. We brought everyone back to religion. We didn't get
all enmeshed in argument and emotion. We just prayed
for God's guidance, and I think that alone helped things
considerably. Now, except for a few, our ministers are returning to the quiet, steady work that in the end does the
most good. The church has been the church, and we have
preserved it as such.

"Now, when you consider, sir, what little influence religion has on people today, I think you have to admit that
this city's clergy has done about all it could. Most of us are
known to be in favor of gradual integration, but we've
managed to go on with the work of the church. And the
Columbus Day prayers made our citizens remember that
religious considerations must contribute to a solution to
the problem.

"And I hope I've told you what you wanted to know,
sir. I can sum it up for you the same way I did for two
young pastors who came to me for advice about all this
trouble. My policy, I told them, is to be firm, but don't

stick your neck out. This thing has not disturbed the program of my church and it's not going to."

IV. A Study in Caution

Mr. Strategy, pastor of Proud Protestant Church, had a standing agreement with his ushers that any Negroes who attended Sunday services in his church would be seated and shown all courtesies. In the fall of 1957 several of his ushers came to tell him they could not sit with Negroes nor willingly usher them into the church. Suave, sincere, refreshing Mr. Strategy gave a characteristic answer: "That's all right, I understand. Just find someone to take over your ushering duties until you feel you can return. Our policy will continue unchanged." (The ushers themselves had set the policy, under provocation by the minister. No Negroes have come.)

Mr. Strategy is a pastor in one of Little Rock's most popular denominations, and his own church has a particularly proud heritage. From its membership has come a striking number of public servants in high office, of whom the members are justly proud. Some of its laymen have been effective leaders in church work at state and national levels. They have also pioneered in establishing co-operative lay activity across denominational lines. There is also quiet pride in that Proud Church fuses into a co-ordinated unit a large membership that ranges from the city's wealthiest citizens to those for whom the church extends support. Although it is among the elite of churches in the community, it is amazingly and refreshingly free from snobbery.

In the early days after nine Negro students entered Central High School, students from Proud Church took the lead in befriending them. For example, they invited

Negroes to dine with them in the school cafeteria. They became objects of pressure from segregationists and their overtures of friendliness stopped. Mr. Strategy tried through small groups, seminars, and personal contacts to maintain these friendly gestures; he also asked his youth workers to do likewise. He failed, but he tried.

Like only a small number of his ministerial colleagues, Strategy did not mince words when he dealt with the approaching integration at Central High School from his pulpit shortly before school opened. He told his congregation that the Christian faith demanded more of them than that they acquiesce in a social pattern that heaps indignities on Negro citizens. He invited his listeners to try placing themselves in the position of those who are the victims of discrimination. He exploded what he termed "myths" that some people used to defend their bigotry. He gave unqualified praise to the gradual integration plan of the local school board, and he presented evidence from the New Testament to show that integration is the only defensible position for a Christian.

At the conclusion of the service, an elderly personal friend and a member of his congregation for many years told him at the church door: "Preacher, that was a very good sermon. The only thing wrong with it is that it just ain' so." Generally though, the sermon had a "marvelous reception"—especially from the younger members.

Strategy is one of the fifteen local ministers who issued a protest against Governor Faubus' action only a few hours after the governor had called out the National Guard. He feels strongly that the governor followed a lawless course of action against the best interests of the community and the state.

And yet, Strategy has not discussed the community's

race problem from his pulpit since that eventful day the National Guard turned away Negro students seeking to enter Central High. Nor has he issued statements to or through the press. Nor is he publicly perceived by either whites or Negroes as an active or effective pro-integration minister. Nor has he publicly proposed ameliorative action, commented on the arrival of Federal troops, condemned intimidation in the high school, challenged his members to seek constructive solutions within a desegregated framework, nor taken any of the other actions some think he might have taken to express the revulsion he felt at the turn of events after school opened. Many people think the failure to peacefully integrate the high school means little to him. Liberals in the community feel he has let them down.

Frightened? Hardly. Segregationist? Impossible. Shy? Not at all.

Actually his cautious behavior expresses a rational philosophy of the ministry. As a matter of simple tactics and techniques, Strategy believes it is unwise to make pronouncements in the heat of temper. He believes that hasty actions and angry words can all too easily alienate those you want to influence. Actions and pronouncements during the heat of tension must be considered against a long-range program. They can easily do more harm than good. If a minister has done his work well in the months and years of calm, his members will not require a special tempo on his part to know their religious obligations during crisis. He further feels that a minister's primary responsibility is to his members rather than to the community. The pastor must keep an "upper tension" on his flock as they grow in religious stature and social awareness, but he should not expect sudden and dramatic transformations. There is a long road ahead.

An efficient and persuasive person, a minister beloved by his people, Strategy has accumulated a significant amount of respect, prestige, and affection in the community as in his congregation. He used very little of it last fall. In a city whose liberals were disheartened and unassured, when certain ministerial voices said loudly that God is a segregationist and went without effective rebuttal, Strategy might have rallied an efficient body of citizens to assert liberal convictions based on moral imperatives. He is, perhaps, better qualified than any other local minister for such an effort. Yet he did not do it. Not from fear of losing his job, nor fear of criticism, nor for distaste for the effort itself. Not because he is illiberal, but because he believes that his influence must be preserved until it can be employed with maximum impact.

Strategy has excellent contacts with public leaders, in both the city and the state, whose behavior during the crisis he regards as contrary to the Christian imperative. Regarding these leaders he says: "They need help and I can help them. I intend to help Governor Faubus and others like him. When the time comes, I will, but I wouldn't be able to help them if I had said things that alienate them from me and made it impossible for me to get them to listen." It is clear that with such people his philosophy stands to receive its acid test.

V. A STUDY IN COURAGE

A menacing crowd surrounded Little Rock's Central High as the first week of school began. When the Negro students approached the school for the first time, Mr. Action was on hand. In fact, he led the small group of white and Negro adults who faced the crowd with the children.

Later, an exasperated parishioner and personal friend asked him, "Did you have to do it, Robert?"

The question begged the answer. Yes, Action "had to do it," as he has to do everything else that he believed might bring about effective educational integration in his city. For he, like very few others in Little Rock, publicly supported integration and did everything in his power to achieve its peaceful acceptance. A sympathetic family grew concerned, and many of his closest ministerial friends let him go it alone.

Mr. Action, to the consternation and unbelief of his many detractors, truly fits the "voice from the old South" description given him by a local newspaper. Descendant of the Confederate dead and of slaveholders, born and raised in a Deep South state, servant of the South's people for many years, he has a fervent love for his region and its people. For his racial views he has suffered the abuse of his homeland, and he speaks feelingly of how his efforts in the cause of racial justice disassociate him from a tradition and a people he loves. He does not fully understand the vigor of their caustic remarks, and their remarks are the more caustic because he was one of their own.

It is no accident that Action was president of the biracial Greater Little Rock Ministerial Association when the crisis broke. For he does not stand alone among his ministerial peers in believing that a segregated society cannot secure racial justice and equality. Many colleagues agree with him. But unlike most of his integrationist colleagues, Action was neither cautious nor compromising in his approach to Little Rock's crisis. As the tense September of 1957 began, he issued an official appeal to all members of the ministerial association to urge their congregations to peacefully comply with the Federal Court orders. When

Faubus suddenly flung his soldiers around Central High School to maintain segregation, Action helped to initiate at once a denouncement of this maneuver by fifteen prominent local ministers. And after Negro leaders requested his aid, he gathered up the small band of ministers who escorted the Negro children on their first attempt to enter the school. This done, he aided in organizing and moderated a state-wide, interdenominational meeting of ministers which released a religious proclamation concerning the crisis.

When the violence burst forth in late September, he requested, as the ministerial association's executive head, forthright measures from the mayor and the chief of police. The following day, President Eisenhower sent Army paratroopers into the city, and Action publicly praised the move. He was virtually the only local leader to do so. And, unlike many Little Rockians, he was concerned about the conflict's international implications. Thus, he tape-recorded a short talk for the Voice of America, which was translated into twelve languages, including Russian.

His public activity did not keep him from dealing with the community's racial problems in his own pulpit. Action was one of the very few clergymen in the city to preach repeated sermons explicitly supporting integration as a Christian imperative.

In October, Action joined with other religious leaders to organize the city-wide prayers for peace. After these prayers, most of the ministerial participants ceased their integrationist activity completely. But Action continued unabated. He became the local chairman of the Goodwill Scholarship Fund, a trust set up "to reward youth of Little Rock Central High showing a belief in fair play." He helped organize and later headed a small group of white and Negro leaders which meets each week in an effort to maintain at least one open channel of communication between the races.

At the invitation of various church organizations, Action has flown to distant parts of the nation to describe in detail the difficulties of his community. And he has continued to make local pronouncements—criticizing a "voluntary segregation" plan or praising Negroes for their nonviolence—that receive wide community attention. In June of 1958, when Ernest Green became the first Negro graduate of Central High, Action and Dr. Martin Luther King sat with the Green family throughout the tense troop-guarded ceremony.

In short, Action has done everything that he could think of doing to support racial integration in Little Rock. But he has constantly faced stern opposition. Pressures, some subtle, some blatant, have been applied to him, but to little avail. Those closest to him grow tense in concern for his safety. Relatives in other states have expressed their displeasure at his views. He has been told that some he loves "deeply regret" the position he has taken. Some members of the ministerial association have said that Action is a publicity seeker. And letters to the editors of the local papers select him out as their favorite target for abuse.

More important, perhaps, are the pressures from his own congregation. Financial pledges and attendance at Downtown Protestant Church declined sharply. One faithful member expressed her displeasure and then said defiantly: "No preacher is going to run me off from my church." Laymen asked him to please preach "just a spiritual sermon," and others admonished him that the church should not engage in controversial issues. A financial stalwart complained that Action's racial activities "take time away from the work he's supposed to be doing" and added tellingly: "This is not exactly what his congregation pays him for."

This opposition from the congregation is stern and serious. It might be even worse were it not for Action's warmth, charm, and refusal to become provoked at his detractors. Many of his parishioners, even older ones who almost to a man favor segregation, remain loyal to him. "I just can't go along with you," blurted out an elderly woman member on Sunday morning following a sermon on integration, "but I certainly think you are a sincere man, and I love you, Mr. Action."

There probably are but few ministers in Little Rock's major denominations who have not felt at least an occasional twinge of conscience when they compare their own cautious ineptness to the risks and abuse Action has endured. For he *is* the voice of conscience for his colleagues no less than the city itself. And perhaps, as so often happens, he has found that it requires more courage at such a time to face one's friends than to face one's enemies.

The blow that hurt the most came in a letter from a close boyhood friend in the Deep South. Having read of Action's activities in the Little Rock crisis, he chided his friend bitterly: "Judas betrayed a Man; Benedict Arnold betrayed a nation; and you, my friend, have betrayed a race!"

Characteristically, there was a plaintive quality, an element of true pathos, in the calm answer Action gave his friend: "I have full respect for your sincerity and integrity and hope that at some time in the future we may renew the ties which were so strong between your family and mine in days gone by. . . . May God's richest blessing rest on you now and always." But there are some things he cannot have, and he has made his choice.

The Fellowship of Class

David W. Barry

Our Protestant churches in the city are on the whole not community-oriented or neighborhood-oriented, but group-oriented. The membership is a selective voluntary membership, and association by choice. What is the basis of this association, the nature of the choice that people make in affiliating with one church rather than another? Our American cities are accumulations of people from almost every racial and national and religious stock on the face of the earth, with a strong emphasis on those of European origin, and more recently those of African origin; and also in the Southwest those of Spanish-American origin, and on the West Coast, many of Asiatic origin. The city drew to itself all the different religious and national strains that went to make up America and dumped them all together in a small area.

What must be emphasized is that every group brought its religious tradition to the city with it, and often created new traditions as well. St. Louis in the heart of America is a good illustration. It was settled by the Protestants of British-American origin: the Presbyterians, Methodists, Baptists, Episcopalians, and somewhat belatedly the Congregationalists. With the later German immigration came

Reprinted from *The City Church* (January-February, 1955), pp. 5–8. Used by permission of the author and the Department of the Urban Church, National Council of Churches.

the continental European churches: Lutheran and Evangelical, with their own internal divisions; and the Roman Catholics in some strength. A small migration from southeastern Europe, chief among them the Italians, brought their religious culture later in the century. The Civil War split several denominations into northern and southern branches: Presbyterians and Baptists have representatives in St. Louis of both traditions, and the Methodists did also before their reunion. The Negroes migrated from the South with their own brands of Methodist and Baptist religion. Then came the fundamentalist-modernist controversy to create new splits in existing churches. Finally came the great migration from rural areas and the southern states, bringing in a variety of newer sects indigenous to those areas. And this splintered Protestantism is at work in a city where a united Roman Catholicism is very strong and Judaism is well represented.

As the Protestant churches and church people moved into city situations from their relatively homogeneous village origins, they made stubborn and persistent efforts to preserve the identity of each religious and social group. The typical Protestant church, while in theory preaching a gospel to all mankind, in practice appealed to the particular minority that was sympathetic to its point of view and historical background. Every division of Protestantism in the wide stretches of the country was transplanted to the concentrated populations of the city, where the divided character of our faith sticks out like a sore thumb. And this stubborn adherence to one ethnic group has lasted down to this day; only within the last two decades, for example, have the German Lutherans made serious efforts to reach beyond the German community for constitutents.

AN EGG BEATER IN THE MELTING POT

But no matter how much the local Protestant churches
wanted to remain homogeneous, the facts of city life were
against them. We used to have a good deal of talk about
the city as a "melting pot," but it is not until about the
third generation in America that it becomes one. The first
generation of each in-migrant group settles in clusters, and
the second generation, while usually moving out to somewhat better neighborhoods, manages to maintain considerable unity as a group. But by the third generation, the
melting pot has done its work. The third generation selects
their homes, marriage partners, friends, jobs, largely on the
basis of income, ability, and preference; and national origin
is a very remote factor in any of these. Our cities are becoming third generation, heterogeneous in every local
area, but particularly in those areas where young couples
settle and raise families. Visit any low- or medium-priced
housing development or housing project and you will see
this. They are not solidly German, or Italian, or British-
American, or solidly anything; they are not solidly Protestant or solidly Catholic, except in some cases where the
Catholic Church has deliberately colonized its people. The
newer communities are coming to be pretty good cross
sections of the city, at whatever economic level they represent. The older nationality communities have begun rapidly to break down as the first generation passes on.

There are even promising signs that our Negro ghettos
will one day break down and the Negro population will
disperse itself through our cities on the basis of income
and preference rather than race. Until recently we have
been able to think in terms of Italian churches for Italian
communities, German churches for German communities,

Negro churches for Negro communities, Congregational churches for Yankee communities—to that extent our group specialization in the Protestant churches made sense. But not any more. The entire city, with its many diverse elements, is being laid at the doorstep of every Protestant church in the city.

The Protestant churches on the whole, I think, have done their best to resist this process, and indeed so have the Roman Catholic churches. Our religious institutions have tended to be the last strongholds of the foreign language cultures or for that matter the various early American cultures, such as that of New England or that of the pre-Civil War South. We who belong to the older established Protestant groups, torn between our evangelistic duty and the need to keep our historic constituencies relatively pure, generally solved our problem by creating a series of foreign language ministries which served their purpose and have now largely disappeared as the American-born children of these immigrant groups have disappeared into the anonymous urban mass.

We are raising a new generation in our cities, and it is a generation among whom the national origin of their parents is much less important than the fact that they live in today's city, attend the same public schools, watch the same television shows, compete for the same jobs, belong to the same unions. I was in Brooklyn not long ago with a group of young people who attended the same high school and the same church. It happened that a couple were Negro, one was Puerto Rican, one was Italian, and one German—all born and raised in Brooklyn. As I watched them and listened to them it came to me suddenly that there was literally no difference in the speech and accent of any one as against any other. There was an accent, all right, but it was a Brooklyn accent—with my eyes closed I could not distinguish the slightest trace of what I was accustomed to think were Negro speech habits or Puerto Rican or Italian.

This incident highlights the fact that the old ethnic divisions have begun rapidly to diminish as the basis of human association in the city. World War II, the draft, and the tremendous mobility of our population greatly accelerated this process. Where these divisions are associated with skin color, of course, the barriers break down more slowly. Even here, though, there is rapid change.

Social Stratification

But as these divisions based on national origin have diminished in importance, others have emerged to take their place. What the sociologist talks about these days is something called social stratification, the social class structure of American society. This America of ours, it appears, in spite of two and a half centuries of vigorous equalitarian social and political doctrine, seems to have something of a hierarchical structure in its social groupings; there are upper, middle, and lower classes; indeed, according to the most widely known student of social class, the gradations are upper-upper, lower-upper, upper-middle, lower-middle, upper-lower, and lower-lower. And every study that has been made has consistently shown that the Protestant churches are neatly arranged on this scale from upper to lower in terms of the constituency they serve. The Congregationalists, Episcopalians, Presbyterians, are upper class; the Methodists and Lutherans are middle class; the Pentecostals and Nazarenes and many Baptists are lower class.

Now this matter of social class is rather subtle, and if it is understood only superficially it can be dismissed much too lightly. To say that the Congregational churches are upper class does not mean that they are solidly composed of business and professional men. Any Congregational pastor knows they are not. On the other hand, neither do they reflect accurately the composition of the community. If business proprietors and managers are, say, 10 per cent of a community's working population, they are likely to be 20 per cent of the Congregational membership. I don't know how many times I have been told by a minister that his church is a "cross section" of the community. This attitude reminds me somewhat of the business firms in this state who, when the FEPC law was passed, hastily hired one or two Jews so that when the enforcement officers came around they could say, "Of course we don't discriminate—see, here is our Jew." There are upper-class Protestant churches that seem to maintain a few captive workingmen and one or two captive Negroes for just this purpose.

Statistics, of course, must be considered here as something like the "odds" at a race track. What they mean is that the odds are good for a Congregational church to succeed in an upper-class community, but the odds are poorer for success in a community of laborers. The reverse would be true of, say, a Nazarene church. An able and imaginative minister, of course, can beat the odds. On the other hand, national Home Mission agencies in their "high-potential" programs have to play the odds in allocating their limited funds for church extension—unless pastors can develop and demonstrate new skills and techniques in building strong churches in supposedly "unfavorable" communities.

UPPER-BRACKET LEADERSHIP

But the operation of social class in our churches goes to a much deeper level than statistics on membership occupations. It is even more influential in terms of leadership and orientation. Whom do we seek out for top leadership positions in the church? Whom do we send as lay delegates to General Council? I am willing to bet that nine times out of ten it is a business or professional man; if it is not a business proprietor or owner or someone from the upper levels of management and sales, it is an educator or a lawyer or a physician. Or possibly it will be wives from the same social class. Almost never is it a laborer, even a labor leader; seldom is it a farmer, and certainly never a tenant farmer; nor is it except in the rarest cases a railroad conductor or a policeman or the owner-manager of a gas station. Yet most men in the nation work at such jobs as these, and few Christians would deny that their witness is as valuable in our top ecclesiastical gatherings as that of the man whose income is in the upper brackets, or whose education is at the postgraduate level.

I am aware of the argument that only top-bracket men are free to travel to week-long meetings of church bodies. I would comment only that the Nazarenes and Pentecostals and Churches of Christ and Jehovah's Witnesses do not seem to have unusual difficulties in securing lay participation from the lower social brackets.

But more fundamental even than leadership is the matter of denominational orientation. Being myself a fairly standard product of middle-class Presbyterianism (incidentally any given American is said to consider himself middle class; it is poor form to be at one or the other extreme), it has been only gradually and over a period of years that I have come to have some understanding of the ways in which the values and standards of our churches are entangled with the values and standards of our status in society. And I think that perhaps I have seen this more concretely in our Christian education literature than anywhere else.

I have been exposed to a good deal of denominational literature in my past and present. It seems to me that there are certain assumptions implicit in this literature about the audience for which it is written. It seems to assume a normative family situation as one with two or three children living in a single-family house with some modest space around it, with a father who comes home at night from working in an office. They live in a community where teachers are pleasant, policemen are friendly, and a fairly decent neighborhood spirit exists. The problems of the children are primarily those of adjustment to other children of like circumstances and learning basic principles of behavior and morality. In the literature they are expected to learn, for example, that Negroes and Italians are children of God and are just as good as they are. The children go to high school to prepare for college, and to college to prepare for a business and professional career, and they will be married sometime after graduation from college or postgraduate work.

Now the point I want to make about this literature is that it is directed to the needs of a specialized class in America, and one that is by no means preponderant in our cities. If we are under the impression that such a family is typical, it reveals the limits of our own associations. In the first place the family situation itself—father and mother and two or three children—probably represents less than half of our city families. In the second place, if father comes home from an office, the family is still less representative. To go on, if this is a single-family home in a nice neighborhood, it still further restricts the number of families who can identify this situation with their own. In the large city, not all teachers are pleasant, and not all policemen are friendly, depending on what neighborhood you may live in. The neighborhood spirit is likely to be a phenomenon only of the residential areas at the edge of the city. So far as the children's needs are concerned, in some communities, problems of children may be described more accurately in terms of survival than adjustment—not always physical survival, but emotional and psychological and moral and intellectual survival certainly. And while it is nice for our children to learn to be nice to Negro and Italian children, it is very clear, is it not, that literature written with this message is not written *for* Negroes or *for* Italians? Examine our literature in terms of whom we are told to direct our Christian attitudes *toward,* and you will find a good many implicit assumptions about the social class that is expected to read it. And as for education, I am told that the number of youngsters taking out working papers before they finish high school is on the increase, most urban youth do *not* expect to go to college, and of course very few go on to postgraduate business and professional study. As to marriage, a great many city young people are already married by the time our Christian educators assume they are ready for premarital guidance. Our very term for this group—the "college age" group—reveals our presuppositions about young people from eighteen to twenty-two—they are supposed to be in college.

Now please understand that I approve heartily of single-family housing and friendly policemen and college education and a good job in the business or professional

world. But the point I want to make is that this whole
complex of values is still in urban America something that
must be described in terms of privilege and privileged
classes. The circle of privilege has widened tremendously
in the past fifteen years, but it is still the experience of
only a minority in urban society, and as soon as we assume
these privileges as characteristic of the experience of our
church constituency, we have restricted sharply the area
of our ministry.

CLASS STRUCTURE ALIEN TO THE GOSPEL

And likewise, we can often confuse these values seriously
with the values of the gospel we preach. I know of a
Christian neighborhood house director who for ten years
in raising money for his program told over and over the
story of the young son of an Italian bricklayer whom he had
helped and encouraged to go to college and medical school
and who became an outstanding physician. The Presbyterian elders applauded him and gave him a slice of
their missionary budget. Now there is nothing in either
the Old Testament or the New, so far as I know, that says
our mission is to make professional men out of promising
young children of the working class. And yet this is a
theme that has appeared again and again in our missionary
literature to reveal the class bias.

Some of the more amusing sociological literature in this
field has to do with the way in which people describe their
own class and others. In one national study, a sample of
people were asked: "What do you think are the criteria or
characteristics that put someone in the upper classes?"
Members of the "upper classes" gave a long series of
answers, including education, family heritage, ability,

achievement, good character, leadership, power, influence, prestige, high-ranking occupation or position, dress, and intelligence. But members of the "working" class had a much shorter answer: *money*. On the other hand, when asked to describe the attributes of the "working" class, members of the "upper" class said: "Low income"; while members of the "working" class said: "We work for a living." And "upper class" and "middle class" alike seemed to have a surprisingly uniform opinion of the "lower" class as a rather despicable group characterized by poor character, low morals, drink, crime, lack of ability, low intelligence, shiftlessness, lack of ambition, while members of this "lower" class, speaking for themselves, said that poverty and lack of education put them in this class.

The social hierarchy exists in America and is a real factor conditioning attitudes. There are undoubtedly other scales on which people could be arranged in a way that would give us interesting information; I should like to see, for example, scales devised to arrange people in a hierarchy of happiness or personal influence or creativity or family stability or good deeds. But the hierarchy we know something about, the one the sociologists have done some analysis of, is the hierarchy of social class, and it is intimately related to our church structure in America.

We have recently completed a study of New Haven which included among other things a 5 per cent sampling of the entire city and an arrangement of the families in the sample by religion and social class. Congregationalists, as is usual in New England, were solidly established at the top of the social hierarchy. We also conducted a large number of depth interviews within our sample, our basic purpose being to discover the effectiveness of radio and television when used by the churches to communicate their message.

One revelation from these interviews I want to pass along to you, and I can do it by describing a familiar pattern of misunderstanding. Picture the minister standing in front of the microphone or camera to deliver a sermon to the broadcast audience. He is identified as a Congregational minister. To him this means simply that he is a representative of one of the great Protestant traditions. He is innocent of any class bias; he sincerely wants to preach a gospel to all who will hear it. But what does "Congregational" mean to the people who have tuned in?

To the workingman, it may mean a representative of the "bosses," and often very paternalistic bosses.

To the uneducated, it may mean a representative of the "intellectual snobs" at the university.

To the successful Jewish businessman, it may mean a representative of the group who have excluded him from the "best" social clubs.

To the poor man, it may mean a representative of wealth and—to his mind—exploitation.

And this millstone of class hangs around the neck of the Congregational minister—himself innocent of such prejudices and unaware that they are attached to his person and position—and builds a barrier against his communication to the very people he may want most to reach. You cannot tell me that this is not a handicap to the preaching of the gospel.

And it is a handicap to the practice of the gospel. We have all read enough of psychology or, for that matter, of the New Testament itself, to know the emotional and psychological and moral cost of maintaining a position in society which is privileged, which excludes any large groups. And equally there is a cost in the waste of lives and the destruction of family relationships when the goals and ambitions and strivings of the parents are wrongly ori-

ented. We documented also in our study the demoralizing
effect upon a family of concentration on the external symbols of upward class mobility—the supervisory and white-
collar job, a home in the "right" kind of community, membership in the "right" church. And at the working-class
level particularly, the *Protestant* families were ridden by
these frustrations much more often than the Catholic.

The class structure is an alien intrusion into the Christian
fellowship; it is a condition of our existence in American
cities today, but not a necessary condition. And every
church and every pastor who manages—as some have managed—to defy the strictures of class and conduct a ministry
to people of many kinds in terms of their spiritual condition and need rather than their family background and
current state of prosperity has brought the church a little
closer to a recognizably Christian witness.

Protestant-Catholic Tensions in Pluralistic America

Will Herberg

My purpose in these sessions is to discuss the problem of religious tensions in American life. It is surely unnecessary to stress how important, indeed how urgent, this problem is at the present time. Religious tensions are, in fact, the most pervasive kind of tensions in our society, having their effects and repercussions in all areas of American life.

All kinds of issues appear that require careful analysis and evaluation. However, we never really get to the heart of the matter if we limit ourselves merely to a discussion of the particular issues in controversy between the religious groups, for by restricting our consideration strictly to the issues we are in danger of overlooking the social and cultural situation out of which these issues emerge and which endow these issues with their characteristic virulence. Without seeing these issues in their larger historical and cultural setting, we cannot even rightly understand what they are about.

Therefore, I have a kind of triple task here: to uncover the historical-sociological background of the current situation of tension; to describe the group attitudes engendered by these background factors; and to assess the various

Reprinted in abridged form from *Yale Divinity News* (November, 1960), pp. 3–11. Used by permission of the author. This article is a summary of several lectures delivered at the Yale University Divinity School.

religio-ideological and religio-social issues in this context.

I

Let us examine first the historical-sociological background factors—the context in which the Protestant-
Catholic tensions of which we are so anxiously aware in
contemporary America have emerged. The fundamental
fact about American society against which we must try
to interpret contemporary Protestant-Catholic tensions is
the restructuring of American society from the "land of
immigrants," where identity was defined in terms of ethnicity (what Americans call "nationality"), into what
might be called the "triple melting pot," where identity is
defined in terms of religious belonging. This is the great
transformation that has been taking place in the past thirty
or forty years, and accompanying it has been a corresponding change in the religious structure of American
society.

Until quite recently, the kind of religious belonging that
normally went along with being an American was Protestantism. Protestantism was, in fact, America's unofficially
established religion. Today, the kind of religious belonging
that normally goes along with being an American is being
either a Protestant, a Catholic, or a Jew. America has
thus been transformed within the past generation from
a Protestant nation into a three-religion country. Our unofficially established church today is the trifaith system of
Protestant-Catholic-Jew.

The effect of all this upon Protestant-Catholic relations
has been double. It has made for both the mitigation and
for the exacerbation of these tensions, operating in different directions in a rather complex way.

How it has made, or rather is making, for mitigation should be obvious. Catholicism is now a recognized part of American religion, one of the three great faiths. That means that it is an *American* religion, no longer a foreign importation to be abandoned in the process of becoming an American. Furthermore, Catholics are today increasingly good, middle-class Americans—"Our kind of people." Within the past generation, American Catholics have gone far from the peripheral, foreign, lower-class status that had so long been theirs to become a nuclear middle-class American community. In the long run, a change such as this is bound to make for the easing of tensions. But in the short run, these very factors tend to operate in the opposite direction. Let us now examine the short-run effects.

Because of the structural changes in American society to which I have called attention, Protestants are today facing the threat of loss of accustomed status. And this is true everywhere, even in those areas of the country that are overwhelmingly Protestant; perhaps the threat is most acutely felt precisely in these areas, and the reaction is most violent. However distasteful this reaction may be to many of us, we should try to understand it. It is simply a fact that the special status Protestants have enjoyed throughout American history—as long as America was a Protestant nation—is now being subverted, and the Catholics seem to be those who are doing the subverting. Faced with the threat of loss of accustomed status, American Protestants, especially those of the older generation, have become anxious, sometimes even frantic. They feel themselves dispossessed of what is rightfully theirs. Once, America was theirs, their home, belonging to them of right and of fact. Now, in the three-religion America that has emerged, they are merely one of three tenants. Catholics and Jews, especially Catholics, have moved in on them and taken over. No wonder they feel frightened, embittered, and resentful.

A generation or two ago, there were plenty of Catholics around, of course, but where were they to be found? At the margin of society, laborers and servant girls. And the Protestants, who felt so much at home in the nuclear institutions of the community, didn't worry much about them. Today, the middle-class American Protestant, wherever he turns, finds Catholics all around him, everywhere, in all of the nuclear institutions of the community. He begins to feel not only dispossessed, but surrounded, overwhelmed. He begins to develop nightmares of vast Catholic growth and imminent Catholic domination.

Now, these nightmares are no more than nightmares, if you go by the facts. The Protestant-Catholic ratio in this country has not changed substantially in forty years. In certain periods, Protestants have moved ahead faster; in other periods, it has been the Catholics who have moved ahead. Both have grown; but Catholic growth has seemed more formidable and threatening. In the first place, Catholic advances have been in urban and especially suburban communities; and secondly, this Catholic advance has come as an incursion into middle-class American society, which Protestants had always thought of as their natural and rightful preserve.

As a result of this collocation of circumstances, Protestants in this country seem to be developing what the editorial writer of *The Christian Century* some years ago (October 29, 1955) called "Protestant paranoia." This is an attitude of intense and morbid suspicion, a sense of imminent threat, an overpowering belief that they are the victims of a vast conspiracy engineered by "Rome."

Now, let us look at the other side, the Catholic side. American Catholics have their problems too in this situation. But their problems are of an inverse character. American Catholics have recently achieved real status, and they naturally are afflicted with what sociologists call status anxiety—the anxiety of those who have recently moved up and are very anxious about preserving their new status. They are easily tempted to self-assertiveness and overcompensation. They tend to develop what *The Christian Century* editorial writer, in the article referred to above, designates as "Catholic claustrophobia." Catholics tend to feel "closed in," discriminated against, barred from the seats of prestige and power, denied the social recognition to which they feel that their newly acquired status entitles them. They, too, develop their frustrations, hatreds, and resentments; and these too we should try to understand.

But, after all, this is the short-range picture. The long-range picture may be quite different, because in defining the long-range picture new factors enter of decisive importance. These factors all flow out of the generational differences that both Protestants and Catholics show in their group attitudes.

These generational differences are already significant. Protestant opinion about Catholics, or for that matter, Catholic opinion about Protestants, is very different if you take those under thirty-five or forty years of age than if you take those over forty. Recently, an opinion survey was made of a sizable New England community in which religious group tensions seemed to be rising at an alarming rate. The main issue seemed to be the parochial school situation, but other discontents and grievances were involved. The most interesting thing that was discovered was probably the marked cleavage in opinion between Protestants under thirty-five and those over. The latter, the older generation, were deeply disturbed, and expressed their state of mind in such formulas as these: "The old

American principles are being destroyed," "Democracy is being subverted." The younger Protestants, however, simply couldn't understand what the shouting was about. They did not feel threatened, nor did they see the American way being overthrown. Why the difference? The mind of the Protestants of the older group had been formed under the older conditions, when America was still a Protestant nation. Naturally, they felt that what was going on was a subversion of everything they held dear. The younger generation, on the other hand, had had their outlook formed in an America that was a three-religion country. What was happening in their town did not arouse much apprehension in them; on the contrary, they found it quite natural. Catholics were no different from anybody else, they felt, and they articulated their attitude in the well-known formula, "After all, we're all Americans!"

The same generational difference is reflected in public opinion polls on a Catholic for President. The younger voters uniformly show a considerably lower percentage avowing anti-Catholic sentiments than do the older voters. The tendency of these varying attitudes is obvious: older-generation attitudes make for the exacerbation of religious tensions; younger-generation attitudes make for their mitigation. The former define the short-run situation; the latter, the long-run. Both are important, but it is the long run that is decisive.

In the short run, however, we have a situation of growing tension. In this situation, both Protestants and Catholics, and Jews, too, of course, see themselves as minority groups, confronting the others in the characteristic posture of minority-group defensiveness.

What does this analysis add up to? It adds up to at least three conclusions, which may perhaps be formulated this way: first, the religious tensions we have been discussing emerge out of certain deep-going social and cultural changes in American life and may best be understood in relation to these trends and changes; secondly, the process is by no means uniform, unleashing as it does forces working in opposite directions; and thirdly, the significance of the particular issues in controversy between Protestants and Catholics can be properly assessed only within this historical-sociological framework, although these issues are undoubtedly real and important on their own account.

II

Keeping in mind the main points in this analysis, let me now turn to an examination of American Catholicism as it really is, in contrast to the appearance it often presents in the minds of American non-Catholics, both Protestants and Jews.

I have isolated a number of conceptions held by non-Catholics about American Catholicism, and I want to present them to you for consideration. In speaking of these conceptions as "appearance in contrast to reality," I do not mean to suggest that they are entirely false. On the contrary, they often contain a modicum of truth, but even this truth, when seen out of context, can be misleading. My purpose is to subject these beliefs and concepts to a critical examination to see what the facts really are, and how much truth, and what kind of truth, they contain.

Is Roman Catholicism Ideologically Monolithic?

The first charge in the indictment is that American Catholicism is ideologically monolithic. This is not the case for Catholicism anywhere, least of all in America.

Let me enforce this point by quoting from an unim-
peachable authority, by no means pro-Catholic, F. E.
Mayer, the Missouri-Synod Lutheran historian. Mayer
writes: "The Roman Church is the most dogmatic, and
at the same time the least doctrinal church. There is a
fixed dogmatic limit, but within this limit there is room
for divergent and often contradictory opinions. There is
probably no church which has the capacity for harboring
so many widely divergent points of view as the Roman
Church." (*The Religious Bodies of America,* pp. 30, 36.)

The Jesuit journal *America* agrees. "There are today," an
editorial in a recent issue (March 10, 1956) points out,
"well over 30 million Catholics in our land. By background,
education, occupation, and national origin they differ
profoundly from one another. There is probably a greater
pluralism among American Catholics than exists within
any comparable group in the world."

Is there a Catholic "line"? Yes, within very narrow limits.
There is a Catholic "line" on defined dogmas of faith, but
these defined dogmas of faith can be formulated in very
brief compass. Beyond the limits thus defined, there is
the greatest possible diversity of opinion and the widest
range of views. And no wonder, with American Catholics
so diverse in their ethnic origin, cultural background, class,
and economic status.

Not only is there no Catholic "line"; there is no centralized Catholic hierarchy in America at all. Each diocese is
directly related to the Holy See, and again there is the
widest diversity among bishops and dioceses. Some measure of uniformity on certain matters is achieved through
the National Catholic Welfare Conference, but even this
is quite limited and often more apparent than real. Nothing
anywhere near ideological monolithism is to be found
among American Catholics.

Is Roman Catholicism Institutionally Totalitarian?

The second charge often made is that American Catholicism is institutionally totalitarian. The notion here is that Catholicism is institutionally totalitarian because the Catholic Church claims total jurisdiction over the life of the believer, and the hierarchy dictates the attitudes and decisions of the faithful on everything. Now, in a certain sense there is truth in this. The Christian church as such demands the whole of man. It makes a total claim. It is therefore "totalitarian" in that sense.

But it is wrong to assume that the Catholic Church as an institution makes a total claim. Catholic theologians have long distinguished the two "perfect societies"—the state and the church, each autonomous with its own right to existence and its own field of operations. In America, above all, there has never been any claim to the total life of the faithful on the part of the church. In fact, if you want to criticize the Catholic Church in America, you ought to criticize it from the other direction: it has only too often failed to exercise its proper authority over the life of the faithful in combating notorious abuses in social, political, and economic affairs.

If you want to pursue the question a little further, you might make the point that the Catholic Church in its very nature is hostile to totalitarianism. Totalitarianism, as a political system, does indeed make a total claim upon society and the individual, allowing nothing to escape its supervision and control. But this is precisely what the Catholic Church cannot tolerate. The church, on grounds of natural and divine law, insists, for example, on the prior right of the family and itself in the upbringing and education of the children. This no totalitarian state can allow: to give up the children, the rising generation, is to give up everything. Conflict with the church is therefore inevitable, as all recent history shows. This is not the case with all Protestant groups. Some Protestant groups are so "spiritual" they make no claims at all, so long as they are permitted to pray in silence. Therefore the totalitarian state can tolerate them as long as necessary. But it cannot tolerate the Catholic Church.

Is Catholicism Undemocratic?

The next count in the indictment runs: Catholicism is undemocratic. The ecclesiastical regime is monarchical rather than republican or democratic; the Catholic ethos is authoritarian; the church is ready to flout the democratic will of the people on certain questions. Let us examine these charges.

Here I find a total misunderstanding of what American democracy means. American democracy prescribes no particular kind of church regime, and no church regime is more "American" than another. American democracy makes no such pretensions; it does not claim the prerogative to prescribe the right way in all areas of life. Such a claim would make democracy a totalistic ideology, would destroy its democratic character, and turn it into an idolatrous faith. The monarchical regime, in one form or another, has been the Roman Catholic Church regime since the early Middle Ages. Whatever one may think about it, no one has the right to denounce Roman Catholics as "undemocratic" or "un-American" on that account.

As to "authoritarianism," it is true that among considerable groups of American Catholics the authoritarian spirit is quite pronounced. American Catholics vary widely in ethnic origin and degree of acculturation. Obviously Catholic groups who still retain the old ethnic culture are going to be more authoritarian in the internal organization of family, community, and the like than other Americans are. As they lose their ethnicity and become more acculturated, they tend to take on American patterns, which may or may not be better, but are certainly less authoritarian.

In general, I should say the ethos of American Catholics is not very different from the general American ethos, given equality of condition, the same kind of ethnicity, and the same degree of acculturation.

It is charged that Catholic spokesmen have insisted that they would not hesitate to defy the popular will in certain extreme circumstances where the will of the majority comes into conflict with the divine or natural law. For example, if the United States were to decree compulsory sterilization as the Hitler regime did, Catholics insist they would defy and resist the law, even though 95 per cent of the people were for it. Now, this seems to me not only right, not only proper, but thoroughly democratic in our sense of the term. Because our kind of democracy recognizes a majesty beyond itself. We have God to obey, not man. Therefore our kind of democracy recognizes the appeal to conscience. The notion that democracy means that everyone must conform to the majority will in every area of life, as a matter of conscience, is thoroughly despotic. When Catholics insist that they might be compelled to defy the popular will in certain extreme circumstances, they are insisting upon what to every Christian should be simply a matter of course.

Is the American Catholic Church a Power Organization?

The last charge against American Catholicism that I am going to consider is perhaps the most serious. It is that the church is really a power organization, and is indeed power-mad. What is the reality?

Under American conditions, all special-interest groups,

and churches are ecclesiastical special-interest groups, are power groups, and must be so, if they are to survive as social institutions. The Catholic Church is no more so than some other church groups. The Catholic Church has a special problem, however. It has the problem of defending minority ethnic groups through the church.

Now, in a situation like this it is perfectly obvious that the church will be led to accentuate its power strivings. However, I must add to this that there is a great uneasiness among American Catholic thinkers in this matter. Father Murray and others have written quite candidly about it. The matter is not an easy one to deal with.

I cannot leave this part of my remarks without emphasizing that just as non-Catholic Americans have their false image of American Catholicism, so American Catholics have their false image of American Protestantism. It works both ways, and when I speak to Catholic groups I generally make a special effort to get them to become aware of the grotesque misconceptions they frequently harbor about Protestants and Protestantism in this country.

Protestants, Catholics, and Jews in America are usually neighbors and friends, co-operating in most social and civic enterprises as fellow Americans. Yet, they are almost totally ignorant of each other's religious community life. They harbor the strangest suspicions and misconceptions in this sphere, threatening the mutual confidence and understanding without which a pluralistic society such as ours cannot survive. These suspicions and misconceptions are a source of confusion also in our religious understanding, for they tend to obscure the real differences between the religious groups and to replace these real differences with false images and false issues.

CHAPTER VIII

URBAN CHURCH AND
COMMUNITY CO-OPERATION

INTRODUCTION

Despite conflicting interests in urban society, no community could exist without a high degree of co-operation and consensus. Just as conflict is not inherently evil, however, so co-operation is not inevitably good. A group of business firms co-operating to fix prices is illegal. Whether co-operation is good or bad depends largely on the ends toward which such action is directed.

In the context of this chapter, co-operation implies positive mutual help. The selections portray the co-operation of church and community to meet human needs. The church that is concerned about community needs cannot play a lone game; it must co-operate with other community agencies. Co-operation does not imply that churches abdicate their responsibility by turning housing needs over to the public housing authority, the jobless and the "hard-core families" to social caseworkers, the alcoholics to the AA.

The urban church cannot withdraw from human needs, although it acknowledges that many community agencies have expert professional knowledge and resources that are not present in the church. Pastoral responsibility in the city entails community co-operation and the recognition of common concerns and unique contributions so that churches and community agencies may be mutually helpful in serving the urbanite.

"The Pastor and Community Resources" is written by

Charles F. Kemp, Distinguished Professor of Practical Ministries at Brite College of the Bible, Texas Christian University. The author notes that a new sense of co-operation between churches and social agencies is emerging. To serve the needs of urban man, the pastor must know what social services and facilities are available, how to refer people to specific agencies, and how to interpret the work of these agencies. As an ally of social welfare agencies, the church is not shirking its distinctive role to interpret the meaning of life as a whole. Rather, it enables the church to perform its task more adequately.

In "Urban Church and Co-operative Planning," Clifford C. Ham, lecturer on the faculty of Wesley Theological Seminary, argues that the church can serve the community through "community-centered planning." Churches have a stake in long-range, comprehensive city planning as well as an important role to play. Churchmen must be involved as citizens in the planning process. The most effective planning is done co-operatively with all the churches and public and private agencies working together.

J. Archie Hargraves suggests in "The Local Church and Juvenile Delinquency" that delinquency is one of the pressing problems of our day. The author, now on the staff of the Board of Home Missions of the Congregational Christian Churches, contends that the local church can be a focal point for effective action against juvenile delinquency. He calls for unity of action, for church-neighborhood co-operation. Although the church can work directly with youth, it must also prepare the neighborhood so that adults will come to relate to young people. As prerequisites for such a program, the local parish must understand its task, be able to marshal community resources, and implement a relevant and redemptive program. The author concludes with an account of how a group of churches in a high delinquency area is seeking to cope with the problem co-operatively.

The Pastor
and Community Resources

Charles F. Kemp

There have been three stages in the churches' relationship to social service: First, the period when they did it all —or almost all; second, a period of separation; third, the one we are now entering which is marked by a trend toward co-operation. This trend toward co-operation is coming from both directions. Co-operation between social work agencies and between such professions as medicine and social work has long been accepted; in fact, it is recognized that a worker in any one of these fields is ethically committed to get a "client" or a "patient" to the person or service that can do him the most good. The church has often been ignored in this process, but there is a new realization that spiritual resources are as important as any other resources, that "man does not live by bread alone." There is a rediscovery on the part of the social workers of the fact that social welfare and the church have common roots and common purposes, and can do much together. Pastors also are becoming aware that here is a resource, not a danger; that only as they work with these other groups can they render the fullest service to their people.

This does not mean the pastor no longer needs to be

Reprinted from *The Pastor and Community Resources,* by Charles F. Kemp, Department of Social Welfare, National Council of Churches (The Bethany Press, 1960), pp. 19–33. Used by permission of the author and The Bethany Press.

concerned about problems of a welfare nature or that he
does not have an important function to fulfill in helping
people who are confronted with problems of human need.
Quite to the contrary, a large portion of his time may be
spent in such areas. He cannot avoid it. The question is,
Does he handle it well, or inadequately? There are now
many resources to help him. He either utilizes them or he
doesn't. The church must meet the needs of men; to do this
it must work *with* these other agencies or other professions.

There are two basic principles that govern such work;
one grows out of the other. (1) The good of the individual
is the primary concern. This being the case, (2) all resources must be utilized. A pastor should not attempt what
someone else can do better.

Other agencies do have resources; other workers do have
skill and techniques that the pastor does not have. Furthermore, these special services are increasing all the time.
For example, there is much more help available for older
people than there was just a few years ago. Much is known
now about vocational rehabilitation that is of very recent
origin. Voluntary groups like Alcoholics Anonymous provide a unique service to alcoholics that few individuals or
churches can fulfill. One of the minister's chief tasks is to
get the person to those who can help him the most. Wayne
Oates says, "The pastor needs to ask himself in every situation of pastoral care and personal counseling, 'Is this
parishioner in need of help other than the specific ministry
that I am commissioned and equipped to give?' "[1]

This is not an indication of weakness or of inadequacy;
rather, it is a sign of wisdom and strength. In fact, one
might say the more mature and intelligent the pastor, or
social caseworker, or other specialist, the more effective is
his use of other services. The pastor may not have the
(*a*) time, (*b*) training, or (*c*) resources to meet all of the

needs of some people. Some problems require a great deal of time. This is certainly true of the alcoholic and of family problems. If the pastor is not able to give it the time it deserves, he is obligated to see that the persons involved find someone who can. Some areas require special training. The pastor is not trained to serve as a psychiatrist; he is not qualified to give mental tests as the psychologist is; he does not have the special training that is necessary in such fields as vocational rehabilitation or special education. He does not have the resources that some agencies have. He does not have as many resources for finding a man a job as the employment service does; he does not have facilities for caring for transients as the Salvation Army does; he cannot administer funds as the local public welfare office can.

The Pastor's Duty to Know Community Resources

The pastor is frequently placed in a position in which it is important that he know the resources that are available in his community. One study conducted a few years ago in a town of some 30,000 people asked the question, "Where do the people turn in time of need or stress?" A very large percentage said that in time of trouble they would go to their church. A social worker, commenting on these findings, was quite surprised and somewhat disturbed. He was disturbed, not because they went to the church but because he feared the pastor would not know the resources that were available or might not make the effort to secure adequate help.

It is not meant to be critical to point out that many ministers do not make use of all of the community's services that are available. They do not mean to be negligent, or to deprive their people of some help that they need—they simply do not know of all the available resources.

The pastor, for the good of his people, has the obligation to be informed about community resources. This may be a difficult task, especially in larger cities. There is a great variety of agencies, public and private, local, state, and national, all providing different services; nevertheless, the very number increases the possibility of securing help.

The pastor must know not only agencies in general (such as are described in the textbooks on an introduction to social work); he must know also what particular resources are available in *his own* community. All communities differ. The services that are available in Chicago, Cleveland, or New York are quite different from the services that are available in a small town in Minnesota or a county-seat town in Wyoming, for example.

He does need to know the over-all pattern of community resources as such. He also needs to know what exists in this town where his people live and work. He must know more than what agencies exist. He should know the people who operate them, what their effectiveness is, what are their attitudes and point of view, what they are prepared to do and what they can't do. There is no point in requesting a service that an agency is not prepared to give, or which may even be forbidden by law.

One of a pastor's first tasks is to become acquainted with these men and women who work in these other fields. Successful referral and interprofessional co-operation is a result of mutual acquaintance and understanding. It works most effectively when the pastor and the social worker, or doctor, or teacher, or whoever it may be, know each other and understand the role or position the other expects to fill.

A pastor should be able to answer such questions as these:

Where do you go if a man wants a job?

Where do you go if a transient wants a meal and a room for the night?

Where do you go for help for an alcoholic?

Where do you go when parents wonder if their child is retarded?

Where do you go if a husband and wife are having difficulty and it seems to be a deeper problem than the pastor feels adequate to handle?

Where do you go if a family does not have sufficient clothing to send a child to school?

Where do you go if there is an older person who needs nursing-home care but does not have the funds to provide it?

Where do you go if a boy wants to study for the ministry but isn't sure whether or not he has the intellectual capacity to finish college?

Where do you go to find help or a foster home for a neglected child?

Where do you go to find help for a family that needs legal assistance but cannot afford to hire an attorney?

How do you find out if a person or a family has been consulting other agencies?

THE PASTOR AS A GUIDE AND INTERPRETER

The pastor can do much not only to guide people to the agencies that they need but to interpret the agencies for them. Many people, especially older people or children or those who have had few educational opportunities, do not know about them or what their particular functions are. In a large city the very complexity of social agencies makes it even more confusing. Without some guidance a person may not find the one he needs. There are many people barely managing to get along, or struggling with some difficulty or handicap, who are unaware of the fact that there are people with special training and resources available to help with a problem like theirs. There are others who do not avail themselves of such services because of a sense of embarrassment, a natural hesitation or timidity, a fear of what such an agency may do, investigations they may make, etc.

The pastor's function is not to perform the service, but to recognize the need, to provide information so people can know what the possibilities are, to help create the atmosphere by which such help will be desired and accepted.

Some people do not understand the purposes or procedures of a complex agency. Here the pastor can help to interpret. He should not discuss the details of the other agency's procedures. That is their business. The pastor should be careful not to oversell or to depreciate an agency; rather, he should interpret so that the parishioner understands and knows what to expect. To do this he must be familiar with its functions himself.

There may be occasions when the pastor will make the initial contact or when he will go with the person on the first visit. Probably everyone approaches a social agency with some hesitation or apprehension. There are some who feel that to seek such help is an admission of failure, or that to apply for financial assistance is a cause for embarrassment. There is almost always a bit of uncertainty. They wonder what their reception will be, what questions they will be asked, what they will do. At such a time it is well to have someone just "standing by."

Sometimes the intake procedures of an agency are rather complex and confusing; in fact, they can become almost bewildering, especially to the very young, or to older people, or to the foreign born. Such a simple matter as helping an older person fill out a questionnaire at a welfare office may be a little thing, but it helps.

The pastor should not take over the responsibilities for his people. Those who can should be permitted to make their own contacts; but for the immature, the dependent, the aged, those for whom it is very difficult, he can render a real service by preparing the way with a letter or phone call and, when need be, accompanying them on the first visit. This has a further value, for it enables the pastor to become acquainted with the worker who will be dealing with his parishioner and paves the way for future co-operation when that seems advisable.

SOURCES OF INFORMATION

Where can a pastor secure reliable information about the agencies in his community? Some denominations maintain their own local welfare agencies which will gladly help their pastors with consultation and information. If a pastor lives in a city where there is a community welfare council or a community chest, he will find there a directory of agencies. If he lives in a small community, he may have to gather this information for himself. The social workers are usually the best informed about community resources and will be glad to lend assistance either in providing general information or in helping to find the right agency for some specific need. Also, the state department of child welfare and the state department of health can supply him with a list of many community agencies. Sometimes a council of churches can be of assistance. Councils in larger cities often have departments of welfare which gather such information for pastors. An older pastor who has been in a community for some time can sometimes provide valuable information and can perhaps evaluate services from a pastor's point of view.

A Continuing Pastoral Relationship

In most situations a pastoral relationship to an individual or family who come to the pastor for help should be continued no matter what other resources are used. There may be exceptions, where it is best for the specialist or some agency to take complete charge of the situation, but they are exceptions. In the vast majority of cases the best procedure is for the pastor to assist the person in securing the help that is needed and for him to continue his relationship as a pastor. Finding specialized resources does not eliminate a pastor's responsibility. He may be instrumental in getting an alcoholic to join the AA or in seeking the help of a physician, but this does not eliminate the responsibility he has as a pastor. He may make arrangements for an older person to get old-age assistance, but he still has a service to render as a pastor. His task is to find the best help available—then he is free to serve as a pastor and to make the contribution he is uniquely prepared to make.

Dangers and Problems

It is only realistic to point out that working with other agencies does not solve all of the problems; in fact, it has some dangers, and can create some problems of its own. It can be a means of dodging responsibility. Some pastors are too quick to shunt a person off to someone else rather than to take the time or to make the effort to work with him.

There is always the danger, in making a referral, that the

person who is being referred may not understand. For him it has an element of rejection. He may feel the pastor is not interested in him as a person, or does not want to spend the time. The very fact that someone else is suggested may cause undue alarm.

We must recognize that the people in a few agencies may not welcome co-operation with the clergy. This attitude, fortunately, is diminishing. The agency workers may not understand or appreciate the approach of the church. Others may have had unfortunate experiences in attempting to work with the clergy in the past and are conditioned against such a co-operative approach to human problems.

There may be times when the pastor and the social agency may disagree as to what is best for an individual or a family.

The pastor must recognize that some individuals and some agencies do much better work than others. Some workers are better trained and better qualified than others. Some agencies are more effective in one community than an agency by the same name in another community. In this manual we must speak in *general* terms. In any given community the pastor must be *specific*.

Many of these agencies and specializations are new. They are still in the process of experimentation. They often have limitations of budget and inadequate, untrained personnel. Some do not have the attitudes of humanitarian concern a pastor might prefer. We should remember that pastors and churches are not perfect either. These same criticisms can and have been directed at the church.

NEED FOR CLOSER CO-OPERATION

All that we have said thus far emphasizes that closer co-operation between all groups must be developed. The concept of a group or "team" approach has long been accepted by other professions. Doctors, nurses, social workers, psychologists, and others work together in a variety of settings and circumstances. The pastor is not often thought of as a member of the team. There is a trend in that direction. More and more of the people in these other professions are willing to accept the pastor as a member of the team. The activities of a co-operative pastor will encourage that trend.

The place to begin is at the point of training—both theological and otherwise. The clergy should be trained to use the resources of social agencies. Social workers, doctors, nurses, psychologists, need to be taught to use the resources of religion and the church. Part of this is the responsibility of the schools. Part of it is the responsibility of the pastor in the local church. Most young people enter these other humanitarian professions with a high sense of idealism; many times they are searching for a personal and professional philosophy of life. They often have a very real sense of spiritual values and a personal commitment to service. The pastor who has them in his church should see their guidance as a real opportunity. He should cultivate their friendship, keep in contact with them through their training as much as he would the young man or woman who is studying for the ministry, religious education, or the mission field. These people, too, are preparing to serve.

The pastor can do much to foster good relationships in the community by serving on boards and committees of such groups and by encouraging his people to do so. It is time-consuming work, but the pastor has a contribution to make; he has a point of view that needs to be expressed; he has some familiarity with group processes. Furthermore, he expects busy people to take time to serve on his boards and committees; here is his chance to render a similar service to others.

In such activities he gains a firsthand knowledge of the services and procedures of the agency. He also becomes personally acquainted with the workers, which opens the door to much more effective referral (both ways) and co-operation in specific cases.

The very best thing a pastor can do to increase co-operation is to do a good job with the actual cases with which it is his responsibility to serve. When other workers recognize that the pastor understands his own role in the total community program, when he shows an intelligent, informed, sincere concern for the personal needs of people in specific cases, then they will be much more likely to welcome co-operation or even to seek it, as the case may be.

The Minister's Unique Contribution

The pastor should never forget that the church and the minister have a unique contribution that no other agency and no other profession can make. The church deals with religious faith and with man's relationship to God and to his fellow men. The church does not fail or relinquish this task when referral is made; rather, it becomes free to fulfill its own major responsibility which no other agency can do in quite the same way.

People's deepest needs have not been met when their material requirements of food, shelter, or clothing have been cared for. It is important that people should have health, but it is even more important that life should have meaning and value. Man's deepest requirements have not always been met when he has been provided with medical care or vocational opportunities. Man needs health and employment, but he also needs a sense of purpose, a spirit of self-forgetful service, and a sense of worth. It has been said, "Science has added years to life; the church must add life to the years." This is not meant to imply that other professions and agencies do not add "life to the years." It is not to say that they do not add meaning and purpose to life. Many of them do and very effectively. It is to say— this is the church's specialty.

Man's deepest needs are for faith, purpose, devotion, and understanding of spiritual resources, a sense of the reality of prayer and worship, an awareness of the acceptance of God, the assurance of forgiveness, the ability to love God with all one's heart, mind, soul, and strength and to love one's neighbor as oneself. This is the task of the church.

Some people may come in contact with many agencies. They may be receiving the help of more than one agency at the same time. Some agencies are designed to meet a specific need. They may deal with one aspect of life— physical, economic, or otherwise. These agencies are de- signed to meet particular needs, to help people overcome their weaknesses and handicaps, and to solve some of their problems. The church is deeply grateful for all such groups and their contributions. The church deals with life as a whole; it presents an overarching purpose in which all else finds meaning. It is the church which deals with man's ultimate destiny, which provides spiritual resources that strengthen and sustain an individual in all of the expe- riences of life.

The pastor, too, is a specialist. He is a representative of the whole historic Christian tradition. He, too, has special resources at his disposal—the insights, the understanding, the guidance of Christian teaching; the healing, lifting, strengthening power of worship; the supporting, enriching, enabling experience of Christian fellowship; the challeng- ing, demanding call to self-forgetful service; the sustaining, comforting, empowering experience of Christian faith. These have been tested and proved throughout the centuries.

A CHALLENGE TO OTHER WORKERS

The minister has much to receive from others who minister to the needs of people. As we have pointed out earlier, they have resources, skills, and contributions to make that he cannot make. This is a great help to him as he strives to minister to the needs of his people. He can learn much from these other workers as he co-operates with them in their combined concern for the welfare of people. He can learn much from them about human nature and the methods by which people can be helped. In fact, this is one of the best of all procedures to sharpen one's own insights and improve one's own techniques.

The pastor also has something to offer these other professional people. They too become discouraged. They may wonder if their efforts are worth-while. They too have tensions which need to be relieved and problems which need to be solved.

Many of these people are in a pastor's congregation. He has the opportunity and responsibility of helping them to find and to keep the awareness that theirs is a Christian vocation.

This emphasis on the sacredness of all constructive work has had a renewed emphasis in recent years. If there are any occupations to which this applies more than to others, it is those vocations which deal directly with meeting the problems and enriching the lives of people. The pastor should help such workers to have a sense of "calling," of commitment, of Christian service. They should be helped to grow in the realization that all people are children of God and that their work is sacred in his sight.

Urban Church
and Co-operative Planning

Clifford C. Ham

Too often our churches get bogged down with the maintenance and advancement of the institutions, forgetting the
general welfare of the community. We "oil the wheels of
the machine" and too frequently spend most of our time
keeping it going. But the emphasis can be placed upon the
community to the benefit of both church and community.
It is imperative that good church planning consider not
just the institution but the community through what could
be called "need-centered" or "community-centered" planning.

A young pastor in Philadelphia related how he had directed his congregation out the rear door of his church
building, one Sunday morning, into an alley of slum houses
never visited by the church members. After visiting in
homes (which replaced the usual sermon), the members
met, prayed for forgiveness, and began planning a community-centered program, a program based upon the needs
about the church.

In order effectively to serve the community, a church
group must understand the community and its people. The

Reprinted from *The National Lutheran* (April, 1961), pp. 8–9.
Used by permission of the author and the National Lutheran
Council.

only effective way to do this is to involve the citizens themselves in the planning.

Invite the residents of the neighborhood to meet with a planning committee; involve them in the study and analysis; have them participate in the decision-making process. This is a slow, but sound, democratic basis.

Set Your Goals Properly

Goal-setting is an integral part of planning. It is difficult, if not impossible, to plan ahead if one does not know his ultimate objectives. How can one measure the effectiveness of an operation unless it can be compared to objectives?

But, there are at least three time dimensions for these goals. The following categories are suggested:

Ultimate Ends—those goals which will not be attained in our lifetime, similar to values, or principles. These might be: love, justice, brotherhood, universal peace. These are the ends toward which we continually strive. Whenever we adopt shorter-range goals, they should be in the context of the ultimate ends.

Goals—the long-range goals which may be attained in our lifetime, but not in the immediate future. Such goals, for churches, might be: integrated churches; adequate and modern facilities for worship or education; well-trained clergy.

Objectives—short-range goals, which may be attained in a year, five years, or ten years and which move us in the direction of longer-range goals.

As in all planning, goals must be continuously re-examined, and then either reaffirmed or redirected. Goals should never become fixed for all time, immutable. Not only should goals change, but our standards should be raised as our goals change. Thus, in urban renewal even as we eliminate the most substandard 10 per cent of housing, we know that there is another 10 per cent of housing which has become the worst.

A Realistic Forty-Year Program

Churches infrequently plan for short terms, but increasingly they must learn to plan for longer periods. In our cities today, programs are being carried out which will set the pattern of development for many years in the future.

The urban renewal program sets the physical framework for a community for at least forty years. The church, adjusting its plans to an urban renewal program, will have a fairly accurate prognostication of the number of dwelling units in the neighborhood for the next four decades, and similarly a close estimate of the expected population.

The kind of dwelling units built will indicate the types of households, the number of children, the age of the families, and a range of income limits. Whether schools, playgrounds, recreation centers, or other community facilities are available will determine to a large extent the basic characteristics of the population.

It is, then, fully realistic for the church to have a long-range, forty-year program.

Co-operative Planning Is Most Effective

The most effective planning will be done co-operatively with other churches, health and welfare agencies, and the public services, and using all available resources of the community.

Too often church programs are based upon the limited

resources available in a local church even though public and semipublic agencies are set up to serve all institutions in the community.

In Baltimore a church set up a planning committee which met regularly, studied diligently, and finally recommended a weekday children's program for the church. When resource leaders were brought in at this phase of the process, the urban renewal community worker was forced to point out that there were very few children in the neighborhood, and that the proposed urban renewal program would make the area even less attractive to families with children.

Similarly, while it seems somewhat apart from their normal functions, the urban renewal community workers in Baltimore have aided churches in setting up Homemakers' Clubs for mothers; we call them "Tenant Education" programs while the church stresses "Family Life Education," but they are the same.

In one renewal project several church urban-renewal committees have been set up with the resources of public and private agencies. These churches have been able to use agency resources to plan a Neighborhood Population Questionnaire for advice on building and program and for guidance on the role of the church in the city.

As part of this co-operative planning process, the churches of Baltimore of all faiths, and in co-operation with the Urban Renewal Agency, have arrived at a policy stating the relationship between churches and the Renewal Agency. This clearly states the involvement of the church in renewal and its role of evaluation and criticism of renewal programs. It also makes clear the part of churches in renewal areas and the need for a religious ministry.

In Washington, D.C., churches of all faiths are planning

co-operatively to ensure that the large Southwest Redevelopment area is adequately churched. Together these churches have developed a far better plan than they could have alone; and, by working together, they have achieved some major concessions from the public agency.

COMPREHENSIVE PLANNING CALLS FOR STUDY OF THREE AREAS OF CHURCH LIFE

Comprehensive planning requires that all of the aspects of church life be considered in the allocation of scarce resources. Three areas of church life and their interrelationships must be studied: the buildings; the program, including staff; and finances.

Long-range and short-range plans can be formulated for each of these areas, but they must be co-ordinated and interrelated in order to prepare for the totality of church needs.

How can buildings be best utilized for programs? How can financing be distributed equitably between program and building needs? What is the relation between staff and program? Comprehensive planning must help church leaders move from departmentalized thinking into a broader concept of need.

There are several areas of church life today where this approach is urgently needed. On the local level one problem is the mounting cost of buildings.

An increasing share of the local church budget is being allocated to building, with a declining share for ministerial support and a smaller share of the total budget for benevolence and mission giving today than previously.

Are we overspending for buildings? for our elaborate new sanctuaries? our social halls which will seat the entire congregation at one time? If we allocated more money for program, including staff, would the goals of the church be attained as rapidly? or not at all?

The careful presentation of such alternatives should be done by a planning advisory group.

THE CHURCHES MUST HELP IN CITY PLANNING

Before this subject is concluded, it is important to point out also that cities and other governmental agencies are today making decisions which frequently ignore comprehensive planning. Parks are taken for highways; funds are used for highways which might be used more effectively for schools, parks, or urban renewal. And urban renewal projects are planned and carried out on a project approach generally without a broad comprehensive plan for the city. We are rebuilding our cities with no clear goals—no real concept of the city we are creating.

Churches have an obligation to evaluate these plans and proposals, and to suggest the ideal city of the future from the religious point of view. But we can hardly do this until we have considered the future carefully and planned for mankind ourselves. Too often, as suggested earlier, churches adjust themselves to the urban change, rather than motivating the change itself or directing the change. But again, this calls for long-range and comprehensive planning.

The Local Church and Juvenile Delinquency

J. Archie Hargraves

Juvenile delinquency is one of the most important problems confronting our culture, striking as it does at the very heart of that sacrosanct institution, the family. Few people, however, are in agreement as to the definition of juvenile delinquency or as to its cause, relationship to other factors, and treatment.

These differing diagnoses need not concern us too much at this point. The important thing is neither to discuss learnedly the problem nor to analyze it in a general setting, for when speaking of delinquents we speak of particular children who are part of particular families that live in particular neighborhoods.

Juvenile delinquency is a neighborhood problem because it involves flesh-and-blood people who live next door or across the street. Ideally, the local church can be the decisive instrument in combating delinquency on the neighborhood level.

In making these statements, we are suggesting an approach often overlooked in the general babble of abstract opinions and involved plans of procedure which arise out of the widespread concern about the situation. We suggest coming down from the hilltop of abstraction to the valley of the neighborhood where heterogeneous people exist in

Reprinted from *Christianity and Crisis* (January 6, 1958), pp. 180–183. Used by permission of the author and the publisher.

the nearest approximation of face-to-face relationships (outside of the family) that we have left in city culture.

The inner-city church, today, instead of being the inclusive fellowship which manifests God's grace, is often a strictly sociological manifestation of man's pettiness, disinterest, and lack of involvement. Yet if it works for true understanding of itself and its mission, the local church can be the focal point for effective action against juvenile delinquency. The effectiveness of the church depends on three things: how well it understands itself and the problem, how well it marshals its resources, and how willing it is to develop and implement a relevant and redemptive program.

A few observations in regard to two of these principles should be made before we describe the program undertaken this summer by a group of churches in a high-delinquency area in Brooklyn.

The Need for Understanding

For the local church to assume responsibility in this area it is necessary that it have a profound understanding of itself as a living manifestation of the church of Christ and not limit its focus to the four walls that enclose the worshiping congregation on Sunday morning. It has to seek a new community orientation that implies it will cease existing for itself and will come to share its particular concerns, techniques, and love with the whole neighborhood so that all may advance together.

It has to be a church that proclaims time after time that its primary God-given function is not to mend gaps in its administrative "setup" but, through concrete preaching and witnessing, to wrestle with the life-and-death problem

of making a Christian environment and of redeeming
human lives.

Understanding itself in this way, the church can move
toward an understanding of the problem of delinquency on
an equally profound level. This is not a simple task, for
even the experts may not have such a profound understanding. Indeed, as new incidents of delinquency are
given wide and sensational coverage in the press, many
experts lose their perspective by espousing recommenda-
tions merely for increased services and facilities. However,
in centering its approach on the area it serves, the church
recognizes that a more creative solution than a mere sat-
uration of services and facilities is required.

More than anything else, consensus and involvement of
indigenous people are needed, for obviously no one is more
familiar with the problem of delinquency and no one understands the delinquent better than a resident of a high-
delinquency neighborhood. All these people need is a
direction and a focal point, and the local church is aptly
suited to provide both. To these people, the local church
can bring a factual picture of delinquency and can show
them the interrelatedness of all the factors which complicate the problem. The church can work to secure agreement that the problem needs the full attention of all local
persons and organizations, thereby achieving for it "crash
priority."

But the church must also have insight into the make-up
of teen-age life before it can present a plan of action to
alerted people. Teen-agers become delinquents often because they are alienated—nothing to belong to, no place
to go, no one to understand them. They are the perennial
outsiders in all social units. Because one third of them cannot read adequately, school is a torture and a bore, and

they wait only until they reach the age at which they can be released—still too young for a responsible job, too young to belong to political institutions.

Alienated from everything—from status, rootage, tolerance, and love in the family—teen-agers seek reconciliation in a fellowship of their own age and interests. In depressed areas this emerges as the gang, the recognized symbol of their own teen culture, with its own *mythos* and vocabulary, an entity whose existence must be taken into account by those adults who work with them.

The local church can move to meet the challenge offered by the gang in two ways. First, it can minister directly to teen-agers in their main areas of concern in such a way that they can be stimulated to assume some responsibility for solving their own problems. Secondly, it can minister to them indirectly by reorienting their parents and the adults they know in face-to-face relationships. If adults can be persuaded to befriend the teen-agers and become involved in their daily life, the hub of the problem will be reached.

This is especially true in the inner city where teen-agers need to be brought in contact with more wholesome people of the local neighborhood in order that they may have more adequate hero symbols to which to aspire. The tragedy is that it is usually "Louie the Lip," the local big shot, who takes time with them and shows interest. To displace the existing prototypes of aspiration with more suitable symbols, it should be the merchant, the doctor, the tailor, the hard-working craftsman who shows concern and understanding and establish themselves as mentors.

Finally, the local church has to learn that it does not have all the answers—that other people and organizations have much to contribute. Most inner-city churches grossly underestimate the leadership and personnel resources in their neighborhoods. Any program that realistically grapples with the problem of delinquency and seeks its solution will bring out hidden reservoirs of leadership.

MARSHALING RESOURCES

Not only does effective combating of delinquency require understanding, it also involves the marshaling of the church's resources in the proper proportion and at the right time. There are five resources necessary for adequate programing: leadership and personnel, program, budget, facilities, and imagination.

Given the key resource of imagination, more of the other resources can be secured than we might anticipate. The leadership resource is as available in the inner city as in the suburbs if it can be tapped and challenged. Leadership does not occur in a vacuum, and dynamic followers who can play creative second fiddle are needed. Even some money can be attracted by relevant programing. The important thing is to determine what needs to be done and then move to do it, utilizing all of these factors.

For example, some facilities are necessary, but the particular form they should take is seldom thought through very carefully. Huge centers for children, even though they are being built every day, do not appear desirable in terms of the present trend toward decentralized neighborhood social activities—smaller groups in smaller places.

We may even go so far as to say that even though physical facilities assume some importance in programing, they are currently overrated. Human relationships, as we have emphasized before, are much more important. Facilities can always be improvised by converting store fronts, using garages, basements in homes, and whatever else is available. Certainly local churches can make more imaginative use of the facilities they now have. They should concentrate on imagination and program and order the other factors from this basis.

PROGRAMING

In order to discuss concretely the details of programing, we shall cite the program adopted by the group of churches previously mentioned in the Bedford-Stuyvesant area of Brooklyn.

These churches set up a pilot area in that borough and within it carefully delineated the area of geographical responsibility for each church.

Each church was encouraged to hold a general membership meeting and come to a real decision about making the war against delinquency a major thrust for the year. The church also sought to involve each member personally by assigning him a specific job in getting the program off the ground.

The next step was to call in the various block organizations and plan with them how the assigned area might best be penetrated. After this, the church and block organizations did a public information job, saturating the neighborhood with facts using every conceivable publicity medium. The purpose here was to arouse interest and to stimulate discussion of ways to combat delinquency.

A further step was for members of the church and block clubs to go from house to house and from block to block seeking leadership, money, and facilities, trying to find children and teen-agers who wanted to be involved and to determine what activities they desired.

These steps made a "crash" impact upon the respective neighborhoods. Residents began discussing not the extent of the problem but the part each could play in its solution.

As a result, several of the churches came up with bold and imaginative approaches that could be readily implemented. One of the churches, Nazarene Congregational, has put the following three-pronged program into effect.

(1) *A "Godparent" Program.* After the people discussed what they could do, they decided to focus on the relationship between adult and child. Efforts were made to get adults to respond to this challenge and relate themselves to a child who needed their help, interest, and love. Each adult promised to spend a few hours a week with the child, working at a hobby, enjoying recreation, worshiping together, seeking resolution of problems, and just plain relating.

Putting this plan at the center of its worship and educational life, the church gave it a firm liturgical basis by blessing and hallowing each relationship as part of its corporate worship. All organizations and fellowship groups discussed it and followed through.

Although the church did the actual job of relating the children to adults, short-term objectives and long-run goals were set in co-operation with block organizations as procedures were determined and the "godparents" trained in their new roles.

From this plan, the church developed a summer program involving over 200 children and 31 "godparents." At present, problem children from the area are being referred to the church by the courts and schools for integration into the program.

(2) *A Remedial Reading Program.* As we have already noted, one of the contributing causes of juvenile delin-

quency is the inability of many children to read. It is a well-known fact that one third of New York City's school children read below their grade level; the same number never read children's books.

After a careful consideration of the facts available concerning this facet of the general problem, the people of Nazarene's neighborhood decided to start remedial reading classes. Now, three teachers and thirty children are part of such a program which meets twice weekly. As more teachers are added, more children can be helped.

(3) *"Outposts" in Store Fronts.* It was soon recognized that while this church was doing a commendable job with the children it was reaching, it was not reaching enough. The church felt it needed to involve people on a small neighborhood scale in more intimate group activities with children they knew. Decentralized group activities seemed part of the answer.

The people worked out a plan to rent store fronts to be used as youth and children's centers and as a means of access to the hard-core families (the families that constitute 1 per cent of the population and produce 75 per cent of the delinquency) that are so difficult to reach.

The store front will serve as a "hangout" for children by day and for teen-agers by evening. It hopefully will encourage their interests in wholesome activities and will be kept up to date in terms of teen-age tastes—i.e., no ancient dance records! Since the teen-agers will be partly responsible for fixing it up and keeping it in order, it will be *their* place.

Because the store-front center will be located in the middle of things, it will afford access to two types of teen-agers that are difficult to reach: those in street-organized gangs and those "lone wolf" or drifting individuals.

The store-front outposts have been conceived of as a means to provide young people with a well-supervised "hangout" as well as a means by which parents may be enlisted "to do things" with their children.

Through the help of the Hart Foundation, the first of these centers has been secured. The church eventually plans to sponsor, in co-operation with block organizations, at least four more centers of this type.

This program in the Bedford-Stuyvesant area is just one example of what neighborhood churches might be doing. The plan developed and carried out by the Nazarene Church is not cited here as a final answer; it is given only as a series of suggested steps. The steps, however, are simple, involving all the people who want to be involved and penetrating much further than do the saturated service approaches.

The way outlined calls for faith, understanding, compassion, imagination, and commitment. In short, it calls for all the members of the church and all the residents of the neighborhood to involve themselves deeply in sharing together their attempts to solve a crucial problem of our culture.

CHAPTER IX

THEOLOGY
AND THE URBAN CHURCH

INTRODUCTION

Understanding the nature and purpose of the church is a fundamental task. No matter how astutely the urban churchman may comprehend the sociological pressures in a community, the varieties of religious groups, the processes of conflict and co-operation, he is ultimately driven to the theological question: what is the significance and mission of the church?

The church is a divine-human community which bears witness to the love of God in Christ Jesus. Its basic task is to proclaim the gospel of Jesus Christ everywhere in the city so as to call men to Christian faith and fellowship, to nurture them in that faith so that they might serve the community and the world.

A prime requisite for spiritual renewal is the church's deepening awareness of its essence as a witnessing community. The church that forgets it has a gospel to proclaim and a mission to perform will fail to bear abiding fruits. The church exists to serve the world. It will hardly become a servant church if it has an "edifice complex."

The selections in this chapter remind us of the centrality of the gospel as the raison d'être *of the church. At the same time we are cautioned that any significant penetration of urban culture will come through theological understanding and rediscovery, on the one hand, and sociological awareness, on the other. The ability to relate theological thinking and sociological analysis will greatly enhance the urban churchman's efforts to fulfill his responsibilities in the city.*

"*The Theology of the Urban Church*" *is written by Howard G. Hageman, minister of the North Reformed Church in Newark, New Jersey. The author argues that Protestantism's abandonment of transitional urban areas may be traced to a theologically inadequate conception of the nature and task of the church. Although there is no unique theology of the urban church, its special plight accentuates the need for sound Christian theology. The congregation is the "body of Christ." It lives not merely for its believers, but also its mission is to witness to God's redemptive love.*

"*The Mission of the Church in a Mobile Society*" *is a report prepared by the Department of Evangelism of the World Council of Churches. It warns against the imprisonment of churches in their own organizational structures, while neglecting the essential nature of the church as one, holy, catholic, and apostolic. In today's urban and mobile culture, the church must be flexible in order that its witness may be expressed in all areas of life. The openness of the church to sociological insights will aid in the performance of its mission and witness.*

In "A Theological Approach to the Inner-City Parish," Robert McAfee Brown, Auburn Professor of Systematic Theology at Union Theological Seminary, sees the inner-city parish as the challenging front-line activity of the church. He sets forth three theological concerns that are particularly relevant in this situation: the sacraments of the church, which dramatize God's unconditional love for men and his activity in the mundane and the commonplace; the doctrine of the incarnation, which encourages our involvement in the total life and problems of men by its forceful understanding of God's involvement in the human situation; and the church as koinōnia, which redeems men from loneliness into fellowship and community, into relationship with God and neighbor.

The Theology
of the Urban Church

Howard G. Hageman

In the year 1876, The Washington Square Reformed Dutch Church in New York voted to disband, "owing to the moving away of the class of population in this quarter whose needs are met by such a church." Whatever else may be said about the decision, we have to thank the man who recorded it for his honesty. At least he made no attempt to gloss the situation over. Without knowing it, he stated as bluntly as possible the real reason for the failure and flight of the Protestant churches from the city. Over most of the churches which we have abandoned could well have been written the words, "owing to the moving away of the class of population in this quarter whose needs are met by such a church."

Now it would, of course, be possible to examine these words economically and sociologically—an interesting and important task. But my purpose is to examine them Biblically and theologically in the hope that we may thereby come to some deeper understanding of the mission of the church in the city.

I should like to begin by pointing out that there are within Protestantism two competing and in many ways contradictory ideas of the church. There is first of all the

Reprinted from *The City Church* (May-June, 1959), pp. 2–3, 10–11. Used by permission of the author and the Department of the Urban Church, National Council of Churches.

idea of the church as a parish. Wherever in Europe there was a state church, this was the prevalent idea. Every congregation has rigidly established geographical bounds. Within this area, the congregation has complete religious jurisdiction. To move out of the neighborhood is *ipso facto* to move out of the congregation. To a greater or lesser degree, the church assumes religious responsibility for everyone living within its parish boundaries.

On the other hand, there is the idea of the church as a society, as a "gathered community." Membership in this society has nothing to do with geography, but is entirely a matter of personal decision. Although in theory the decision is a religious one, in fact it is often influenced by a variety of factors. But whatever these may be, the church, by this concept, is a voluntary society composed of those who are there because they want to be there.

Initially, most of the denominations in this country were, by virtue of their relationship to churches in Europe, developed by the parish system. In many instances it is possible to find maps indicating the geographical limits of a congregation or definite districts assigned to its office-bearers as late as the middle of the last century. But soon after that time, and in many places much earlier, American Protestantism went over to the concept of a "gathered community" and the parish idea was almost entirely abandoned. In many places churches of the same denomination were built around the corner from each other serving not an area but a constituency without relationship to any area. Today this has come to be our idea of a congregation.

It is not now a question of the relative merits of these two ideas. The important thing is that our flight from the city is the direct result of our understanding of what a congregation is. The Washington Square Church had no hesitation in leaving Washington Square when the time came because they never really had any relation to Washington Square. The building happened to be there; the congregation was from anywhere. When Washington Square ceased to be a convenient meeting point, the only sensible thing to do was to go elsewhere. As a business must follow its clientele, so the meetinghouse must follow its society.

Illustrations of the same development are so numerous in the story of American Protestantism in any city that we can safely conclude that we have touched on one of the theological reasons for our failure in the city. It is our concept of what a congregation is. Having committed ourselves, perhaps unwittingly, to the idea that a congregation is a society of like-minded believers, we must logically place our church buildings at whatever points our societies find most convenient and desirable. The flight from the city can therefore be said to be the result of our theory of the nature of the congregation.

But surely there is another reason for our failure. Not only have we given a wrong answer to the question, What is a congregation? but we have an equally wrong answer to the next question, What is a congregation here to do? Though it is difficult to know exactly what people a century ago thought a church was for, there is one striking fact of history that gives us at least a good clue.

A century ago (and indeed more recently than that) almost every Protestant church in every major American city was pewed; i.e., the major part, if not all, of the space available in the sanctuary was taken on a rental or purchase basis. That was the usual method of church financing. Churches measured their property in terms of the size of their waiting lists for pews, and one sure sign that the time had come to move was an ever-increasing list of pews to rent.

Leaving to one side the merits and demerits of the new pew system, think of it as a very honest answer to the question, What is a congregation for? The obvious answer is, For itself; for the spiritual benefit of its members. The very pewing of a church indicates that you expect nobody else, save an occasional visitor. The church is here to edify its members, baptize and instruct their children, comfort and sustain their sorrowing, visit their sick, lay to rest their dead. It is a kind of religious service station operated for the benefit of those who support it; the minister, a kind of chaplain to those who value and maintain his services.

To be sure, these same congregations had missionary interests, sometimes considerable ones. They were often generous supporters of the denominational program. Often they supported missions on the other side of the tracks. But this missionary interest was something detached from the life of the congregation itself. It was a department within the church. People gave to national and foreign missions or to a mission on the lower East Side; some even gave time to teach in the mission Sunday school or do volunteer work. As they saw it, the congregation had a very necessary missionary department; but it was not itself a mission.

When, therefore, the area in which the congregation was located became blighted, it was abandoned. Many times, a mission was left in the area, sometimes in the very building which the congregation had forsaken. Church and mission were so fatally divorced in the idea of what a congregation is for that one had to leave before the other could take over. Both could not be in the same place at the same time.

To take but one illustration out of scores of possible ones, the Broome Street Reformed Church flourished in New York from 1823 to 1860 when it followed the northward trend to 34th Street. At the last service in the Broome Street building, the minister had this to say: "But we are now the victims of peculiar change. Remorseless time has made especial havoc in our midst. Who can but sigh as he beholds the fairest portions of our city, once inhabited by the good and the great, now abandoned to filthy lucre, natural pollution, and moral degradation? But most of all to be deprecated is the removal of our churches. We cannot but regard this as vandalism, necessary though it is."

One would have imagined that the natural pollution and moral degradation of the area would have been a compelling reason for the Broome Street Church to stay put. But no; a necessary vandalism takes it northward to 34th Street. But soon after the removal, the City Missionary Society began work in the Broome Street Tabernacle, in essentially the same area abandoned by the church! The church went after the good and the great in 34th Street while the mission could and did remain to struggle with the sin of the surrounding Sodom.

In short, our idea has been that congregations are for those who believe; missions for those who do not. With the exception of finances, the two never belonged together. History has taken its revenge. In more instances than could be accounted for by mere chance, the mission, related to its community and responsible for it, has survived while the congregation which once fostered it has become extinct. The survival of these missions long after the death of the parent church raises a good many helpful questions.

If we are to stay in the city, these are the questions which we must rethink. What is a congregation? What is a congregation for? We have been driven from the city because our answers have been inadequate and mistaken. We shall remain in the city when our answers are those written into the very heart of the gospel.

The best answer to these questions will be found in one of St. Paul's favorite metaphors for the church—"the body of Christ." In the twelfth chapter of I Corinthians there occurs an extended discussion of the meaning of this metaphor, beginning in the twelfth verse with the assertion that "just as the body is one and has many members, and all the members of the body, though many, are one body, so it is with Christ." The last phrase is startling. We should have expected "so it is with the church." But it lies at the base of our answers about the congregation to note that for St. Paul there is a sense in which Christ and the church are virtually interchangeable terms.

The discussion then continues with the statement that into this body, which is Christ, anyone, regardless of his racial or cultural background or economic condition, is received by baptism. After pointing out the necessity of all the members for the proper functioning of this body, the apostle concludes with the direct statement, "Now you are the body of Christ and individually members of it."

Remembering that it was a congregation to which these words were originally addressed, we could answer our question about the congregation with these three propositions drawn from St. Paul's discussion:

a. The congregation, as the body of Christ, is the organ through which Christ himself is at work in a particular community.

b. The concern of this body must be limitless. As the body of Christ, the congregation can set no barriers to its membership save the single one of baptism and faith in its Lord.

   c. In this body everyone has a job to do. The failure
     of any member to do his job weakens the whole
     body's effectiveness.

In the fourth chapter of his letter to the Ephesians
St. Paul has a similar discussion. Many of the themes are
those which we have already heard in Corinthians. The
only new theme is that introduced in the sixteenth verse
. . . (that we may) "grow up in every way into him who
is the head, into Christ, from whom the whole body,
joined and knit together by every joint with which it is
supplied, when each part is working properly, makes bodily growth and upbuilds itself in love."

Here is the additional idea of Christian growth which is
clearly not an individual thing, but the growth of an entire
community. And just as clearly, the insincerity or indifference of a single member can retard the Christian development of an entire congregation. To our previous three
propositions, then, we must add a fourth:

   d. It is only in the body of Christ that one can realize
     the full potential of God's redemption in Christ, the
     full development of the whole personality into the
     likeness of Christ.

Can we apply these somewhat theoretical statements
to the situation in the city? It would result in such statements as these:

1. A Christian congregation in any part of a city is
Christ at work in that part of the city. To abandon the
congregation is to remove the organ through which he
works in that place.

2. No congregation can ever withdraw because of the
changed population in its neighborhood. The body of
Christ involves every kind of man. The weaker and inferior
members are just as important as the stronger and superior.

3. To survive in the city, a congregation must be a func-

tioning body in which every member takes his part. The ministry of the church can never be left to a paid staff of professionals.

4. An area without a congregation is deprived of the full gift of God's redemption in Christ. Only in a congregation can men and women grow up into Jesus Christ in all things.

5. While the congregation is a gathered society, it must have a definite relation to a particular area for which it assumes responsibility for Christian life and growth.

The techniques of the matter remain to be discussed. But important as they are, they are no substitute for a firm grasp of the essential. And the essential is not only that the gospel be preached unto all men, but that all men be given the opportunity to grow up in it in the holy fellowship of a congregation. Any program of urban evangelism which omits membership in the congregation, omits the one term which the New Testament deems essential.

Our second question is, "What is a congregation for?" We have already begun to answer it by defining a congregation. But we can extend our answer by looking at a few words from the first epistle of St. Peter. "Ye are a chosen race, a royal priesthood, a holy nation, a people for possession, that you should proclaim the praises of him who has called you out of darkness into this amazing light." (2:9)

I shall not do more than observe that the charge of the New Testament is not to "win others to the amazing light," but to "proclaim the praises of him who has called us into it." St. Peter uses four terms to describe the congregation, each term drawn from the Old Testament, each term a purposive term. They are all ways of saying that God has laid a charge upon the congregation, given it a mission—witness and proclamation.

Too often this charge is conceived too cheaply. An occasional revival, an annual campaign of visitation evangelism, a service held now and again in the rescue mission by the Men's Bible Class—these are poor substitutes for St. Peter's requirements. The total impact of the entire gathered community upon its community—that is what the apostle is talking about. Not the impression left by the Sunday service alone, but the impression left by the whole congregation on Wednesday is the question at hand. Here in a particular place we, the body of Christ, are set to show the glory of our Redeemer by our redeemed lives.

In short, wherever a congregation is found, it must be a colony of heaven, a living demonstration of those relationships of man to God, and of man to man, which are the creation of God's redeeming grace in Christ. That is the congregation's mission and purpose. The congregation is eschatological; it presents the world with a token and sample of what life is like, in all of its relationships, in the Kingdom of God. Of course, the congregation has its imperfections, its spots and stains. As a human organization, it is always under judgment. But as the body of Christ, it is the fellowship in which grace triumphs and love reigns as they do not in the world outside.

What is the congregation for? It is here to proclaim by its life together what the redeeming love of God in Christ can do in the actual situation of human life.

Now obviously, all of this relates just as much to a congregation in rural Iowa as to a congregation in New York or Chicago. In that sense, there are not urban churches and rural churches. There is only the church, one body with one task. In that sense, there is no theology of the urban church. It is only that the plight of the urban church makes it more imperative that we should remind ourselves of the Biblical teaching about the nature and mission of the congregation.

But at the same time, it is well to recall the strange fascination which the Bible, in many ways a rural book, has with the city. Not only is there Jerusalem, the city of the great king in the Old Testament; not only was the city a place of strategic importance in the mission of St. Paul in the New Testament; most of the visions of the future take the form of a city.

For here we have no continuing city, but we seek one to come. And I saw the holy city, coming down from God out of heaven. Blessed are they that do his commandments that they may enter in through the gates into the city.

Between that city of God which shall be and these cities of ours which are now, there stands only the Christian congregation—the colony of the city of God in the cities of the world—living and witnessing until his Kingdom come and his will be done in earth as it is in heaven.

The Mission of the Church in a Mobile Society

Department of Evangelism,
World Council of Churches

The nature of the church has been determined by the gospel of which it is a part, and by the Lord who is its head. The organizational structures of the church necessarily express its nature. Yet these structures must not be identified with the nature of the church. They are determined in part by the cultural pattern of the society in which they are set. In part they are determined, under the guidance of the Holy Spirit, by the nature of the mission which has been given to them. Therefore, the renewal of church structure must not become a concern isolated from the renewal of the total life and mission of the church. Its structural renewal is God's gift to a church struggling to become more faithful to its unique task, rather than a conscious attempt to change existing structures. There is a structure of the church which must be maintained because it is an essential expression of the nature of the one, holy, catholic, and apostolic church; but there are also structural elements of present church life which need to be changed because they are antiquated.

It is not only in one area that these structural changes are called for. In the form of the congregation, both in

Reprinted in abridged form from *A Theological Reflection on the Work of Evangelism,* World Council of Churches, Division of Studies, *Bulletin* 5 (November, 1959), pp. 30–36. Used by permission of the Division of Studies, World Council of Churches.

multistructural and in multiracial societies; in the constitutions of denominational churches; in the varied relationships within the foreign missionary movement; in the way that Christian service institutions are governed; in the involvement of churches in culture and their place within the nations—in all these and other aspects of the church's life changes are necessary. No attempt is made here to deal with the whole range of these problems. Only one set of them is dealt with which is of immediate urgency for evangelism, which also reveals the depth of the many issues to be faced.

A. A MOBILE AND MULTISTRUCTURAL SOCIETY

Man in an industrial society is neither an isolated individual, nor an anonymous mass-man, nor a member of just one group and milieu. He is a member of many quite different smaller and larger groups. In modern industrial society there are few homogeneous groups left, i.e., groups in which the geographic and social dimensions fall together, in which people live and work and spend their leisure time in the same place. Modern life is characterized by the falling apart of the geographic and social dimensions of life and therefore by the increasing importance of "activity groups" (at work and during free time) and "neighborhood groups" which alone are really touched by the traditional parish structure of many churches.

Within this extremely multistructural and mobile society, not only is the diversity of groups important for the churches, but also the fact that in all these different types of groups there are different levels of community life. For example, within the geographic dimension a man is not only influenced by the administrative sector of the town, which corresponds to the limits of the local parish, or by the group of people from which a congregation is gathered; he is also influenced by many much smaller units (e.g., the family, the neighborhood, etc.) and many much larger units (e.g., the region, the nation, the continent).

How can the church reach men in these different groups and levels of society? And what sort of worshiping community and what forms of worship are capable of arousing spiritual awareness in them? It is here that the problem is most acute. How can the forms of worship be so changed, without emasculating historic forms of worship, that for the many the veil may be lifted, and it may be true that "we all, with unveiled face, beholding the glory of the Lord, are being changed into his likeness from one degree of glory to another."

Many churches today are too preoccupied with maintaining their organizational structures to spare energy for their real evangelistic task. This is true for churches in the West, and acutely so for the younger churches, where structures appropriate to the West have been transplanted into a totally different society.

One example is seen in the traditional economic structure of the younger churches. The churches require an ordained ministry, places of worship, and related institutions. When the financial support of a full-time ministry, property, and institutions become the main problems of church life, they become a hindrance to the essential life of the churches. Under the economic pressure to which the churches are subject, their dependence upon foreign aid tends to become chronic, their fear of social and political change induces them to adopt a policy of supporting the *status quo*, and their absorption with their own economic preservation deprives them of the energy to fulfill their mission or the courage to exercise their prophetic function in the world.

Another example, common among the younger churches, is a monolithic and authoritarian structure which derives in part from the age of missionary paternalism. Too often, every activity of the Christian community is kept under the direct control of the minister or of official ecclesiastical organs, with the result that lay initiative perishes, and the churches become ingrown and dominated by the clergy.

Such conditions have called forth new forms of church life. Perhaps one of the most radical is that of the "non-church" groups in Japan, which form a strongly missionary-minded lay movement based on a high academic standard of Biblical knowledge. Because it denies the sacramental nature of the church, it does not have ordained pastors, but the groups are led by Biblical scholars, most of them having other work during the week. Regular Sunday meetings concentrate on exegesis of the Bible. There are seldom financial or administrative difficulties, and concentration on Bible study and prayer gives power to the individuals to witness to Christ during their weekday life. This movement is one of the most indigenous forms of Christian community in the country, and its challenge to the churches is increasing.

To what degree does this movement give an answer to the general problem, or is it an escape from it?

B. The Clash of Structure

What happens when the self-preserving structures in which some churches are imprisoned clash with the structures of a society to which the churches have been insensitive is illustrated in the whole history of "foreign missions," and also in the following example.

A study made of a typical suburban community near New York City revealed a dynamic community life among the Roman Catholics, the Jews, and the Protestants, with a high degree of participation based on a recognition of common responsibility for community welfare. Despite the usual problems of suburbia (conformity, materialism, etc.) this was a good example of people trying to solve the human problems of living together in a multiple society.

Later, the churches moved in with structures of social and "activity" groups, which not only divided the community but apparently diverted concern from the problems of common citizenship to the preservation of denominational life. Each denomination began to do things of its own—discussion groups, sewing circles, baseball teams, etc. The study showed that where there was formerly some integrity and honest secularity, there was now a false spirituality. The consequence was less interaction among members of the community with consequent degeneration in human relations. The churches had taken over at last!

What has happened here? Competitive denominationalism based on self-preservation and fellowship narrowly conceived has resulted in a false "Christianization" of the legitimate structure of life in a pluralistic society. Instead, should the laity not have been dispersed into the structure of the community to live as citizens of the Kingdom in the affairs of "secular" life? Their service to their neighbors, their gossiping of the gospel within the pattern of suburban life, should not have been made impossible by the structures which the churches brought into the community. Admitting the difficulty of divided churches, still should not every Christian service, that truly ministers to the world rather than to itself, discover something of the unity of the body of Christ and witness to that unity in the community it serves?

C. KNOWLEDGE OF SOCIAL STRUCTURE

Any consideration of the changes in the structures of church life which are required by the task of evangelism today should use the social sciences as a valuable instrument for the church. The social sciences obviously are not competent to reveal either the true life and mission of the church or the true origin and purpose of society. Nor should one suggest that the Holy Spirit is bound by sociological laws.

But the social sciences can be useful in two respects. On the one hand, they can show more realistically the present state of the churches, removing dangerous illusions and confronting Christians with the facts of the imprisonment of the churches in their own structures. On the other hand, they can make the churches sensitive to the changing social structures of the society in which they have to witness. One cannot really serve those whom one does not know. Fundamental facts, such as the high mobility of many societies, the emancipation of women, the impact of night shifts and Sunday work, the international exchange of workers, and the need for civil rights and social justice, for racial, ethnic, and caste minorities have not yet been sufficiently recognized by local, regional, and national churches. Neither have the older churches in their missionary work in Asia and Africa been sufficiently aware of the breakdown of the old structures of tribal communities, of the rapid social and economic changes taking place in rural and urban life, or of the spirit of nationalism and the resulting new political climate. Realistic analysis of these and other factors of the social scene, and of the position of the churches in relation to them, will greatly assist evangelism in this present time.

D. Toward Flexibility in Church Structures

In the New Testament the same term for the church (*ekklēsia*) is used for a house church (like the church which came into being in the house of Philemon), for a local congregation (like the church in Corinth), for a regional church (like the church in Asia Minor), and for the church universal of all countries and peoples and periods. It is always the same reality that is being referred to, for where Christ is, there is the church.

This New Testament use of the same term for the same reality, appearing in different environments with different structures, is significant. Indeed, the same reality of the one, holy, catholic, and apostolic church can appear in the structure of the house church, which assembles the Christians of one street, and in a "Kirchentag" which assembles the Christians of one large region. It may appear in a local parish, nurturing the Christians living in the same place, or in a brotherhood, nurturing Christians who, because of their mobile profession, cannot be members of a geographically determined parish. It may appear in the work of a team of laymen and clergy, working in the midst of an industrial center; or in an *ashram* in India; or where non-Christians are gathered for prayer and Bible study in the house of a convert.

This is to say that the church's mission must be conducted with flexibility. Varied forms of organization and strategy are required. Christian laymen, for instance, are already living and working in places which organized missionary work does not yet reach. What is necessary here is that these laymen should be trained and built into a fellowship. Again, the churches need mobility in meeting the demands of populations which are in constant motion, whether to new housing areas or summer holiday resorts. At another level, the churches must discover, on the basis of sound sociological analysis, ways of presenting the gospel at key points in the social structure. Not all of these manifestations of the reality of Christ's church will show forth all the marks of the church, but it is essential that they all recognize themselves as of the church and within it.

E. The Bond of Peace

In facing up to this problem of the church and its structures in society, Christians are continually aware of the fact of their disunion. Here is a failure to participate fully in bringing God's message of salvation to the world. A penitent awareness of this fact and unceasing prayer for the realization of God's gift of unity to his church must mark all Christian work. In a church which is not only divided by denominational boundaries, but in which its mobile and multistructural character has given rise to tensions between traditionalists and pioneers, constituted church congregation and free movements, every opportunity must be sought to overcome the indifference, ignorance, and rivalry which so often mark the church's evangelistic witness. Above all, there is need for Christians to pray for one another, and so maintain bonds of mutual sympathy and concern which the Holy Spirit can use to lead the churches into a full realization of their oneness in the body of Christ.

A Theological Approach to the Inner-City Parish

Robert McAfee Brown

In one of the most maltreated lines in modern literature, T. S. Eliot reminds us that the greatest treason is "to do the right thing for the wrong reason." There are probably many wrong reasons for being concerned about the inner-city parish.

However, in briefest outline, here are some of the *theological* concerns which it seems to me are right reasons behind one's approach to the inner-city situation.

1. *The Concern of the Church for the Sacraments of Baptism and the Lord's Supper.* I begin with this in face of the possible implication that the most important thing the church does is to maintain its own life of worship. While this is true, it is most decidedly untrue if it leads to the implication that worship is separated from the rest of life. It seems to me that churches which take seriously the fact that to them has been bequeathed the holy privilege and duty of administering the sacraments will see their task in the inner-city situation in a way much more profound than those for whom the sacraments are merely perfunctory ceremonies.

Consider what we do in the baptism of a child. We are acting out the fact that God has claimed this child for his

Reprinted from *The City Church* (November-December, 1957), pp. 2–4, 8 and 15. Used by permission of the author and the Department of the Urban Church, National Council of Churches.

own; that this child is one on whom the stamp of God's fatherly concern has been placed long before the child is even remotely aware that there is a God or that God gives two cents what happens to him. It sets the child forth as one claimed by God—not by virtue of the child's worthiness or the child's response, but simply by virtue of the fact that the child is one of God's children whom he has created and whom he therefore loves. That fact, which is at the center of the gospel and is at the heart of the baptismal act which the church performs, says something to you about those kids who break into the parish house on Saturday night, or the boy who gets caught up in the vicious cycle of dope, or the girl who loves too often and too well, or the old man who can't hold down a steady job and whose good intentions in the new one vanish the first time there is a coincidence between his weekly pay check and a friendly neighborhood bar. It says that these people are people whom God loves in a very special way and that his love is not conditional upon their goodness but is there from the very start, offered to them at the very beginning of their lives. It says that when your church has so accepted them, it can never put them out. It says that even if on occasion you must be harsh and judging, your harshness and judgment must be harshness to heal and judgment to save.

Or consider what the church is affirming in its celebration of the Lord's Supper. Among other things it is saying that the most ordinary, secular, mundane objects and actions can be vehicles through which the real presence of the risen Lord is made known to the people. A hunk of bread and a sip of wine are more eloquent transmitters of God's presence than the noblest Gothic nave or the most beautiful religious painting. The ordinary, the commonplace, is in this sacramental act of the church made sacred and holy. (This should, incidentally, furnish some consolation for those of you who do not labor in noble Gothic naves, the singing of whose choirs is far from inspired, who have no beautiful stained-glass windows, and for whom the closest you come to a beautiful religious painting is a Sallman's *Head of Christ* which was purchased by your predecessor.) The point is that God has taken lowly things and made of them the conveyors of the highest things.

This says worlds to us about the outlook which must characterize our attitude toward our inner-city parishes. The fact that the setting may be mean and rude and squalid does not mean that God is far off. On the contrary, if we take seriously the meaning of the Sacrament, he is particularly near at hand. The Sacrament spells out what must come to define our attitude to the ordinary, the unexciting, the monotonously worldly and earthy, the things which are so much the stock in trade of inner-city life.

Let us see the Lord's Supper as a parable of our situation. The elements of bread and wine are brought forward and placed upon the table. In this act all of our immediate situation is being offered up to God. The day-to-day routine, the dingy office, the repeated calls at precinct headquarters, the frustrating encounters with the Catholic priest—all of these things are lifted up and presented to God, offered to him, placed upon the table of the Lord. Out of them, God gives us something back. He gives us back the bread and the wine, the day-to-day routine, the dingy office, and all the rest. But now they are no longer just the bread and the wine and the dingy office. Now these same commonplace things have become vehicles through which the risen Christ is seen to be in our midst. Now we receive back, not apart from them, but precisely in and through them and in no sense without them, the power and strength of the risen Lord, entering into our bodies and invigorating our lives so that Christ is *present* in the day-to-day routine (and the people who interrupt it). The dingy office is the place where he dwells; the precinct headquarters is vibrant with his presence; and even in the difficult Catholic priest we can see one for whom Christ died.

It would seem to me that without some such perspective one would slowly lose one's sanity in the inner city. If this sounds to you like rhapsodizing, let me simply say that if it is not deeply true, then we have been kidding ourselves for a good many centuries about the meaning of the sacraments in human life.

2. *The Doctrine of the Incarnation.* A second area of theological concern is all tied up with right where you are. It is the fact which guarantees that the Christian faith is not vague speculation but is just about as concrete and specific as God or man could ever get. It asserts that God is not like some absentee landlord who dwells a long way off from his tenants, unconcerned about their plight, but that on the contrary, God is so radically concerned about the destiny of men on earth that he has done the astonishing thing of becoming man himself, "in-fleshed," to be quite specific in the human situation, sharing with us to the very nailprints the plight and lot of the human situation. No far-off deity this, but one who took the form of a servant and dramatized his love by total identification with those in need, bearing their burdens, taking upon himself the weight of their wrongdoing, dying to show that the love he brought to them was not a distant love or an unconcerned love but a love which realized that concern means involvement and that involvement means willingness to suffer alongside the other, rather than staying aloof from the other.

This forever gives the lie to the notion that Christian faith is abstract or remote from the most desperate human situations. Right where people are is where Christ is. Just where human need is greatest, there you find him most surely. In the place where people are most severely broken on the wheel of living is the place where his cross is most deeply planted.

For us, this clearly means a kind of total involvement with our own situation, a recognition that the church of Christ must not refuse to follow where its Lord himself went. It means that just as in him God totally involved himself in the plight of the people of first-century Palestine, and even specifically of Jerusalem, so we, as those who are today Christ's church, must seek to do the same in our situation in twentieth-century America, and specifically in our city. It does not mean we do exactly the same things he did but that *we have the same total concern he did.* We may not be called upon to upset the money-changers in the Temple, but we may be called in his name to become involved in the politics of the ward or at the very least to get our people involved. We may not be called upon to feed the five thousand with five loaves and two fishes, but we may be called upon to work upon the welfare agencies to see that needy families have enough food to stay alive. What I am trying to say is that if we take seriously the incarnation—God's involvement in our human situation— then we have to take *every* aspect of that situation seriously; we cannot be unconcerned about politics or city budgets or efficient ambulance service. For these are all part of the realm which Christ's presence in the incarnation makes holy, and they are all part of the realm which Christ's atonement on the cross redeems.

3. *The Doctrine of the Church.* One could show how

the doctrine of creation means that matter is good, that God thinks so because he made it. Thus, new housing projects, sewage disposal plants, and hospitals are all within the orbit of God's concern and, therefore, within ours. Or one could show how the Christian doctrine of man, stressing both the devilish side of human nature and the possibilities in human nature, for which theologians use words like "sin" and "the image of God," gives us the resources which guard us against a premature despair and a too naïve optimism when we deal with our parishioners. However, for purposes of time and clarity, I want to speak of one aspect of the Christian doctrine of the church. This is the recognition that the Christian church at its best is a *koinōnia*, a fellowship. As such, it is doing no more than being faithful to the Christian gospel, which is that men are redeemed by Christ from loneliness into fellowship, into community, into relationship not only with God but also with their neighbors.

A good deal of sentimental nonsense is written and spoken these days about "Christian community." It is sentimental or nonsensical not because the idea is all wrong, but simply because it has been misunderstood. Community, in Christian terms, is not so much a thing we set out self-consciously to achieve as it is the inevitable by-product of a true relationship to Christ. To be close to Christ but isolated from one's fellows is simply a contradiction in terms. And it is this dimension of community which the inner-city church can inject into the lives of people who are crowded terribly close to one another and who were never lonelier in their lives. We have seen studies which show that with all the advantages which the new housing projects bring in terms of basic cleanliness, creature comforts, and the like, these also introduce into the lives of people a sense of isolation which they did not feel in the old flats and tenements. People who remain isolated, whose lives continue to be lonely and empty, either go mad or begin to create new kinds of communities. The kids join street gangs. The adolescents taste the pleasures of dope and cannot escape. The men begin to make the rounds of the bars. All of them are seeking something—a sense of belonging, an identity in relation to other people, perhaps even a little recognition.

This situation is the great challenge and opportunity of the inner-city parish as well as the measuring stick by which its ineffectiveness in many areas is shown. For what these people are rather desperately looking for, we've got! At least we've got it in principle. We've got a situation where supposedly there is neither Jew nor Greek, bond nor free, male nor female, Negro nor Puerto Rican, Park Avenue nor First Avenue, ditchdigger nor organization man, lost generation nor beat generation, for all are one in Christ Jesus . . . and of course you immediately say: "We haven't got it; that's a theologian's pipe dream of the church. Now if you would just come up to Bedford Avenue or down to 66th Street or out to Throggs Neck. . . ."

My point is precisely that this is one of the things which lays such an exciting responsibility upon the inner-city parish. For you are in a position to achieve a greater portion of this than is going to be granted in our day and age to Westchester and Port Washington or Englewood because you are living in rapidly changing areas where the old prejudices don't maintain themselves as easily; you are faced by the fact that you open up your doors to Puerto Ricans or you shut them forever; you are faced by people who are so hungry for a real sense of community that they will be willing to re-examine some of their old stereotypes so that the need for community may be filled. The Lord can use even sociological pressures to praise him, and you are on the growing edge of these sociological pressures. If you see what these can potentially do to your church as a true *koinōnia*, you may be inclined in the not-too-distant future to redefine sociological pressures as the hand of God moving across the face of the city and stirring his children up so that they can settle down. And you will see that the church must meet *this* challenge, or it will not deserve to live; it will only deserve to die.

The possibilities of trying new things to meet the new situation are almost endless. You are on the growing edge of the most exciting situation in the contemporary Protestant Church scene. Not in our day and age will this ever be second best. It's the real firing line.

NOTES

CHAPTER I. THE SETTING: URBAN LIFE AND URBAN CULTURE

1. Oswald Spengler, *Der Untergang des Abendlandes,* IV (München, 1922), p. 105.

2. *Ibid.,* p. 106.

CHAPTER IV. RENEWAL IN INNER-CITY CHURCHES

1. For additional case studies of inner-city churches, cf. Ross Sanderson, *The Church Serves the Changing City* (Harper & Brothers, 1955); and Walter Kloetzli, *The City Church: Death or Renewal* (Muhlenberg Press, 1961).

2. George E. Todd, "Inner-City Consultation" (The United Presbyterian Church in the U.S.A., April 13, 1959), pp. 1–6.

3. David W. Barry, "The Successful Inner-City Church," *The City Church* (November–December, 1959), p. 7.

CHAPTER V. URBAN SECT AND CULT MOVEMENTS

1. The Church of God and Saints of Christ is to be distinguished from such groups as the Commandment Keepers, who are also called "Black Jews." The latter was founded by a Fallash or Ethiopian Jew who had an orthodox rabbinical training. This group has synagogues in Harlem, New York, and in other American cities. See Elmer T. Clark, *The Small Sects in America* (Abingdon Press, 1937), p. 163.

2. Robert A. Nisbet, *The Quest for Community* (Oxford University Press, 1953), p. 7.

3. Erich Fromm, *Escape from Freedom* (Holt, Rinehart & Winston, Inc., 1941).

4. David Riesman, *The Lonely Crowd* (Yale University Press, 1950).

5. Nisbet, *op. cit.,* p. 11.

6. Will Herberg, *Protestant—Catholic—Jew* (Doubleday & Co., Inc., 1955).

7. André Brien, "Les petits communautes soustenance de la Foi," *Etudes*, Paris, Vol. 279 (November, 1953), pp. 168–186.

8. George A. Hillery, "Definitions of Community: Areas of Agreement," *Rural Sociology*, XX (June, 1955), pp. 111–123.

9. R. M. MacIver, *Community* (The Macmillan Company, 1936), pp. 110–131.

10. R. M. MacIver and Charles H. Page, *Society* (Holt, Rinehart & Winston, Inc., 1939), p. 293.

11. Ferdinand Toennies, *Fundamental Concepts of Sociology*, tr. Charles Loomis (Monthly Review Press, 1940), p. 40.

12. A. B. Hollingshead, "Community Research: Development and Present Condition," *American Sociological Review*, XIII (April, 1948), pp. 136–146.

CHAPTER VI.   DILEMMAS OF URBAN CHURCH ORGANIZATION

1. Paul Harrison, *Authority and Power in the Free Church Tradition* (Princeton University Press, 1959), p. 136.

2. Philip Selznick, *TVA and the Grass Roots* (University of California Press, 1953), p. 256.

3. Philip Selznick, "An Approach to a Theory of Bureaucracy," *American Sociological Review*, VIII (1943), p. 48.

4. Emil Brunner, *The Misunderstanding of the Church* (The Westminster Press, 1953), p. 17.

5. Jacob Taubes, "Community—After the Apocalypse," in *Community*, edited by Carl J. Friedrich (Liberal Arts Press, Inc., 1959), p. 113.

6. H. Richard Niebuhr, "Religious Institutions—Protestant," *Encyclopedia of the Social Sciences*, Vol. 13 (1934), p. 267.

7. *Management Audit of the American Baptist Convention* (American Institute of Management, 1955), p. 1.

8. *Ibid.*

9. Elizabeth Nottingham, *Religion and Society* (Doubleday & Co., Inc., 1954), p. 56.

10. Robert T. Handy, *Home Missions* (American Baptist Convention, n.d.), p. 9.

11. Kenneth Boulding, *The Organizational Revolution* (Harper & Brothers, 1953), pp. 3–4.

12. Reinhard Bendix, *Max Weber: An Intellectual Portrait* (Doubleday & Co., Inc., 1960), p. 301.

13. *Ibid.*, p. 313.

14. *Ibid.*, p. 314.

15. Robert Michels, *Political Parties* (The Free Press of Glencoe, 1949), p. 189.

16. The relationship between charisma and the rationalization or secularization of charisma is a complex one. It is tempting to suppose that there was a period in the life of the church of "pure charisma," a pneumatocracy. If one begins with this assumption, then the history of the church may be conveniently viewed as a decline of charisma. This is essentially the framework of Rudolf Sohm, from whose analysis Max Weber formulated his own concept of charisma. Here I would have to agree with Harnack that there are legal and "constitutional" elements mixed in with charismatic authority almost from the beginning. Thus history is not the arena for an inevitable decline of charisma, but rather the scene for a continuous interplay between law and spirit. For a further discussion and exposition of Sohm's conception, cf. Walter Lowrie, *The Church and Its Organization* (Longmans, Green & Co., Ltd., London, 1904); James Luther Adams, "Rudolf Sohm's Theology of Law and Spirit," *Religion and Culture: Essays in Honor of Paul Tillich*, edited by W. Leibrecht (Harper & Brothers, 1959); and W. D. Davies, *A Normative Pattern of Church Life in the New Testament: Fact or Fancy?* (James Clarke & Company, Ltd., Publishers, London, n.d.).

17. Ernest Q. Campbell and Thomas F. Pettigrew, *Christians in Racial Crisis* (Public Affairs Press, 1959), p. 127.

18. Philip Selznick, *Leadership in Administration* (Row, Peterson & Company, 1957).

19. See also the discussion in Joseph H. Fichter, S.J., *Southern Parish*, Vol. 1: *Dynamics of a City Church* (University of Chicago Press, 1951), Ch. 2, "What Is a Parish?"

20. The term "institutionalized group" used by Florian Znaniecki seems to combine both concepts used above, "superimposed association" and "institutionalized association." His

360 CITIES AND CHURCHES

definition denotes "groups which are essentially co-operative products of their own members, but whose collective functions and statuses are partly institutionalized by other social groups." See his article, "Social Organizations and Institutions," in Gurvitch and Moore, *Twentieth Century Sociology* (Philosophical Library, Inc., 1945), p. 212. Hiller's concept of the "institutional group" is partly similar to our concept of the parish as a "superimposed association" in that the cultural system of the church provides a common value-orientation for the members of the parish. See his article, "Institutions and Institutional Groups," *Social Forces*, 20 (March, 1942), pp. 297–306.

21. See Joachim Wach's article, "Sociology of Religion," in Gurvitch and Moore, *Twentieth Century Sociology*, p. 428.

22. See Everett Clinchy's article, "The Efforts of Organized Religion," *The Annals of the American Academy of Political and Social Sciences* (March, 1946), p. 128.

23. Pitirim Sorokin, *Society, Culture and Personality* (Harper & Brothers, 1947), p. 127.

24. William Thomas and Florian Znaniecki, *The Polish Peasant in Europe and America* (Alfred A. Knopf, Inc., 1927), I, p. 275.

25. John D. Donovan, "The Sociologist Looks at the Parish," *American Catholic Sociological Review* (June, 1950), p. 68. Wach similarly says that "religious communities are constituted by loyalty to an ideal or set of values which is the basis of their communion," "Sociology of Religion," *loc. cit.*

26. D. W. Brogan developed a similar analogy in his article, "The Catholic Church in America," *Harper's Magazine*, 200, pp. 40–50, where he says that the Catholic Pastor is like the postmaster who holds the local franchise for all postal transactions.

CHAPTER VIII. URBAN CHURCH AND COMMUNITY CO-OPERATION

1. Wayne E. Oates, *The Christian Pastor* (The Westminster Press, 1950), p. 141.

BIBLIOGRAPHY

These suggestions for further reading are arranged according to the theme of the chapters in this book. They include articles and books from which selections might have been made were it not for space limitations and their greater accessibility.

I. THE SETTING: URBAN LIFE AND URBAN CULTURE

Burgess, E. W., *The Urban Community*. University of Chicago Press, 1925.

Fortune Editors, *The Exploding Metropolis*. Doubleday & Co., Inc., 1958.

Lee, Robert, "Urban-Rural Development in the U.S.A.," *Background Information*, Department of Church and Society, World Council of Churches, June, 1960.

Meyerson, Martin (ed.), "Metropolis in Ferment," *The Annals*, November, 1957.

Petry, Ann, *The Street*. Houghton Mifflin Company, 1946.

Rodwin, Lloyd, and Lynch, Kevin (eds.), "The Future Metropolis," *Daedalus*, Winter, 1961.

Tunnard, C., and Reed, H. H., *American Skyline: The Growth and Form of Our Cities and Towns*. Houghton Mifflin Company, 1955.

Vidich, Arthur, and Bensman, J., *Small Town in Mass Society*. Princeton University Press, 1958.

Weber, Max, *The City*. The Free Press of Glencoe, 1958.

Wickham, E. R., *Church and People in an Industrial City*. Lutterworth Press, 1957.

Winter, Gibson, *The Suburban Captivity of the Churches*. Doubleday & Co., Inc., 1961.

II. RELIGIOUS CONCEPTIONS OF THE CITY

Clark, Dennis, *Cities in Crisis*. Sheed & Ward, Inc., 1960.

Dynes, Russell R., "The Urban Religions," *Dynamic Urban*

Sociology, ed. by William E. Cole, pp. 191–210. Stackpole Co., 1954.

Lenski, Gerhard E., "Religion and the Modern Metropolis," *Review of Religious Research*, Summer, 1959.

Miller, Kenneth D., *Man and God in the City*. Friendship Press, 1954.

Reiss, Albert J., "In Mass Society: What Is the Future of the Church?" *National Lutheran*, April, 1961.

Spike, Robert W., *Safe in Bondage*. Friendship Press, 1960.

Wickham, E. R., "The Encounter of the Christian Faith and Modern Technological Society," *The Ecumenical Review*, April, 1959.

Williams, Charles, *The Image of the City*. Oxford University Press, 1958.

III. The Church Faces the Changing City

Fordham University Publications, *The Church in the Changing Community*. Fordham University Press, 1957.

Hallenbeck, W. C., and Brunner, Edmund de S., "The Influence of Environment on Churches," *American Society: Urban and Rural Patterns*, pp. 480–487. Harper & Brothers, 1955.

Kincheloe, Samuel C., "The Behavior Sequence of a Dying Church," *Religious Education*, November, 1929.

Kloetzli, W., and Hillman, A., *Urban Church Planning*. Muhlenberg Press, 1958.

Leiffer, Murray, *The Effective City Church*. Abington Press, 1961.

Seifert, Harvey, *The Church in Community Action*. Abingdon Press, 1952.

White, Hugh C., "Detroit Industrial Mission Faces the World of Work," *The Witness*, August 20, 1959.

Yinger, J. Milton, "Religion in Urban Society," *Unsolved Issues in American Society*, ed. by R. W. Kernodle. College of William and Mary, 1960.

IV. Renewal in Inner-City Churches

Allan, Tom, *The Face of My Parish*. Harper & Brothers, 1957.

Ehle, John, *Shepherd of the Streets: The Story of James A. Gusweller*. William Sloane Associates, Inc., 1960.

Hargraves, J. Archie, "The Inner City Ministry," *The City Church*, January–February, 1957.

Meyers, Kim, *Light the Dark Streets*. The Seabury Press, Inc., 1957.

Russell, Letty, Allison, Clyde, and Little, Daniel, *The City— God's Gift to the Church*. Board of National Missions, The United Presbyterian Church in the U.S.A., 1961.

Sanderson, Ross, *The Church Serves the Changing City*. Harper & Brothers, 1955.

Shope, John H., "A Strategy for Combining Suburban Strength with Inner-City Opportunity," *Strategies for City Churches*. Evangelical and Reformed Church, June, 1956.

Southcott, Ernest W., *The Parish Comes Alive*. Morehouse-Barlow Co., Inc., 1956.

V. URBAN SECT AND CULT MOVEMENTS

Berger, Peter L., "The Sociological Study of Sectarianism," *Social Research*, Winter, 1954.

Daniel, Vallel, "Ritual and Stratification in Chicago Negro Churches," *American Sociological Review*, June, 1942.

Fauset, Arthur, *Black Gods of the Metropolis*. University of Pennsylvania Press, 1944.

Holt, John B., "Holiness Religion: Cultural Shock and Social Reorganization," *American Sociological Review*, October, 1940.

Lincoln, C. Eric, *The Black Muslims in America*. The Beacon Press, Inc., 1961.

Marty, Martin E., "Sects and Cults," *The Annals*, November, 1960.

Niebuhr, H. Richard, *The Social Sources of Denominationalism*. Holt, Rinehart and Winston, Inc., 1929.

Wach, Joachim, "Church, Denomination and Sect," *Types of Religious Experience*. University of Chicago Press, 1951.

Yinger, J. Milton, "The Rise and Functions of Sects," *Religion, Society, and the Individual*. The Macmillan Company, 1957.

364   CITIES AND CHURCHES

VI. Dilemmas of Urban Church Organization

Dynes, Russell, "Relation of Community Characteristics to Religious Organization and Behavior," *Community Structure and Analysis,* ed. by Marvin Sussman. The Thomas Y. Crowell Co., 1959.

Fichter, Joseph H., *Southern Parish,* Vol. I: *Dynamics of a City Church.* University of Chicago Press, 1951.

———, *Social Relations in the Urban Parish.* University of Chicago Press, 1954.

Gustafson, James, "An Analysis of the Problem of the Role of the Minister," *Journal of Religion* (34), 3, 1954.

Harrison, Paul, *Authority and Power in the Free Church Tradition.* Princeton University Press, 1959.

———, "Church and Laity Among Protestants," *The Annals,* November, 1960.

Kloetzli, Walter, *The City Church: Death or Renewal.* Muhlenberg Press, 1961.

Lee, Robert, *The Social Sources of Church Unity.* Abingdon Press, 1960.

Musselman, G. Paul, *The Church on the Urban Frontier.* The Seabury Press, Inc., 1960.

Nuesse, C. J., and Harte, T. J., *The Sociology of the Parish.* Bruce Publishing Company, 1950.

Schuyler, Joseph, *Northern Parish.* Loyola University Press, 1960.

Thompson, R. H. T., *The Church's Understanding of Itself: A Study of Four Birmingham Parishes.* S.C.M. Press, Ltd., 1957.

VII. Urban Church and Community Conflict

Bennett, John C., *The Religious Concern with Politics.* National Conference of Christians and Jews, 1960.

Coleman, James, *Community Conflict.* The Free Press of Glencoe, 1957.

Fletcher, Verne H., "Collective Dimensions in Interracial Behavior," *The City Church,* September-October, 1960.

Hager, Don J., Glock, Charles Y., and Chein, Isidor (eds.), "Religious Conflict in the United States," *The Journal of Social Issues* (12), 3, 1956.

Hunter, Floyd, *Community Power Structure.* University of North Carolina Press, 1955.

Kane, John, "Protestant-Catholic Tensions," *American Sociological Review* (16), May, 1951.

Pope, Liston, "Religion and the Class Structure," *Class, Status and Power,* ed. by Reinhard Bendix and S. M. Lipset. The Free Press of Glencoe, 1953.

Robinson, Allyn P., "Catholics in the Community," *American Catholics: A Protestant-Jewish View.* Sheed & Ward, Inc., 1959.

Shippey, Frederick A., *The City Church and Social Class.* Methodist Board of Missions, 1958.

Underwood, Kenneth, *Protestant and Catholic: Religious and Social Interaction in an Industrial Community.* The Beacon Press, Inc., 1957.

VIII. URBAN CHURCH AND COMMUNITY CO-OPERATION

Chakerian, Charles G., *The Churches and Social Welfare.* The Hartford Seminary Foundation Bulletin, Fall, 1955.

Department of the Urban Church, National Council of Churches, "Co-operation for Neighborhood Renewal," *City Church Study Kit # 2,* 1960.

Harper, E. B., and Dunham, Arthur, (eds.), *Community Organization in Action.* Association Press, 1959.

Hostetler, H., and Greene, Barbara, "The Relation of the Parish to Social Agencies," *The City Church,* March-April, 1955.

Ross, D. Reid, "Churches and Public Agencies," *Journal of Housing,* June, 1959.

Ruoss, Meryl, "The Churches and Urban Redevelopment," *The City Church,* May-June, 1957.

Spike, Robert W., "Social Work in a City Parish," *Religion and Social Work,* ed. by F. Ernest Johnson. Institute for Religious and Social Studies, 1956.

Warren, Roland, *Studying Your Community*. Russell Sage Foundation, 1955.

Webb, Robert and Muriel, *The Churches and Juvenile Delinquency*. National Council of Churches, 1957.

IX. THEOLOGY AND THE URBAN CHURCH

Folliet, Joseph, "The Effects of City Life Upon Spiritual Life," *The Metropolis in Modern Life,* ed. by Robert M. Fisher. Doubleday & Co., Inc., 1955.

Fukuyama, Yoshio, "The Theological Implications of Mobility," *Christian Unity in North America,* ed. by J. Robert Nelson. The Bethany Press, 1958.

Handy, Robert T., *Members One of Another*. The Judson Press, 1959.

Matson, Theodore E., *Edge of the Edge*. Friendship Press, 1961.

McPhail, David P., (ed.), "Renewal in the Churches," *Union Seminary Quarterly Review,* March, 1961.

Raines, Robert A., *New Life in the Church*. Harper & Brothers, 1961.

Rauschenbusch, Walter, "The Church as the Social Factor of Salvation," *A Theology for the Social Gospel*. The Macmillan Company, 1917.

Webber, George W., *God's Colony in Man's World*. Abingdon Press, 1960.

Weber, Hans-Ruedi, "The Church in the House," *Laity Bulletin No. 3,* April, 1957.

Welch, Claude, *The Reality of the Church*. Charles Scribner's Sons, 1958.